NEW
TESTAMENT

David Stone

TEACH YOURSELF

NEW
TESTAMENT

Cover: Ronald Sheridan (The Ancient Art and Architecture Collection)

.

Long-renowned as the authoritative source for self-guided learning – with more than 30 million copies sold worldwide – the *Teach Yourself* series includes over 200 titles in the fields of languages, crafts, hobbies, sports, and other leisure activities.

Library of Congress Catalog Card Number: on file

First published in UK 1996 by Hodder Headline Plc, 338 Euston Road, London NW1 3BH

A catalogue for this title is available from the British Library

First published in US 1996 by NTC Publishing Group, 4255 West Touhy Avenue, Lincolnwood (Chicago) Illinois 60646 – 19975 U.S.A.

The 'Teach Yourself' name and logo are registered trade marks of Hodder & Stoughton Ltd in the UK

Typeset by Transet Limited, Coventry, England.
Printed in Great Britain by Cox & Wyman Ltd, Reading, Berkshire.

Impression number   10 9 8 7 6 5 4 3 2 1
Year   2000 1999 1998 1997 1996

CONTENTS

This book is dedicated
with nostalgic affection and grateful thanks to
Raynes Park High School
in celebration of its 60th anniversary.

Acknowledgements

The author wishes to thank the following for their invaluable assistance in the preparation of this book: Gerald Beauchamp, Curate of St Luke's & Christ Church, Chelsea; Colin Gale, sometime Lay Assistant at St Jude's Church, Courtfield Gardens; Corinne Smith, Librarian at Wycliffe Hall, Oxford and David Wenham, Tutor in New Testament at Wycliffe Hall, Oxford.

1

INTRODUCING THE NEW TESTAMENT

Getting our bearings

For nearly 2000 years the collection of documents which we know as the New Testament has exercised a profound fascination for people from all over the world. It's a book which has proved to be one of the foundations of Western culture and continues to be the object of rigorous academic research and study. But the New Testament is much more than simply an object of scholarly study and interest. Together with the Old Testament it forms the Holy Bible, a book which millions of people believe to be not only *'inspiring'* but also divinely *'inspired'*. As part of the sacred Scriptures of the Christian religion, the writings which make up the New Testament are seen by many as the 'word of God' as well as the 'words of men'.

Looked at from this perspective, the title *Teach Yourself the New Testament* may perhaps promise more than it can deliver! The reason for this stems from one of the basic characteristics of the Christian Faith, namely the affirmation that God is not an object to be studied but a person to be encountered. When discussing why he taught in parables in Chapter 4 of Mark's Gospel, Jesus is recorded as pointing out that certain aspects of his message are a 'secret' which is hidden from those who want merely to be spectators and only revealed to those who are prepared to commit themselves actively to him. That's why this book should perhaps be more accurately, if somewhat inelegantly, entitled *Let Yourself be Taught the New Testament!* Indeed, the experience of many Christians is that God 'speaks' to them through the Bible in ways which transcend the purely academic – and may even lead them to reject such methods of study altogether as 'dry and dusty'. We shall look at this in more detail in Chapters 8 and 9.

One other distinctive feature of the way Christians use the New Testament is a growing emphasis on the value of studying with other people, so much so that group Bible study is becoming identified as one of the major leisure pursuits of our day! Many Christians affirm the enormous value of such group study in complementing and enhancing their own private use of the Bible. It's not so much a case of teach *yourself* as teach *yourselves* the New Testament.

A further point to make at this early stage is that the New Testament should not be studied in isolation. There is much to be gained from looking at other works of ancient literature, both from Jewish and pagan sources. More than that, from a Christian perspective, the Old Testament is just as much a part of the Scriptures as the New. To study the New Testament without adequate reference to the Old is bound therefore to lead to distortions in Christian teaching and belief. A companion volume in this series, *Teach Yourself the Old Testament*, is available to assist students in this further field of study.

This present book is designed as an introductory guide to the background and contents of the New Testament and aims to set out some of the main ways it has been studied and thought about using the different methods of biblical criticism. The aim is to provide a basic foundation on which the student can go on to build through further reading and investigation. It's also intended specifically to help Christian believers come to a deeper appreciation of the tools of modern scholarship as well as looking at some of the more devotional approaches to Bible study. Incidentally, even though modern use of the word 'criticism' tends to be negative and critical, this is not the sense in which it should be understood in connection with biblical study. 'Criticism' (derived from the Greek word *krino*, to judge) is concerned simply with making decisions about the Bible based on the available evidence in whichever field we happen to be working.

Of course, it's no good just reading *about* the New Testament. Throughout this book, then, there will be a stream of references to read or look up as we explore what it actually says at first hand. Use a modern version of the Bible if you can. In this book, quotations will usually be from the *New International Version*. It's also often a good idea to compare what different versions say. More details of those which are available will be found in Chapter 5. Bible references will usually look like this: Mt 5:12–13. This short-hand code begins with the abbreviation for the book (see Appendix 1 on page 178). In this case, Mt is the commonly accepted abbreviation for Matthew's Gospel. The number before the colon refers to the chapter, and the number(s) after the colon to the verse(s).

⸻ What is the New Testament? ⸻

The most obvious division in the contents page of any copy of the Bible is into the Old and New Testaments. The word 'testament' comes from the Latin *testamentum*, which is itself a translation of the Greek word *diathēkē*. (In this book, Greek characters will usually be set in their English equivalents.) Latin Bibles are divided therefore into the *Vetus Testamentum* and the *Novum Testamentum*, while Greek Bibles have *hēpalaia diathēkē* and *hē kainē diathēkē*. But what does *diathēkē* mean? While it can mean what we refer to when we talk about someone's 'last will and testament', its more usual meaning in the Bible is 'covenant', a solemn and binding agreement between two parties. The New Testament, then, can be called the collection of the books of the New Covenant. But how does this help us to understand what it's all about?

One of the Bible's most important themes is the nature of the relationship between God and human beings, a relationship which is often expressed through the idea of covenant. On several occasions in the Old Testament, God offers protection and care to his people in return for their loyalty and obedience. The problem with agreements like this is that God's people seem to be unable to keep to their side of the bargain. Indeed, one of the main ways in which the Old Testament writers interpret the history of Israel's mixed fortunes is to see events in the life of the nation as a repeating cycle of rebellion against the covenant, followed by punishment, repentance and restoration. But then comes the promise of something to replace the 'old covenant' and bring this cycle to an end. Under this 'new covenant', God's people would be given a new ability to obey him (Jer 31:31–34).

Christians believe that this promise was fulfilled for the whole of humanity as a result of the coming of Jesus Christ into the world.

Luke's Gospel records Jesus speaking of his death as bringing about the new covenant (Lk 22:20). The Epistle to the Hebrews, written particularly for Christians who have come from a Jewish background, demonstrates how the new is foreshadowed in the old and the old is fulfilled by the new. Basically then, for Christians, the Old Testament covers the time when God's dealings with humanity were governed by the 'old covenant', while the New Testament marks the coming of Jesus and the inauguration of the 'new covenant'.

Though often presented as a single volume or simply as the second half of the Bible, the New Testament is actually a collection of 27 separate pieces of literature. It begins with the four gospels, Matthew, Mark, Luke and John, each of which presents a portrait of the life and significance of Jesus Christ. Then comes the Acts of the Apostles, which tells the story of the first few years of the Christian Church. Acts is followed by a series of letters or 'Epistles' written by early Christian leaders to deal with various issues which arose in the life of the early church. A few, like the Epistle to Philemon, are addressed to individuals, but most are intended to be read by churches or groups of churches in different parts of the ancient world. This is reflected in their title, e.g., Philippians, which, although eventually enjoying universal circulation, would have gone first to Christians in the city of Philippi. Finally comes the Book of Revelation, chiefly consisting of an account of an extraordinary series of mystical visions experienced by the apostle John.

Chapter and verse

The original writers of the New Testament did not divide their work up into the neat chapters and verses we have today. But most ancient manuscripts do divide the text up in order to make it easier for readers to find their way around, and we have evidence of a number of different systems of chapter division. For example, the manuscript known as Codex Vaticanus (which we shall look at in more detail in Chapter 6) divides Matthew's Gospel into 170 sections, while Codex Alexandrinus divides the same Gospel into 68 sections. The different books of our modern New Testament are divided up into 260 chapters (Matthew, for example, has 28) and then further subdivided into nearly 8,000 verses. This modern system of chapters dates back to the thirteenth century and was devised by Stephen Langton while he was a lecturer at the University of Paris. He later became the 44th Archbishop of Canterbury from 1207–28 and is also remembered as one of the people who played a leading role in drawing up the Magna Carta. The division into verses was the work of Robert Estienne, Printer to the French king Francis I. The first New Testament (set out in both Greek and Latin) to be divided into the verse structure we now have was published by him in Geneva in 1551 in his fourth printed edition.

— The canon of the New Testament —

In this section we shall examine the process leading to the formation of the standard list of authoritative books known as the canon of the New Testament. The word 'canon' comes from the Greek *kanōn*, itself derived from the Hebrew *qāneh* whose root meaning is 'reed' (from which we get the word 'cane'). From the uses to which reeds were put, especially in measurement, 'canon' came to indicate 'ruler' or 'standard' and also 'index' or 'list'.

It's clear that the 27 books which make up the New Testament were by no means the only pieces of literature that were circulating around the early Christian churches. Those which survive to the present day include the First Epistle of Clement, the Epistle attributed to Barnabas, the *Didache* (or 'Teaching of the Twelve Apostles') and the Epistles of Ignatius and Polycarp. A number of questions arise from this observation. How was the present form of the New Testament decided? Why did the early Christians feel the need to recognise certain books as authoritative? How did they decide what to include and what to leave out?

Three factors seem to have been important. First, the idea of an approved list of books was inherited from the Jewish religion and what we now refer to as the Old Testament. Here is an extract from Matthew's Gospel in which Jesus is recorded as placing his own teaching on a par with that of the Hebrew Scriptures.

You have heard that it was said to the people long ago, 'Do not murder, and anyone who murders will be subject to judgment.' But I tell you that anyone who is angry with his brother will be subject to judgment... (Mt 5:21–22).

It was only natural, then, for the accounts of what Jesus had said to be placed alongside the Old Testament as equally authoritative for Christian believers. This view is evident within the New Testament itself in the writing of the apostle Paul (see 1 Co 7:10; 9:14; 11:23ff.; 1 Th 4:15). But such recognition was not restricted to the words of Jesus himself. The apostles were treated as his personal representatives and so what they wrote was also seen in these terms. When ambassadors speak officially they do so with the full authority of the rulers they represent. In just the same way, the apostles are seen as speaking in the name of Christ (see 2 Co 5:20). The fact that the writings of the apostles were seen as being on a par with the Old Testament scriptures is suggested by 2 Peter 3:15–16, where the writer reveals his view of the apostle Paul's epistles.

Bear in mind that our Lord's patience means salvation, just as our dear brother Paul also wrote you with the wisdom that God gave him. He writes the same way in all his letters, speaking in them of these matters. His letters contain some things that are hard to understand, which ignorant and unstable people distort, as they do <u>the other Scriptures</u>, to their own destruction.

Early church leaders in the post-apostolic era were quick to recognise a clear distinction between the apostles and themselves. Here, for example, is a quotation from Ignatius, who lived between c.35 and c.110 and became Bishop of Antioch: '*I do not wish to command you as Peter and Paul; they were apostles*' (To the Trallians, 3, 3).

Secondly, Christians faced the growing difficulty of heresy (i.e. serious distortion of their message) as it became clear that not everything which carried the label 'Christian' was authentic. This often happened as a result of the desire to make the Christian faith more palatable for those outside the church by mixing in other philosophical and religious ideas. The problem from the orthodox point of view was that such compromises sometimes went too far by undermining certain key Christian truths and so throwing out the baby with the bathwater. This tension between making sure that people believe the right things on the one hand and making it easier for them to do so on the other lies behind many of the controversies which have often seemed to preoccupy Christians during the last 2,000 years.

An early example, from just before the middle of the second century, is the teaching of Marcion, who gained quite a following with his ideas. He began with the entirely orthodox assertion that Jesus had revealed what God was really like. But then he went on to claim that this bore little or no resemblance to the God of the Old Testament. He therefore rejected any Christian writings which appeared to allow any sense of continuity between Judaism and Christianity. In opposing the developing orthodox consensus, Marcion championed his own canon instead. This consisted of an expurgated version of Luke's Gospel and copies of most of Paul's letters, carefully edited to remove any references to the God of the Old Testament. He wasn't alone. Other unorthodox teachers joined him in producing works in which they tried to claim that their views were in fact identical to the teaching of Christ and his apostles. This was another factor which led to the further definition of the canon, an authoritative list of approved books, against which any other teaching could be assessed and either accepted as truly Christian or rejected as heretical. Marcion himself was excommunicated in the year 144.

A third reason for gathering together what we now know as the New Testament was the activity of groups in the early church like that led by Montanus, who lived in Phrygia (part of what is now north-west Turkey) during the second century. The main characteristic of the Montanists which concerns us here was the belief that rather than be limited by a body of truth set down in the past, God is constantly revealing truth to his people through prophets who speak in his name. Their authority was therefore held to be greater than that of the apostles, whose teaching they superseded. While not wanting to deny completely the value of contemporary prophecy within the church, orthodox Christians felt the need to define the standard of 'once-for-all' truth against which such prophetic claims could be measured.

The precise details of how the New Testament canon was formed are obscure and we rely on the different lists supplied and sources quoted by early writers to give us clues as to how it came together, as well as on early copies of the New Testament. One famous official list to have survived is known as the Muratorian Canon after Lodovico Antonio Muratori (1672–1750) who discovered the document in the Ambrosian Library at Milan. It is now held to date from the fourth century not, as once thought, the second, which means that it is not as authoritative as it was once held to be. Damage to the manuscript makes it impossible to be certain, but it seems to have listed all the New

Testament books apart from Hebrews, James and 1 & 2 Peter. It also includes the Apocalypse of Peter and, from the Apocrypha, the Wisdom of Solomon.

The foundation of the canon appears to have been the four Gospels, the Acts of the Apostles and the 13 epistles of St Paul, a fact confirmed in the writings of several early church Fathers, including Irenaeus and Tertullian. A Syrian Christian called Tatian, who lived around the middle of the second century, took the trouble to harmonise the four Gospels in a work known as the *Diatessaron*, which at least suggests that they were recognised as uniquely authoritative at this time. Many so-called 'Gospels' were circulating among Christians but only Matthew, Mark, Luke and John were received as Scripture. Some of the other New Testament books had a rather rough passage before they gained widespread recognition. Revelation does not appear to have been in widespread use until the third century, and the Epistle to the Hebrews, though in use by the end of the first century (it is quoted by Clement of Rome), was later viewed with suspicion in the Western Church, partly because of uncertainty about the identity of its author. It did not receive universal approval until the fourth century. The distinction between the Western and the Eastern Church is based on the tension between Latin-speaking Christians in the West (e.g. at Rome and Carthage) and Greek-speaking Christians in the East (e.g. at Alexandria, Antioch and Constantinople). Such tensions are reflected today in the continuing rift between the Orthodox churches and the rest of Christendom. As a general rule, church leaders in the East tended to be more open to insights from contemporary philosophy, while those in the West preferred to remain more clearly within the boundaries set by Scripture.

Other contenders for inclusions in the New Testament canon were added at different times (and some taken away again!) until the present consensus finally emerged. The earliest list which corresponds to the New Testament as we now have it stems from Athanasius in his Easter Letter of 367. The first major council of the Church to list the 27 books of the New Testament was the Synod of Hippo in 393. It is important to understand that the leaders gathered at this council did not so much confer canonicity itself as recognise the widespread consensus that had already developed concerning the boundaries of the New Testament. Early Christians sought to acknowledge the authority the books that made up the New Testament already had, rather than seeking to impose authority on them.

In assessing a book's claim to be included in the canon, the basic qualification was that it should have a connection with one of the apostles of Christ, either directly with the apostle himself as the author, or indirectly through one of his immediate disciples. On this basis, Mark's Gospel was included because of its supposed link with the apostle Peter (a point stressed by the second-century writer Papias), while Luke's writings were endorsed by his link with the apostle Paul. The decision about whether or not a work was genuine was made on the basis of how it was thought to conform with orthodox Christian teaching. For example, a work like the so-called Gospel of Peter was excluded on the grounds that, even though it claims to be by the apostle Peter, this is contradicted by its unorthodox teaching.

When it came to the layout of the New Testament, it was universally agreed that the Gospels, followed by the Acts of the Apostles, should have pride of place and that Revelation should bring it to an end. But the arrangement of the other books was subject to considerable variation. In the West, Paul's letters came before the so-called 'catholic' epistles (i.e. those addressed to Christians in general rather than members of specific churches), an arrangement that was reversed in the East. In any event, the books of the New Testament do not appear in chronological order.

– The language of the New Testament –

The New Testament is written in Greek, a language whose origins go back to at least the thirteenth century BCE (Before Common Era). It has a different alphabet from the Latin one on which English is based – even though our word alphabet is itself derived from alpha and beta, the first two letters of the Greek alphabet! The Greek alphabet has 24 letters.

Until just over a century ago, it seemed to scholars that the form of Greek used in the New Testament was very different from the style of classical Greek literature. The German theologian Richard Rothe (1799–1867) went so far as to suggest that New Testament Greek was uniquely the 'language of the Holy Spirit'! Such a view was decisively overturned by the discovery, late in the nineteenth century, of many papyrus fragments and ostraca (pieces of pottery used as writing material) from everyday life in the ancient world. These demonstrate

The Greek Alphabet

Letter	English	Greek small	Capital
Alpha	a	α	A
Beta	b	β	B
Gamma	g	γ	Γ
Delta	d	δ	Δ
Epsilon	e (short)	ε	E
Zeta	z	ζ	Z
Eta	e (long)	η	H
Theta	th	θ	Θ
Iota	i	ι	I
Kappa	k	κ	K
La(m)bda	l	λ	Λ
Mu	m	μ	M
Nu	n	ν	N
Xi	x	ξ	Ξ
Omikron	o (short)	ο	O
Pi	p	π	Π
Rho	rh	ρ	P
Sigma	s	σ or ς	Σ
Tau	t	τ	T
Upsilon	u	υ	Y
Phi	ph	φ	Φ
Chi	ch	χ	X
Psi	ps	ψ	Ψ
Omega	o (long)	ω	Ω or Ω

that much of the New Testament is written in the language of the ordinary people – *koinē* (i.e. common) Greek – rather than the more literary style found in most classical Greek writing. This is important because some commentators have sought to draw subtle inferences about the meaning of the text on the basis of distinctions which only exist in classical Greek from the fifth and fourth centuries BCE. For example, the word for into (*eis*) is sometimes used where, in classical Greek, we might expect the use of the word for in (*en*). But it turns out that the word *en* was on the way to disappearing from the language and that in *koinē* Greek *eis* means both in and into. To follow classical usage and suggest that *eis* should *always* be translated as into is therefore wrong.

The Greek style of the New Testament is far from uniform. Mark's Gospel and Revelation are written in very basic Greek which sometimes crosses the border and appears to become ungrammatical. Other books, notably 1 Peter, Hebrews, Luke and Acts, demonstrate a much higher literary standard.

The earliest fragment of John's Gospel, written in Greek on a piece of papyrus. (Reproduced by courtesy of the Director and University Librarian, the John Rylands University Library of Manchester.)

Being able to study the New Testament in the language in which it was first written is much more rewarding than having to rely on translations. It's beyond the scope of this book to do any more than whet the appetite to the delights of New Testament Greek, and interested students are advised to search out one of the several courses now available, including a companion volume in this series, *Teach Yourself New Testament Greek*.

Questions to consider

1 Do you think the New Testament is 'divinely inspired'? What does this mean?
2 Why is the New Testament called the 'New Testament'?
3 What do we know about how the early church decided on what should be included in the New Testament?
4 What is significant about the style of Greek found in the New Testament?

2

A TOUR OF THE NEW TESTAMENT

The Gospels:

Matthew
Mark
Luke
John

The Acts of the Apostles

Epistles or 'letters':
Romans
1 Corinthians
2 Corinthians
Galatians
Ephesians
Philippians
Colossians
1 Thessalonians
2 Thessalonians
1 Timothy
2 Timothy
Titus
Philemon
Hebrews
James
1 Peter
2 Peter
1 John
2 John
3 John
Jude

Revelation

The best way to become acquainted with the New Testament is, of course, to read it. It isn't the intention of this chapter to dissuade readers from doing this – far from it! Appendix 5 sets out a daily reading plan which will help you to go through the New Testament in six months. It's helpful both to read whole books at a single sitting to get the broad sweep of what an author is saying as well as to study individual sections in greater detail. Such reading can be enhanced by our having some idea of what to look for. So we'll look briefly at what we can expect to find in each of the 27 different books.

The Gospels

The New Testament begins with the four Gospels: Matthew, Mark, Luke and John. The word 'gospel' derives from the Old English for 'good news' and reflects the Christian understanding of the significance of Jesus Christ, whose life they describe.

The first three are known as the 'Synoptic' Gospels because they look at the life of Jesus from a similar viewpoint and have a fair amount of material in common. This is something we shall look at in more detail in Chapter 8.

John's Gospel is rather different. For the most part, he doesn't bother to cover ground dealt with by the others, and even when he does there are usually substantial differences. John provides a more reflective account of events as he ponders their significance in greater depth. Notice that each of the Gospels spends what might seem to be a disproportionate amount of time dealing with the events surrounding the death of Christ. This is reflected in the Christian conviction about the centrality of this event in assessing the significance of his life and place in human history.

The Gospel of Matthew

The Gospel itself does not say who wrote it, but early tradition associates it with Matthew the tax collector (also known as Levi (e.g. Lk 5:27)). In this Gospel, he is mentioned by name only in 9:9 and 10:3. Most (but not all) scholars agree that it was written after Mark's Gospel, probably between 50 and 90 CE (Common Era). Even so, its place as the first of the four is entirely appropriate since, of all the Gospels, Matthew's bridges the gap between the Old and New Testaments most effectively. He shows particular sensitivity to Jewish readers. For example, where the other Gospels talk quite freely about the 'kingdom of God', Matthew, aware of Jewish reticence about using the name of God, uses the term 'kingdom of heaven' instead. Compare Matthew 4:17 with Mark 1:15.

One of Matthew's aims is to show that the new Christian faith fills out rather than cancels out the previous allegiance of those who come from a Jewish background. At several points he illustrates his descriptions of what is happening with quotations from the Old Testament in order to support the Christian claim that Jesus fulfils its predictions about the coming Messiah, the 'Christ' or 'anointed one'. See 1:18–23; 2:1–6; 2:14–15; 2:16–18; 4:12–16; 8:16–17; 13:34–35; 21:1–9; 27:6–7 for examples of these 'formula quotations', as they're often called. Many Jews in Jesus' day expected the Messiah to come and release them from Roman domination, and so part of

Matthew's message is to show what Jesus really meant by the 'kingdom of heaven' and the way he refused to limit it to a purely political dimension.

The structure of Matthew's Gospel may not be immediately apparent simply from reading it. But stepping back allows us to see that much of the teaching of Jesus is set out in five distinct blocks, each ending with the phrase *'when Jesus had finished...'* (5:1–7:27; 10:1–11:1; 13:1–53; 18; and 23–25). Some scholars suggest that Matthew has done this in order to hint at the parallel between Jesus and the great Jewish leader Moses, traditionally seen as the author of the five books which begin the Old Testament.

Despite having a strongly Jewish flavour, Matthew's Gospel also has plenty to say about those who are non-Jews, or 'Gentiles'. He wants his readers to see that Jesus is the Messiah for the whole of humanity, not just for his own people. So he underlines the fact that Gentile women appear in Jesus' family tree (1:1–16), and on several occasions reports Jesus' commendation of Gentiles for having more faith than Jews (e.g. 8:10; 15:21–28). The Gospel ends with the disciples of Jesus being told to take the message of the Gospel all over the world (28:18–20). Matthew's is the only Gospel to refer specifically to the church (16:18; 18:17). The evidence from within the Gospel suggests that Matthew was written in an environment where Jewish and Gentile Christians belonged to the same church, with Jews forming the majority. Many scholars have come to the conclusion that Matthew was written from the area of Syria, north of Israel.

Summary of Matthew's Gospel

1 The ancestry, birth and early life of Jesus (1–2)
2 John the Baptist, Jesus' baptism, the temptations and the beginning of his public ministry (3–4)
3 Teaching block 1: The Sermon on the Mount (5:1–7:27)
4 Jesus at work in Galilee (8–9)
5 Teaching block 2: Instructions for the disciples (10:1–11:1)
6 Some people accept Jesus while others reject him (11:2–12:50)
7 Teaching block 3: Parables about the kingdom of heaven (13:1–53)
8 Deepening conflict with the Pharisees (13:54–17:27)
9 Teaching block 4: How disciples should behave towards one another (18)

10 Jesus travels from Galilee to Jerusalem (19–22)
11 Teaching block 5: The future (23–25)
12 The death and resurrection of Jesus (26–28)

The Gospel of Mark

Again, although the Gospel itself does not tell us, tradition suggests that it was written by John Mark and that he based it both on what he had seen for himself (he could be the young man referred to in 14:51–52) and on what he had been told by the apostle Peter. Mark himself is mentioned on several other occasions in the New Testament (e.g. Ac 12:12; Col 4:10; 1 Pe 5:13). It's also likely that this was the first Gospel to be written and that Matthew and Luke used it when compiling their own (though some scholars think it was the other way round and that Mark used Matthew or Luke: see Chapter 8). A date of between 65 and 70 CE seems most likely. You may notice that 16:9–20 are set in smaller type in many Bibles. This is because manuscript evidence (see Chapter 6) suggests that they were not part of the original Gospel but added later to round off what was otherwise (or has at some stage since become) a rather abrupt ending at 16:8.

Unlike Matthew, Mark seems to have been written for a non-Jewish readership. This is strongly suggested by the fact that he explains religious customs with which Jews would have been familiar (e.g. compare 7:1–5 with Matthew 15:1–2). His writing is full of vivid detail as he rushes from one incident to another (notice how often he used the word 'immediately'!). His Greek style is relatively unpolished and where Matthew focuses on Jesus as a teacher, Mark's main emphasis is on Jesus as a man of action.

The first half of the Gospel tackles the question of who Jesus is and helps the reader to reach the conclusion Mark begins with in the very first verse: that he is the Son of God who has come to establish God's rule on earth. As you read through, notice the different ways in which Jesus exercises authority – even over death itself (5:41–42). Then in the second half Mark focuses on what Jesus came to do: 8:27–31 is a key turning point in the Gospel. As soon as the disciples have realised who he is, Jesus begins to prepare them for the shocking fact of his suffering and death, together with their significance as he prepares to *'give his life as a ransom for many'* (10:45).

But things are not what they seem. For the one who had accurately predicted his own death had also been right about his being raised from the dead (which is what the Bible word 'resurrection' means). God's purposes cannot fail, however many setbacks there may be along the way. As in the career of Jesus, so too in the lives of his followers: the tone of Mark's Gospel would have been then and is now a great encouragement to Christians coming under pressure and facing persecution for their faith. From the choice of stories about Jesus made by Mark, the teaching seems to be directed mainly to the disciples rather than to the world around them.

Summary of Mark's Gospel

1 Introduction: John the Baptist, Jesus' baptism and temptations (1:1–13)
2 Jesus' ministry in Galilee and the surrounding area (1:14–9:50)
3 Jesus' ministry in Judea and his journey to Jerusalem (10)
4 Jesus' ministry in Jerusalem and his visits to Bethany (11–13)
5 The trial and death of Jesus (14–15)
6 The resurrection of Jesus (16)

———— The Gospel of Luke ————

With a total of 1,151 verses, Luke's is the longest Gospel. It's also the only one with a sequel: the Acts of the Apostles. Both were written so that a certain Theophilus (1:3; see also Ac 1:1) could be more certain about what had really gone on in the life of Jesus and the early church. Although some have thought that the name (which means 'friend of God') indicates the Christian reader in general, it's also been suggested that it's a code-name, written in order to disguise the true identity of its recipient, perhaps the emperor Vespasian's nephew Titus Flavius Clemens. The fact that Theophilus is addressed as 'most excellent' implies that he was certainly a person of some standing and probably a Roman official.

With this in mind, it's been suggested that one of Luke's reasons for writing his two volumes could have been to allay fears about the political implications of Christianity and its perceived challenge to the status quo. If tradition is right, then the author of this Gospel is Luke the doctor, friend and colleague of Paul (see Col 4:14; 2 Ti 4:11; Phm 24). From the style of his Greek, he is clearly an educated and accomplished writer. From the way Acts ends so abruptly with the apostle Paul under house arrest in Rome (dated at around 62 CE), and because Luke's writing shows no particular interest in the fall of Jerusalem which took place in 70 CE, it seems reasonable to assume that Luke's Gospel would have been written between 60 and 70 CE.

Luke's chief concern is to show that Jesus is for the world as a whole, going right back to the dawn of time – notice that Luke's account of the ancestry of Jesus goes right back to Adam (3:38). God is interested in everyone, especially those who are looked down on and seen as insignificant by others. Luke makes a point of highlighting Jesus' concern for the poor and helpless and draws attention to his refusal to go along with the conventions of the day, e.g. in his attitude to women and children – see 7:36–50; 8:1–3, 40–56; 9:37–43, 46–48; 10:38–42; 18:15–17. Other special emphases in Luke are the meaning of salvation (e.g. 1:69, 71, 77; 2:11, 30; 3: 6), the joy of praise to God (e.g. 1:14, 44, 58; 2:10, 17, 21), the role of the Holy Spirit (e.g. 1:35; 3:22; 4:1, 14, 18; 10:21) and the importance of prayer (e.g. 3:21; 5:16; 6:12; 9:18, 28; 11:1–13; 18:1–14; 22:32, 44; 23:46). The fact that he also goes on to write a second volume demonstrates his grasp of the fact that the Jesus story is not confined to his life on earth but that it continues on with the history of the early church.

Another theme of particular interest to Luke is that of 'journey', especially the journey to Jerusalem and all it signified for Jesus. It's been noted that whereas for Mark, Christian discipleship is about *being* with Jesus, from Luke's perspective a disciple is one who *journeys* with Jesus. The clearest indication of this is in the Gospel's long central section, sometimes called the 'travel narrative' (9:51–19:45).

Summary of Luke's Gospel

1 Introduction and the infancy narratives (1–2)
2 John the Baptist, Jesus' baptism, family tree and temptations
   (3:1–4:13)
3 Jesus' ministry in Galilee (4:14–9:50)
   The ministry begins (4:14–44)
   Jesus calls his disciples (5:1–6:16)
   Jesus teaches his disciples and the crowds (6:17–49)

Ministry in Capernaum (7–8)
Incidents focusing on the 12 disciples (9:1–50)
4 Jesus travels from Galilee to Jerusalem (9:51–19:44)
Ministry in Samaria (9:51–10:37)
Teaching about prayer (10:38–11:13)
Conflict with the Pharisees (11:14–54)
More teaching and healing (12:1–19:44)
5 Jesus in Jerusalem (19:45–21:38)
6 The trial and death of Jesus (22–23)
7 The resurrection and ascension of Jesus (24)

The Gospel of John

John 21:20–24 indicates that this Gospel derives from 'the disciple whom Jesus loved'. Early traditions identify him as the apostle John (not to be confused with John the Baptist). Most scholars seem to date the Gospel at around the end of the first century, though some scholars – in modern times, most notably John Arthur Thomas Robinson (1919–83) – suggest that it was written much earlier, maybe even before the others.

John's Gospel is very different from the other three, both in structure and style. Jesus comes over as an even more majestic and authoritative figure than in the other Gospels and there is a much greater sense of the drama of conflict between him and the religious authorities of his day. John describes only seven of the miracles of Jesus in the main section of the Gospel, chosen for their ability to serve as 'signs', i.e. events that point clearly to the significance of who Jesus was and what he did (see 2:1–11; 4:46–54; 5:2–9; 6:1–14; 16–21; 9:1–7; 11:1–44). The teaching of Jesus is set out differently too. Whereas the others concentrate on reporting parables and short sayings, John's interest is in much longer discourses whose chief focus is Jesus himself. Central to these is a series of seven 'I am' sayings which offer graphic pictures to illustrate who Jesus is and what he does (see 6:35; 8:12; 10:7; 10:11; 11:25; 14:6; 15:1). Several of the signs and sayings link up directly. Jesus talks about himself as 'the bread of life' (6:35) just after he has miraculously supplied a meal for more than 5,000 people (6:1–14). A blind man is healed (9:1–7) to illustrate Jesus' claim to be 'the light of the world' (8:12). And to support his claim to be 'the resurrection and the life' (11:25), Jesus raises Lazarus from the dead (11:38–44).

John's Gospel introduces Jesus as having been the 'Word of God' from before the beginning of time. This is an idea with roots in the Old Testament and in Greek philosophical thought. It's clear throughout the Gospel that the writer wants to show what Jesus means both for those from a Jewish background and also for those familiar with Greek thought.

Clearly John had access to other material and could have written more (see 20:30 and 21:25). But he limits himself to whatever serves to support his single overall aim set out in 20:31: '...*that you may believe that Jesus is the Christ, the Son of God, and that by believing you may have life in his name*'. Whether or not he made use of the Synoptic Gospels is a question whose answer remains uncertain. One noticeable feature is the way in which John and the Synoptic Gospels 'interlock' by reinforcing or explaining each other. For example, Mark 14:58 and its parallel in Matthew 26:61 (cf. Mk 15:29 and Mt 27:40) report the accusations made against Jesus at his trial concerning his threat to destroy the temple. What would otherwise be a rather obscure reference is clarified by John 2:19–21, which gives an explanation of why such allegations would have been made. Another example is the way that John 6:66–68 helps to explain the circumstances which led Jesus to ask his disciples what they thought about his identity in Mark 8:27 (see also the parallels in Mt 16:13 and Lk 9:18). Similarly, Philip's hesitation when approached by a group of Gentiles who wanted to be introduced to Jesus (Jn 12:21–22) may be explained by Matthew's mention of how Jesus prohibited his disciples from going out among the Gentiles during the time of his earthly ministry (Mt 10:5).

Summary of John's Gospel

1 Introduction (1)
2 Jesus' public ministry (2–12)
3 Jesus' ministry to his disciples (13–17)
4 Jesus' suffering and glory (18–20)
5 Epilogue (21)

The Acts of the Apostles

Luke describes his first volume as '*all that Jesus began to do and to teach*' (1:1). Acts is all about how this continued in the life of the early church. He begins with the ascension of Jesus into heaven following his promise that the disciples would receive the power of the Holy Spirit. This power would enable them to continue what he had begun and spread it all over the world (1:8).

Luke's key priority is to demonstrate just how this happened. The coming of the Holy Spirit at Pentecost is marked by an astonishing expansion in the number of disciples (2:41) and leads to a time of great popularity and further rapid growth (2:47). But the honeymoon period is soon over. Luke soon introduces us to the repeated sequence of progress and setback which continues throughout the rest of what he writes. Opposition from the authorities in Jerusalem leads to the death by stoning of Stephen (the church's first martyr) and the resultant scattering of Christians throughout Judea and Samaria (8:1). This turns out to be counterproductive though, as they simply carry on the work – just as Jesus had said they would (1:8). As Luke reports, they '*preached the word wherever they went*' (8:4). The result is still further growth as the church expands outwards in ever-increasing circles.

It isn't long before another barrier is crossed as they take the message to Gentiles instead of simply confining their missionary efforts to Jews and Jewish sympathisers. But the fact that the Gentiles respond as well leads to a problem. How far should the newcomers be encouraged to follow Jewish customs as they embrace the Christian faith? In Chapter 15 Luke shows how they sort this out and takes care to stress the rightness of the inclusion of the Gentiles, both in its obvious success and in the way it fulfils Old Testament prophecy. To underline further the equality of Jews and Gentiles, Luke shows the striking similarities between the work of Peter (primarily an apostle to the Jews) and Paul (apostle to the Gentiles). To see this, compare 3:2–8 and 14:8–10, 5:1–5 and 13:11, 5:15 and 19:12, 9:34 and 28:8, 10:1 and 13:12, 10:9–20 and 22:17–21, 10:25 and 16:29, 10:44 and 19:6, 12:7 and 16:26.

Meanwhile, Saul (the apostle Paul's Jewish name, which Luke uses until Acts 13:9) is converted while on his way from Jerusalem to stamp out Christian activity in Damascus. The result is that one of Christianity's fiercest opponents becomes one of its most powerful advocates. This is so significant an event that Luke reports it three times (in Chapters 9, 22 and 26).

Judging from his use of the word 'we', it seems that Luke himself accompanied Paul on some of his travels (e.g. 16:10–17; 20:5–21:25; 27:1–28:16) and so writes, at least in part, from first-hand experience. He sets out the details of Paul's missionary progress round the ancient world, his return to Jerusalem and the trials in Jerusalem and Caesarea which lead to his being sent to Rome where, under house arrest, he continues *'to preach the kingdom of God and teach about the Lord Jesus Christ'* (28:31). In keeping with his primary aim of showing how the church spread from the Jewish into the Gentile world, Luke is content to stop here – even though, tantalisingly, he leaves us guessing as to Paul's fate. Tradition suggests that Paul faced execution by beheading in Rome.

Summary of Acts

Acts is divided into six sections, each separated by a short summary statement about the spread of the word and the growth of the church (see 6:7; 9:31; 12:24; 16:5; 19:20).

1 The birth of the church (1:1–6:7)
   Introduction; the ascension of Jesus (1)
   The coming of the Holy Spirit; growth of the church in Jerusalem (2:1–6:7)
2 The start of persecution (6:8–9:31)
   The martyrdom of Stephen (6:8–8:3)
   The church scatters and the word spreads (8:4–40)
   The conversion of Saul (9:1–31)
3 Christianity spreads to the Gentiles (9:32–12:24)
4 Paul's first two missionary journeys (12:25–16:5)
   The first journey (12:25–14:28)
   The Jerusalem council (15:1–25)
   The second journey (15:36–16:5)
5 Paul's continuing journeys (16:6–19:20)
   The second journey concluded (16:6–18:22)
   The third journey (18:23–19:20)
6 Paul's arrest, trial and journey to Rome (19:21–28:31)

The third journey concluded (19:21–21:17)
Paul's arrest and trial at Jerusalem (21:18–23:35)
Paul's trial at Caesarea (24–26)
Paul's journey to Rome and period under house arrest (27–28)

The Epistles

Much of the rest of the New Testament consists of a series of 21 letters (often called by their older name of 'epistle', derived from *epistolos*, the Greek word for 'letter'). Thirteen appear to have been sent by Paul to a selection of churches and individuals, from which they derive their modern titles. The remainder are the 'general' or 'catholic' epistles, so-called because they are not addressed to specific groups or individuals. Three of them are by John, two by Peter and one each by James and Jude. One, the Epistle to the Hebrews, is anonymous. They were written by church leaders who, unable to visit churches personally, kept in touch and passed on vital instruction, sometimes in response to specific questions. This explains why they sometimes read more like sermons than letters, as their writers seek to argue their sometimes complex case.

In keeping with the practice of the time, the New Testament letters begin with the sender's name and a line or two of formal greeting. The main bulk of the letter follows, with personal messages and a final greeting to conclude.

The Epistle to the Romans

Paul's letter to the Romans was intended to pave his way to the capital of the Empire (1:13–15), a visit which he wanted to make on his way to cover new territory in Spain (15:28). The letter was written around 57 CE while Paul was on his way to Jerusalem from Corinth (15:25).

Most of Paul's letters include instructions for dealing with problems that have come up in the life of the local church. But since Paul had never been to Rome, he is unlikely to have been sufficiently aware of any specific difficulties his readers were facing. Instead, he uses his letter to the Romans to set out the essence of what he saw as his mission: preaching the good news (i.e. the 'gospel') of Jesus Christ. A summary appears in 1:16–17: *'I am not ashamed of the gospel because it is the power of God for the salvation of everyone who believes: first for the Jew, then for the Gentile. For in the gospel a righteousness from God is revealed, a righteousness that is by faith from first to last...'*

He begins with the 'bad news' of human rebellion against God and the entirely justified divine anger which makes such salvation necessary. According to Paul, the problem is that human beings have not kept God's law as revealed both in the Old Testament and, for those without access to the Scriptures, through human conscience. Furthermore, we are in any case quite unable to keep it. The turning point comes in 3:21–22: *'But now a righteousness from God, apart from law, has been made known, to which the Law and the prophets* (i.e. what we know as the Old Testament) *testify. This righteousness from God comes through faith in Jesus Christ to all who believe...'* Paul's argument is that God puts us right with himself (i.e. 'justifies' us), not because of what we do, but through faith in what Jesus has done for us in his death on the cross. He goes on to develop the implications of this new relationship with God which the Christian believer now enjoys.

Chapters 9–11 form a section in which Paul wrestles with the fact that the Gentiles have responded more enthusiastically to his message than the Jews. Is it the case that God's past promises to his ancient people have failed? In which case, how can he be trusted in the future? Paul concludes that Jewish rejection of his message is in fact part of God's plan to bring salvation to the whole of humanity and argues that, in the end, his own people will come to accept Jesus too.

Following on from what he has set out in Chapters 1–8 about the new relationship with God which is possible through Christ, the question arises of how it all works out in practice. This is the theme of the rest of the epistle as he begins Chapter 12 with *'Therefore, I urge you, brothers, in view of God's mercy...'*. He deals mainly with relationships within the Christian community but also includes instructions about how Christians should act towards the secular authorities (see 13:1–7). The epistle concludes with a series of personal greetings to people known to Paul. Since he had never been to Rome, some commentators find it surprising that he should have so many people to greet, and suggest that Chapter 16 was originally a separate letter which may even have been addressed to another church altogether, perhaps Ephesus. On the other hand, Acts 18 indicates that two of those referred to in Romans 16:3 (Priscilla and Aquila) had at one stage had to leave Rome and had met Paul in Corinth. It may be that Romans 16 is a list of others in a similar position who had become acquainted with Paul on his travels.

Summary of Romans

1 Introduction (1:1–16)
2 The gospel according to Paul (1:17–8:39)
3 The question about how the Jews fit in (9–11)
4 Living in the light of the gospel (12–15)
5 Conclusion (16)

— The Epistles to the Corinthians —

Paul's relationship with the church at Corinth was nothing if not stormy! The details are uncertain, but it seems likely that he visited the city three times and wrote a total of at least four letters. A possible sequence of events is as follows. The first visit, described in Acts 18:1–8, took place in 50 or 51 CE and led to the founding of the church. Subsequently, Paul wrote the letter referred to in 1 Corinthians 5:9. Some scholars suggest that 2 Corinthians 6:14–7:1 may be a fragment of this first letter. In response to worrying news (1 Co 1:11; 16:17) and requests for advice (7:1), Paul wrote a second letter, probably in 54 CE, which we know as '1 Corinthians'. A subsequent visit is referred to in 2 Corinthians 12:14, 21; 13:2 and was followed by a third 'severe letter' (mentioned in 2 Co 7:8), which in turn led to a fourth letter (our '2 Corinthians') once Paul heard from Titus how number three had been received. Finally, Paul spent three months in Corinth during his third missionary journey (Ac 20:2–3). There has been much debate about whether 2 Corinthians 10–13 belong with Chapters 1–9 or are part of another letter. The latter possibility is suggested by the markedly different tone of Chapters 10–13, and it's been suggested that these chapters may be either a fifth letter or perhaps the third 'severe letter' mentioned above. There is, however, no textual evidence to suggest that 2 Corinthians once concluded at the end of Chapter 9. It may simply be that Paul received bad news about the situation in Corinth while he was writing 2 Corinthians and that the beginning of Chapter 10 marks his fresh response. Arguments that a number of other passages in 2 Corinthians are interpolations have excited scholarly interest but have not been decisively sustained by the evidence.

The city of Corinth was the provincial capital of Achaia. As a port, it was strategically placed for trade and was therefore a significant and prosperous city. It was also a centre for the worship of Aphrodite, the Greek goddess of love, and had such a reputation in the ancient world for immorality that the word 'to corinthianize' (meaning to have sex outside marriage) entered the language. Such attitudes had also infected the church, and so Paul has to deal firmly with the issues involved. As well as dealing with its distortions, he also includes a section on the true meaning of love, which is one of the most famous chapters in the Bible (13). The social background of the church reflected that of the city and was very diverse and led to problems which Paul deals with in what he writes (e.g. 1 Co 11:17–22).

Summary of 1 Corinthians

1 Introduction (1:1–9)
2 Divisions in the church (1:10–4:21)
3 Sexual morality and family life (5–7)
4 Attitudes of Christians to non-Christian practices (8:1–11:1)
5 Church life, especially in relation to worship (11:2–14:40)
6 The resurrection of Christ and its implications for Christian believers (15)
7 Christian giving (16:1–4).
8 Future plans, personal messages and conclusion (16:5–24)

2 Corinthians is a very personal letter in which Paul expresses his deep feelings for those he has led to faith and who seem to him to be in danger of going off the rails. A central theme is his teaching on the joy, pain and responsibilities involved in Christian ministry and leadership. The letter also includes details of a financial appeal which Paul is making in order to help less well-off Christians in Judea and a passionate defence of his ministry against the opposition he has faced from false apostles. A poignant comment in Romans 15:23 ('...*there is no more place for me to work in these regions...*') implies that his pleas for reconciliation may not have been successful.

Summary of 2 Corinthians

1 Introduction (1:1–11)
2 Paul's understanding of Christian ministry (1:12–7:16)
3 Christian giving (8–9)
4 Paul defends his authority (10:1–13:10)
5 Conclusion (13:11–14)

—— The Epistle to the Galatians ——

Scholars have long argued over exactly what Paul means by 'Galatia' in 1:2. Is he using the term *geographically* to refer to the ancient kingdom of Galatia in northern Asia Minor or *politically* to refer to the Roman province further south? Acts 13–14 deal with his visit to a number of cities in the south and the establishment of churches in this area. Acts 16:6 and 18:23 suggest that he may have also gone further north, but we have no evidence that he conducted an extensive mission in the region.

According to the 'South Galatian' theory then, Galatia refers to an area in what we now know as southern Turkey, including the towns of Pisidian Antioch, Iconium, Lystra and Derbe (see Ac 13:14–14:25; 16:1–4). The letter dates from 49 CE and is therefore the earliest of Paul's writings to have survived. Under the 'North Galatian' theory, the letter must have been written several years later, during Paul's third missionary tour.

Whichever of these views is correct, Paul writes to deal with the problems caused by some Jewish Christian visitors whose teaching was leading the Galatians astray. 2:15–16 indicates that the basic issue was their claim that *'faith in Christ Jesus'* alone was not enough: these recent converts needed also to be *'observing the* [Jewish ceremonial] *law'*. Paul's response pulls no punches – as is clear from the beginning of Chapter 3 and 5:12! He argues tightly, drawing extensively from his understanding of the Old Testament evidence, in order to show the way in which faith supersedes the law for the Christian. Not that Christians are free to go off and do what they like. As he goes on to demonstrate in Chapters 5 and 6, the freedom Christians have from Jewish law is not a freedom to go off and sin but rather a freedom *not* to sin and a consequent new liberty to serve God and others instead.

Summary of Galatians

1 Introduction (1:1–10)
2 Paul defends his authority (1:11–2:21)
3 Paul defends his message (3–4)
4 Christian freedom, the law and the Spirit (5:1–6:10)
5 Conclusion (6:11–18)

—— The Epistle to the Ephesians ——

The lack of personal greetings in this letter is at first surprising, given that Paul spent longer in Ephesus than in any other city (Ac 19:8–10). In addition, some of the best manuscript witnesses omit the words 'in Ephesus' in 1:1, and Marcion actually calls this letter 'the Epistle to the Laodiceans'. In the light of these observations, it may be that this epistle was a circular letter, written to all the churches in the Ephesus area of the Roman province of Asia. This is borne out by the fact that Paul deals with no specific questions or problems. Along with Philippians, Colossians and Philemon, this is one of the letters Paul wrote from prison (6:20), probably while in Rome in the early 60s CE. There are strong parallels between this letter and Colossians.

Many scholars have questioned the traditional acceptance of the letter's claim to have been written by Paul. A comparison of the content and style of Ephesians with other Pauline material suggests that the letter may have been written by a disciple of Paul rather than by the apostle himself. On the other hand, it may be that seeking to force Paul into the stylistic straitjacket of his other writings is unjustified and that the letter is genuine after all.

The letter's central theme is the ultimate unity of all things in Christ and the role of the church in demonstrating the power of the gospel to bring together those who would otherwise be implacably hostile to each other – especially Jews and Gentiles (see 2:11–19). Nothing need (or, ultimately, can) divide those who have Christ in common. As with other letters by Paul, the first half sets out the theoretical foundation on which the second half builds the practical implications. Chapters 4–6 deal with relationships within the church and the home, as Paul sets out instructions on how his readers are to put into practice the high ideals of unity to which they are called as the followers of Jesus

Christ. Much of what he writes would have been quite revolutionary, especially the way in which he supports the dignity of women, children and slaves by balancing how they are to behave with how they are to be treated (5:22–6:9).

—— The Epistle to the Philippians ——

Philippi was an important city, founded by Philip II of Macedon in 358–357 BCE, which helped to connect Rome with the East. The Emperor Octavian established it as a military outpost and Roman colony whose citizens, many of them former soldiers, enjoyed the same rights and privileges as if they were on Italian soil. Paul uses this theme of privileged citizenship to illustrate an important truth in this letter (see 3:20). The founding of the church at Philippi, in about 50 CE, is described in Acts 16:12–40. When Paul, Silas and Timothy left, Luke stayed on. Philippi is known to have been a medical centre, and may even have been Luke's home town.

Paul writes in order to thank them for their financial and practical help (2:25; 4:10, 14–19) and takes the opportunity to include encouragement, warning and instruction. He writes while chained up in prison (1:7, 13, 17), but we cannot be sure exactly where or when. The letter to the Philippians is radiant with a joy that clearly enables Paul to rise above the hardships he is facing (the words 'joy' and 'rejoice' are mentioned 16 times). Trace through and see what exactly it is that enables him to feel as he does. It's clear that his relationship with God is so close that he isn't even worried by the prospect of imminent death (1:20–24; 2:17–18). He draws his example from that of Jesus Christ (2:5–11) and urges his readers to do the same, sitting loose to the distractions of this life and focusing instead on what lies ahead (3:17–21).

Summary of Philippians

1 Introduction (1:1–11)
2 News (1:12–26)
3 Encouragement and instruction (1:27–2:18)
4 Plans for Timothy and Epaphroditus (2:19–30)
5 Warnings against enemies and dangers (3:1–4:9)

6 Final thanks (4:10–20)
7 Conclusion (4:21–23)

—— The Epistle to the Colossians ——

Again, Paul writes from prison (4:18), in a letter which has striking parallels with the Epistle to the Ephesians and was probably written at around the same time. It's likely that the church at Colosse (a small town about 100 miles east of Ephesus) was established during Paul's three years in Ephesus (Ac 19:10; 20:31) as a result of Epaphras and Philemon becoming Christians and returning to spread the Christian message in their home area. Paul himself does not seem to have visited the city personally. He now writes in response to news from Epaphras (1:7; 4:12) about how things were going. From what he says, it seems that the Colossian Christians were in danger of being led astray by a form of false teaching known as gnosticism. He writes to encourage them to remain true to what they had originally accepted about the supremacy of Christ (2:6–7), a theme which he develops at length. Read through Chapter 2 and see if you can work out from what he says how the false teachers were attempting to undermine this. Having dealt with what Christians need to avoid, Paul turns in 3:1–4:6 to the other side of the coin as he gives positive instruction on how they should live. As with most of the epistles, Colossians concludes with a series of personal greetings and messages.

Summary of Colossians

1 Introduction and prayer of thanks (1:1–14)
2 Who Jesus is and what he has done (1:15–2:5)
3 Warnings against false teachers (2:6–23)
4 New life in Christ (3:1–4:6)
5 Concluding messages (4:7–18)

— The Epistles to the Thessalonians —

Thessalonica (the modern city of Salonika) was a thriving seaport, the capital of the Roman province of Macedonia in northern Greece.

Founded by the Macedonian king, Cassander, in about 315 BCE, it was named after his wife, a half-sister of Alexander the Great. Since 42 BCE it had the status of a 'free city', governed by politarchs.

The background to these two letters is found in Acts 17:1–9, where Luke recounts details of a somewhat turbulent trip to Thessalonica made by Paul, Silas and Timothy in 50 CE. Opposition from the Jews was so intense (1 Th 2:2) that they were in danger of being lynched and had to leave in a considerable hurry (2:15). Paul's first letter follows a return visit to Thessalonica made by Timothy some months later (3:1–10). If the North Galatian theory is accepted with its later date for Paul's epistle to the Galatians, then this is the first of Paul's surviving letters. Timothy's report was generally positive, but leads Paul to defend himself against his opponents' accusations that he was only in it for the money (2:5). He also deals with specific questions on sexual morality (4:3–8), work (4:11–12) and the return of Christ (4:13–5:11). It's clear from the second letter, written quite soon after the first, that some of his readers had got the wrong end of the stick. They were using the imminence of Christ's return (also known as the 'parousia') as an excuse to stop work and sit back (2 Th 3:6–13). Paul writes to correct this (2:1–4) and to encourage them never to *tire of doing what is right* (3:13) while they wait.

Summary of 1 Thessalonians

1 Introduction and thanks to God (1:1–10)
2 Paul's defence of his ministry (2:1–16)
3 A desire to revisit Thessalonica (2:17–3:13)
4 Pastoral advice (4:1–5:11)
5 Final instructions and greetings (5:12–28)

Summary of 2 Thessalonians

1 Introduction (1:1–2)
2 Judgement to come (1:3–12)
3 Signs of the end (2:1–12)
4 Encouragement (2:13–3:15)
5 Conclusion (3:16–18)

— The Epistles to Timothy and Titus —

These are known as the 'pastoral' epistles since they are addressed to two young church pastors or leaders as individuals rather than to churches as a whole. Many scholars have expressed doubts as to their Pauline authorship on the grounds both of what they say and how they say it. Some of the events referred to are not easy to fit into what Acts tells us of Paul's life, as they suggest that Paul was released from house arrest in Rome, undertook a further journey, and was then put back in prison (from where 2 Timothy was written). It may be that a later writer compiled them and included some fragments of 'genuine' Paul. On the other hand, it may simply be that Paul himself dictated the letters to a secretary (perhaps Luke?) who had more stylistic leeway than usual. (For evidence that Paul was in the habit of dictating letters see 1 Co 16:21; Gal 6:11; Col 4:18; 2 Th 3:17; Phm 19.) Although the style of the letters differs from others known to be by Paul, this can be at least partly explained by the lack of extended theological argument, perhaps not needed in view of the identity of those to whom the letters are addressed. What theology the letters do contain is thoroughly consistent with what we know of Paul.

Paul took Timothy under his wing on his second visit to the latter's home town of Lystra (see Ac 14:8–18; 16:1–3). Titus, though not referred to in Acts, is mentioned on several occasions in the epistles, especially in 2 Corinthians 7–8 and the beginning of Galatians 2, where Paul mentions him as an example of a Gentile convert to Christianity. Both men assisted Paul and travelled with him before being left in charge of churches at Ephesus (1 Ti 1:3) and Crete (Tit 1:5) respectively.

The first epistle to Timothy deals with some of the perennial problems of church leadership: dealing with false teaching (1:3–20), instructions on worship (2:1–14), guidance on the selection and conduct of leaders (3–4) and advice on various pastoral issues (5:1–6:10). The second letter reveals something of Paul's sense of isolation as he faces hardship alone (see 2 Timothy 4:9–18). He is aware that death is near (4:6) and writes to encourage Timothy to continue the good work – enduring the suffering of persecution and striving against the opposition of false teaching. He pictures the life of faith as a relay race: as he nears the end of his leg of the contest (4:7), it's as if he hands the baton on to Timothy and urges him to keep going.

The epistle to Titus underlines Paul's commission to him – *'to straighten out what was left unfinished and appoint elders in every town...'* (Tit 1:5). 2 Corinthians 7:6–16 and 12:18 reveal something of his previous experience in trouble-shooting. In this letter Paul goes on to indicate to Titus the sort of thing he should be teaching, the keynote of which is in 3:14: *'Our people must learn to devote themselves to doing what is good...'* Merely talking about it is not enough (1:10)!

Summary of 1 Timothy

1 Introduction (1:1–2)
2 False teaching (1:3–20)
3 Worship in church (2:1–14)
4 Qualities and duties of Christian leaders (3–4)
5 Pastoral advice (5:1–6:10)
6 Personal instructions (6:11–20)

Summary of 2 Timothy

1 Introduction (1:1–2)
2 The reality of Christian suffering (1:3–2:13)
3 A challenge to Timothy (2:14–4:5)
4 Paul's present situation (4:6–18)
5 Conclusion (4:19–22)

Summary of Titus

1 Introduction (1:1–4)
2 Church leadership (1:5–16)
3 Duties of different groups (2)
4 Exhortations and warnings (3:1–11)
5 Personal instructions and conclusion (3:12–15)

The Epistle to Philemon

This is the shortest of Paul's letters which have survived in the New Testament, with 335 words in the original Greek. Together with Colossians, it was probably brought back by Epaphras when he returned from visiting Paul in Rome. It is a personal appeal to Philemon, a member of the church at Colosse (compare the mention of Archippus in verse 2 with Colossians 4:17) about his runaway slave, Onesimus. Onesimus had met Paul in Rome and become a Christian (verses 10 and 16). Paul now writes to Philemon, together with Apphia (perhaps Philemon's wife?) and Archippus (perhaps their son?) to ask him to welcome Onesimus home again, not so much as a slave (verse 21 implies a request to set him free) but now also as a 'dear brother' (verse 16). Although Paul does not directly attack the evil of slavery, he certainly undermines it by pointing out that all slaves and all free people are equal in the Christian family. Though Paul expounds no major doctrinal themes in this letter, it provides a valuable glimpse of his compassionate humanity and so firmly counters the idea that he was austere and intolerant.

The Epistle to the Hebrews

This epistle has carried the title 'Hebrews' since the second century: it is not in the text itself. But it's highly appropriate since it's clear that the letter is addressed primarily to Jewish (i.e. 'Hebrew') Christians who are contemplating a return to their previous allegiance. It's for this reason that the text is full of allusions to Jewish belief and practice, many of which may be obscure to the modern reader. But it's worth pursuing: Hebrews has a very helpful emphasis on the humanity of Jesus which therefore enables him to empathise with his followers. The author and date are the subject of much scholarly speculation but remain unknown. Early on, the Eastern church thought that Hebrews was written by Paul, a view that the Western church, after initial hesitation, came to share from around the fifth century. Modern scholars are virtually united in discounting this possibility, on the grounds that the letter's style and ideas differ so markedly from those of Paul. Various alternative suggestions have been made – Luke, Barnabas, Apollos, Priscilla, Silas, Timothy and Epaphras to name but seven! – but it seems better to admit our ignorance and agree with the third-century Christian leader Origen's comment that 'as to who wrote it, only God knows'. Given what the letter says about Jewish ritual, many conclude that it must have been written before the destruction of the Jerusalem temple in 70 CE.

The author's main theme is summed up in 4:14: '*...since we have a great high priest who has gone through the heavens, Jesus the Son of God, let us hold firmly to the faith we profess*'. He seeks to establish the superiority of Jesus over what Jews would consider to be other leading contenders. First, angels, generally thought of as superior spiritual beings (1:4–2:18), then Moses, the great leader of the Jewish people (3:1–19), then his successor Joshua (4:1–13), then Aaron the high priest and his successors (4:14–7:28).

His basic perspective is that Jesus has brought about the reality of salvation once and for all in a new 'covenant' or agreement between God and humanity. The result is that the distinctive rituals of Judaism under the old covenant are no longer necessary. Their function, to point forward to what Jesus would achieve, is now fulfilled. To continue in them would therefore be positively unhelpful as it would cast doubt on the validity of what Jesus has done. The need now is for Christians not to slow down and look back to their former allegiance but to persevere, even under the onslaught of persecution, as they look forward to God's final intervention and the day of judgement. This underlines the need for faith, a subject which the author deals with in Chapter 11 as he looks back on a whole series of individuals in Jewish history who held on to the hope of an unseen future in the face of present difficulties.

Summary of Hebrews

1 Christ is the complete revelation of God (1:1–3)
2 The superiority of Christ over angels (1:4–2:18)
3 The superiority of Christ over Moses (3:1–4:13)
4 The superiority of Christ's priesthood (4:14–7:28)
5 The superiority of the new covenant (8–9)
6 The superiority of Christ's sacrifice (10)
7 Faith in action (11:1–13:17)
8 Personal messages (13:18–25)

The Epistle of James

At least three men in the New Testament have the name James. One was a son of Zebedee who, together with his brother John and their fishing colleague Peter, formed the inner circle of Jesus' 12 disciples (e.g. Mt 17:1; Mk 14:33). Ac 12:2 records his execution at the hands of Herod Agrippa I. Another of the 12 was James son of Alphaeus, probably also known as 'James the younger' (Mk 15:40). The third James was a brother of Jesus (Mk 6:3; Gal 1:19) who became leader of the church in Jerusalem. The Jewish historian Josephus records his death by stoning in 62 CE. His clear leadership is reflected in the events of Acts 15 and he is usually thought of as the author of this epistle, probably written around 45–49 CE. One observation that supports this conclusion is the marked similarity between the Greek of the epistle and the speech attributed to James in Acts 15:13–21.

The epistle of James is addressed to '*the twelve tribes scattered among the nations*' (1:1), a title which may reflect the events of Acts 8:1 and 11:19 when persecution forced many Christians to leave Jerusalem. This attractive possibility would also help to explain the markedly Jewish tone of the letter.

In his letter, James concentrates on how Christian faith should work out in practice. *Believing* the right things is all very well, but it's no good unless it leads people to *behave* in the right way as well. This is the major emphasis that runs through the letter with its 60 direct commands, a feature which underlines the similarities between this epistle and the Wisdom literature of the Old Testament.

Summary of James

James is difficult to organise. Like the Old Testament Book of Proverbs and the Sermon on the Mount in Matthew 5–7, it's made up of short sayings which don't seem to be very closely related to one another. The commentator A. M. Hunter has suggested an arrangement of the letter under the following major themes.

1 Trials and temptations (1:2–8; 12–18)
2 Riches and poverty (1:9–11; 2:1–13; 5:1–6)
3 Faith and works (1:19–27; 2:14–26)

4 Controlling the tongue (3:1–12; 4:11–12; 5:12)
5 Patience and prayer (5:7–11, 13–20)

The Epistles of Peter

In his first epistle, Peter writes as a witness of the sufferings of Christ (1 Pe 5:1) in order to encourage those who are themselves undergoing suffering on account of their faith. *'Babylon'* in 5:13 is a code word for Rome and it's likely that Peter wrote this letter from there in about 67 CE, probably not long before his own death. Its first readers were in various places (1:1) located in what is now western and northern Turkey. He addresses them as *'aliens and strangers'* (2:11), technical terms for two categories of second-class citizen in the Roman Empire. 'Resident aliens' were foreigners with permanent residence but inferior social status, or poor people who never achieved full citizenship. 'Visiting strangers' were people without permanent residence, who were living in a country temporarily. The polished Greek in which the letter is written may reflect the style of Silas, who seems to have acted as Peter's secretary (5:12).

His aim is to shift their thinking from the hardship of their present experience to the glory of what they cannot yet see but hope for in the future (see especially 1:3–9). In the light of this, they must not give up but continue to live in a way that reflects their standing as children of their heavenly Father (1:13–16). The rest of the letter indicates how this works out in practice in a variety of different situations.

Although 2 Peter claims to be from the same author (see 2 Pet 1:1 and 3:1), scholars have drawn attention to a marked difference in style which calls this into question. Other factors are the long time it took for the letter to be accepted by the early church and the fact that Chapter 2 is almost the same as the Epistle of Jude. A late date for the letter is implied by the references to the apostles speaking *'in the past'* (3:2), to *'our fathers'* as having died (3:4) and to letters of Paul (3:15–16). On the other hand, the writer's claim to have been an eyewitness of the transfiguration of Jesus (1:16–18; see also Mt 17:1–9) must not be ignored and at least points in the direction of Peter himself being the author. In addition, the early church *did* eventually accept it into the canon of the New Testament. It may be that, as

R. J. Bauckham has suggested, the letter is pseudonymous but that, far from wanting to deceive, the author *intended* his readers to recognise that Peter himself was not the author. But if the author's intentions were so clear, why was there any debate in the early church about whether or not Peter wrote it? The major problem with theories involving a late pseudonymous author is that, as we saw in Chapter 1, the conferring of canonicity depended very much on there being direct links with one of the apostles.

The letter's emphasis is on encouraging Christians to grow in their faith – in the way they behave, with certainty about the reliability of Christianity's origins, alert to the dangers of false teaching and secure in their expectation of Christ's return.

Summary of 1 Peter

1 Introduction (1:1–2)
2 The certainty of Christian hope (1:3–12)
3 Called to a holy life (1:13–2:12)
4 A Christian response to suffering (2:13–4:19)
5 Christian humility (5:1–11)
6 Conclusion (5:12–14)

Summary of 2 Peter

1 Introduction (1:1–2)
2 Called and chosen by God (1:3–21)
3 False teachers (2)
4 The return of Jesus Christ (3)

The Epistles of John

The style of these epistles is very similar to that of John's Gospel. Instead of arguing in straight lines, the writer weaves his ideas in circles, stating and restating them in different ways. Many of the themes (light and darkness, love and hate, truth and falsehood) are similar too. These observations have led many scholars to conclude that the fourth Gospel and these three epistles are the work of the apostle John ('*the elder*' of 2 John 1 and 3 John 1), probably dating from around 85–90 CE. On the other hand, there are significant differences between John and 1 John which have led other scholars to conclude that they are the work of two different authors. Such observations are far from compelling, however, and it is probably better to see the differences as complementary rather than contradictory.

As we've seen, John's Gospel was written to help people towards Christian faith (John 20:31). John's aim in this letter is to confirm the faith of those who already believe and encourage them to live up to their calling. 1 John 5:13 sums up his approach: '*I write these things to you who believe in the name of the Son of God so that you may know that you have eternal life*'. One reason for possible doubt was that some had left the church (1 Jn 2:19) and were encouraging others to join them (2:26). Looking through the letter gives us clues about what this breakaway group must have been teaching (e.g. see 1:8–10; 2:4; 4:2–3; 5:1). In particular, we can trace signs of docetism (the idea that Jesus was a spirit being who only *appeared* to be genuinely human) and antinomianism (the belief that because Christians are free from the demands of God's law they can do what they like). To help his readers stand firm he provides three tests to enable them to distinguish true and false teaching. First, are those who claim to belong to the truth living genuinely Christian lives (e.g. 1:5–10)? Secondly, are they showing true Christian love (e.g. 4:7–12)? And thirdly, do they believe that Jesus was both God's Son and a real human being (e.g. 4:2–3)?

2 John recapitulates many of the themes of 1 John. The '*chosen lady and her children*' (verse 1) probably refers to an individual church and its members. Notice his rigorous attitude to false teachers (verses 10–11).

3 John, addressed to '*my dear friend Gaius*' (verse 1), warns him about the activity of Diotrephes. Problems in the church's relationship with John were being caused by the fact that '*he loves to be first*' (verse 9).

Summary of 1 John

1 Introduction (1:1–4)
2 The nature of true Christian faith (1:5–2:28)

3 The family of God (2:29–4:12)
4 Being certain of faith (4:13–5:12)
5 Conclusion (5:13–21)

—————— # The Epistle of Jude ——————

The New Testament includes references to four individuals with the names Jude or Judas. Two of the apostles were so named: Judas Iscariot (Mt 10:4) and Judas the son of James, also called Thaddeus (Mt 10:3; Lk 6:16; Ac 1:13). Judas called Barsabbas is mentioned in Acts 15:22. Fourthly, there is Jude the brother of Jesus and James (v.1; see also Mt 13:55) who appears as the author of this epistle. He seems to have had no great prominence in the early church and so it is difficult to see why a pseudonymous writer should have claimed him as the author.

The epistle is written in very strong language as Jude and assumes a familiarity with Old Testament events and teaching. Jude had clearly been intending to write positively (verse 3) but was obliged to use his letter to denounce those in the church who were seeking to undermine orthodox Christian faith and practice (verse 4). He ends on a positive note though as he encourages his readers to press on, secure in God's ability to keep them safe.

Summary of Jude

1 Introduction (1–2)
2 Denunciation of false teachers (3–16)
3 Pastoral advice (17–23)
4 Concluding blessing (24–25)

—————— # The Book of Revelation ——————

This extraordinary book, quite unlike anything else in the New Testament, comes from the pen of John (1:4). Early tradition identifies him as the apostle John, one of the disciples of Jesus, author of the Gospel and epistles that bear his name and leader of the church at

Ephesus. This view has been questioned on the grounds that the author of Revelation makes no specific claim to be an apostle. But it may be that he was so well known to his first readers (1:9) that he felt no need to go beyond calling himself simply 'John'. It's true that the style and contents are different from the other writings that lay claim to the apostle John as their author. But many scholars have come up with a number of ways of explaining these without needing to posit two or more different authors.

Revelation (not Revelations, by the way – a mistake which is often made) probably dates from the end of the first century, written when John was in exile on the inhospitable prison island of Patmos (1:9) – a sort of first-century Alcatraz! The main recipients are listed as 'the seven churches in province of Asia', of which Ephesus was the chief city and the main commercial centre. The sites of these seven cities, some of which have been extensively excavated, may be visited in modern-day western Turkey. John describes how Jesus appears to him in heavenly brilliance and dictates a series of seven letters, one for each church in the group (1:9–3:22). The letters are listed in the order of the route which a traveller would take to visit each of their recipients, beginning at Ephesus (which had a fine natural harbour at the time) and ending at Laodicea. Each letter contains a note of commendation (apart from that addressed to Laodicea), a note of reproof and a promise to 'him who overcomes' (2:7, 11, 17, 26; 3:5, 12, 21). Some of what is said about a church's spiritual state reflects the physical circumstances of its host city. For example, 3:16 refers to the Laodicean church being like lukewarm water. This was exactly the problem faced by the citizens of Laodicea. They relied on water being piped to them from nearby hot springs which would inevitably cool down in the process.

John's extended vision continues with a look into heaven (4:1). What he sees is a series of pictures to indicate how God views reality and how things are going to work out in the future. The fundamental purpose of the book is to encourage Christians undergoing persecution. This was probably under the Roman Emperor Domitian (who reigned from 81–96), though a good case can also be made for dating Revelation towards the end of the reign of Nero (54–68). John's message is that their present suffering is not the end of the story: despite the often painful conflict between good and evil, God has the future firmly in his hands.

The powerful symbols used to convey this message are dramatic, even grotesque and, to us, often obscure. Far from being a 'revelation', much of what is written seems to be a 'concealing'! One helpful way to approach the puzzle is to recognise that the style of Revelation is not unique. Parts of the Old Testament books of Daniel and Ezekiel are written in the same way, as is some of the Jewish literature written between the Old and New Testaments. Scholars call it 'apocalyptic' literature, from the Greek for 'revelation' or 'unveiling'. Using such symbolism allows John more readily to encompass spiritual truth in human language. Its very obscurity also means that there is less chance of recrimination should the book fall into unfriendly hands.

Summary of the Revelation

1 Introduction (1:1–8)
2 Seven letters for seven churches (1:9–3:22)
3 Seven seals broken open (4:1–8:1)
4 Seven trumpet blasts of warning (8:2–11:18)
5 God's view of human history (11:19–15:4)
6 Seven bowls of punishment (1:5–16:21)
7 Babylon the prostitute (17:1–19:10)
8 The real conflict (19:11–21:8)
9 Jerusalem the bride (21:9–22:19)
10 Conclusion (22:20–21)

Questions to consider

1 What is a 'Gospel'? What advantages and disadvantages are there in the fact that we have four of them in the New Testament?
2 What role does the book known as the Acts of the Apostles have in the New Testament?
3 What does 'epistle' mean? In what ways are the epistles useful for us today?
4 How would the Book of Revelation have helped its first readers? What impact does it have on you?

3

THE GEOGRAPHY AND HISTORICAL BACKGROUND OF THE NEW TESTAMENT

The New Testament is not some abstract textbook of theology with an index for us to look up the subjects that interest us. Instead its message is rooted in the stories of individuals who lived in the first century. On the one hand, this makes it easier to relate to because it's much more personal, vivid and interesting. But it also leads to a difficulty. After 2,000 years, many changes have taken place, changes which create a gulf between their world and ours. It's true that the landscape, climate and natural history of the Bible lands themselves are similar to how they were in New Testament times. There is much to be gained from visiting the Middle East and the Mediterranean today in order to gain an understanding of certain features of life in the first century. But in other respects, the culture is very different. Things which *we* now take for granted were completely unheard of, while things *they* were familiar with are virtually unknown to us. This is where an appreciation of the background of the New Testament is vital if we are to understand it properly and get the most out of it.

Palestine

The action of the New Testament takes place in the Middle East, with the main focus on Palestine (a word which comes from the Philistines who occupied part of the south-west of the territory). Palestine is a small area (see map on page 202), only 75 miles wide and 150 miles north to south (*'from Dan to Beersheba'* is the way the Bible sometimes describes it, e.g. 1 Sa 3:20). Its disproportionate significance came from its location at the intersection of Europe, Africa and Asia. This made the area a significant artery for trade routes and led to its history in ancient times of being pulled this way and that by the great world powers of each generation – Egypt from the south, Assyria, Babylonia and Persia from the east, Greece and Rome from the west. On top of this, it has had a special status as the 'Promised Land' for the Jewish people, with all the consequences this has had in recent generations for the Palestinian Arabs. The Old Testament describes how God promised the land to Abraham and his descendants (e.g. Gn 15:18–21) and how, under Moses, they were brought back to it after their captivity in Egypt. Because of its significance for the world's three great monotheistic religions – Judaism, Christianity and Islam – it is also known as the 'Holy Land' (see Ps 78:54 and Zec 2:12 for biblical references to this title) while its capital, Jerusalem, is called the 'holy city' (e.g. Ne 11:1; Isa 52:1; Mt 4:5; Rev 21:2).

In New Testament times, Palestine was divided into seven main areas. Running down the centre of the country was the River Jordan, flowing from the Sea of Galilee to the north and the Dead Sea to the south. West of the Jordan, going from north to south, were Galilee, Samaria, Judea and Idumea. To the east were Gaulanitis, the Decapolis (from the Greek for 'ten cities', a loose federation of semi-independent Greek cities created by Pompey in 62 BCE) and Perea.

When thinking about what Palestine was like in the first century, the key word is *variety*. The territory forms part of what is known as the 'fertile crescent', a well-watered area which sweeps in a semi-circle from the Nile valley in the west to the south-east of the Persian Gulf. South of this area is the Arabian desert. Palestine lies on the western edge of the crescent, with the Mediterranean on one side and the desert on the other. Moving from west to east, the traveller would find five distinct landscapes.

First comes the coastal plain. Well watered by a combination of rivers and rainfall, this fertile area formed the main route taken by traders between Egypt in the south and Syria in the north. Its three sub-sections are the Plain of Acco in the north, the central Plain of Sharon and Philistia in the south. The coastline has no good natural harbours. This is one of the reasons why the Israelites were never a maritime people, a fact reflected in their misgivings about the sea which are evident in, for example, Revelation 21:1. Around the time of the birth of Jesus though, King Herod the Great was responsible for building a great artificial harbour at Caesarea, a feature which considerably enhanced the trading opportunities in the area and so led to increased influence and prosperity.

Next comes the central hill country, an outcrop of rough limestone, with Galilee to the north, Judah (including Jerusalem) to the south and Samaria in the middle. Because they regarded Samaritans (see below) as heretics, devout Jews travelling between Judah and Galilee would normally take a long detour via the east of the River Jordan in order to avoid their territory. Jesus is recorded as making an exception to this rule on more than one occasion, notably in Luke 9:51–56 and John 4:3–4. Between Galilee and Samaria lies the Valley of Jezreel (or Esdraelon), just south of Nazareth, the point at which the north–south trade route crossed to the Jordan Valley on its way to and from Syria. Being much more hilly, this whole area was less suitable for farming.

Moving further east, the traveller would reach the Jordan Valley, part of the 4,000-mile Great Rift Valley. Running from the mountains in the north, the River Jordan flows through the Sea of Galilee, a large fresh-water lake at 212 metres below sea level. In the New Testament this is also known as the Lake of Gennesaret or the Sea of Tiberias. The Jordan flows finally into the Dead Sea, so-called because its exceptionally high salt concentration means that it cannot support life. It can, however, support floating objects – even the poorest swimmer would have a hard time trying to sink in it! At 388 metres below sea level, it has no outlet but loses millions of gallons a day through evaporation. Its surface is the lowest point on the earth's surface. The site of John the Baptist's baptisms in the Jordan would have been at one of the fords within a few miles of the Dead Sea (see Mt 3:1–5). The area round the Sea of Galilee, with its flourishing fishing industry, was the location of much of the ministry of Jesus. Further south, between Jerusalem and the Dead Sea, lies the arid wilderness of Judea. The traveller in Jesus' parable of the Good Samaritan (Lk 10:30–36) was going down the steeply descending road from Jerusalem to Jericho through this area when he was attacked by bandits.

East of the Jordan lies the mountainous region known as the Transjordan. The initially steep ascent levels out towards the east into the desert. Its volcanic soil and rainfall combine to make it a relatively fertile area. To the south lies the great trade route known as the 'King's Highway'.

A year in the life...

Unlike our Roman-based calendar which is based on the length of time it takes for the earth to go round the sun, the Jewish calendar is based on the waxing and waning of the moon. The 12 months of the year consist of 29 or 30 days each, regulated according to the lunar cycle of 354¼ days, with an extra month added every now and then to keep up with the solar year of 365¼ days. By New Testament times, the Babylonian practice had been adopted in which the year begins at the time of the spring equinox with the month of Nisan (March/April) and continues with Iyyar, Sivan, Tammuz, Ab, Elul, Tishri, Marchesvan, Kislev, Tebeth, Shebat and Adar. Days began not in the morning but with the sunset of what we would regard as the previous day. This explains how, by Jewish reckoning, the Last Supper (associated with Maundy Thursday) and the crucifixion of Jesus (on what we call Good Friday) occurred on the same day.

The climate marks the two major divisions of the calendar in the rainy season (from October to April) and the dry season (from May to September) during which rain is virtually unknown. But when the rain comes, it certainly comes! Jesus' parable about the impact of the weather on two houses in Matthew 7:24–27 is no exaggeration. After the early autumn rains had softened the ground, planting (mainly of wheat and barley) would take place in November and December. Crops would then be harvested between March and May, once the spring 'latter rains' had swelled and matured the grain.

Related to this annual cycle were the great religious festivals of the Jewish people when those who were able to would come *en masse* to Jerusalem (e.g. see Jn 7:1–4; Ac 2:5). According to Deuteronomy 16:16, all male Jews were required to attend the three great feasts of Passover, Weeks and Booths. By New Testament times, the widespread dispersion of Jewish people made this impracticable, though Jews would attempt to return to Jerusalem for the great feasts at least once in their lifetime. Acts 20:16 records Paul's desire to reach Jerusalem in time for the Feast of Weeks or Pentecost.

The Feast of the Passover comes in April (14th Nisan) and is followed by the seven-day Feast of Unleavened Bread. These holy festivals celebrated Israel's rescue from Egypt under Moses and included the slaughter of the Passover lamb (see Exodus 12) and the presentation

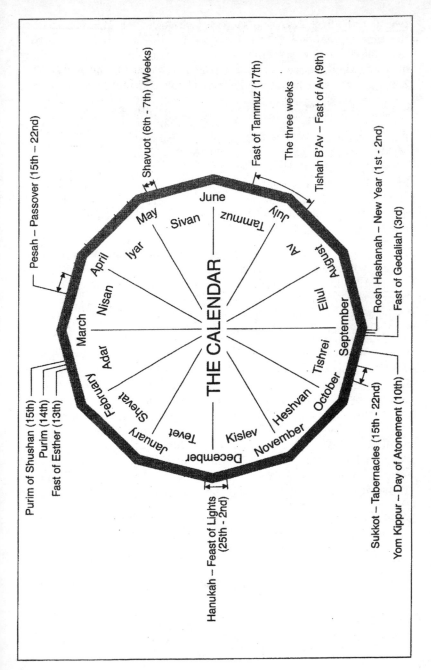

to God of the first sheaves of ripe barley. Mark 14:1 underlines this as the time of year when Jesus was tried and put to death. The New Testament writers see this timing as particularly significant and draw parallels between the death of Jesus, 'the Lamb of God' (Jn 1:29), and the sacrifice of the Passover lamb (1 Co 5:7).

Seven weeks later, on the 6th Sivan, came the Feast of Weeks or Pentecost (i.e. 'fifty days'). This was also known as the Feast of the Firstfruits or Harvest, as the people celebrated the completion of the wheat and barley harvests, (Lev 23:15–21). Pentecost also commemorated God's gift of the Law to his people through Moses at Mount Sinai. Acts 2 records Pentecost as the day when the Holy Spirit was poured out on Jesus' followers with what Christians see as the fulfilment of Jeremiah's prophecy concerning God's law being written on people's hearts (Jer 31:31–34).

Finally, in the month of Tishri came the Feast of Booths or Tabernacles, also known as the Feast of Ingathering (Lev 23:33–44; Nu 29:12–40; Dt 16:13–15). The Israelites were required to live in structures made out of tree branches for seven days as a reminder of their deliverance from slavery in Egypt. At the same time, they celebrated the completion of the vine and olive harvests.

Other important events included the civil new year (the Feast of Trumpets) on 1st Tishri (Lev 23:24f.; Nu 29:1–6). This was also called Rosh Ha–Shanah ('head of the year'). The Day of Atonement, Yom Kippur, on 10th Tishri, was a fast day during which sins would be confessed and the guilt symbolically transferred to a sacrificial goat (Lev 16; 23:26–32; Nu 29:7–11). This is what lies behind the English word 'scapegoat'. The Feast of Hanukkah or Dedication (Jn 10:22) on 25th Kislev celebrated the rededication of the temple in 164 BCE after it had been desecrated by Antiochus IV. The Feast of Purim on 13th–14th Adar celebrated the Jews' deliverance from Haman by Esther (see Esther 9:26–28). In addition, there were special rules for celebrating the seventh year (see Lev 25:1–7) and the fiftieth year of Jubilee (see Lev 25:8–55; 27:16–25).

Invaded!

To understand what life in Palestine was like in Jesus' day, we need to begin at least 600 years earlier when, in 587 BCE, Jerusalem fell to the invading Babylonians. Most of the population was exiled to Babylon and the city devastated. From this point the Jewish state lost its independence and was ruled by successive foreign powers until its autonomy was restored in 1948 CE.

BCE	700	
		Babylonians take Jerusalem, end of kingdom of Judah, 587.
	600	Persians conquer Babylonians, 539.
		Edict of Cyrus, 538; Jews return to Holy Land, Nehemiah builds Temple, Ezra brings the Law.
	500	
	400	Alexander the Great defeats Persians at Issus, 333.
		Alexander conquers Tyre en route to Egypt, 332.
		Alexander dies, 323. Alexander's generals divide empire, Seleucids rule Mesopotamia. Ptolemies rule Egypt.
	300	Four Syrian wars, 276–217; power struggle between Seleucids and Ptolemies to control Syria and Phoenicia. Seleucid rule of Holy Land.
	200	Beginning of Maccabean revolt, 167.
		Pompey captures Jerusalem, extends Roman rule to Holy Land, 63.
	100	Herod the Great, 37–4.
		Life of Jesus, c. 7 BCE – c. 29 CE
	0	Pontius Pilate, governor of Judea, 26–36.
		Paul begins missionary journeys, c. 44
CE		First Jewish Revolt against Rome, 66–73.
	100	Second (Bar Kokhba) Jewish Revolt against Rome, 132–135; ends in complete Roman victory, Jews dispersed.

The Babylonian Empire itself collapsed in 539 BCE and was superseded by the Persian Empire under the rule of Cyrus. Persia was much more lenient towards the Jews and allowed them to return to their own country and worship as they wished. The Old Testament interprets these events as evidence of the hand of God at work in a pagan ruler on his people's behalf (see 2 Ch 36:22, Ezr 1:1–2, Isa 44:28–45:13). Two hundred years later, Alexander the Great (356–323 BCE) came to power and ended the Persian control of Palestine by defeating the forces of Darius III at the Battle of Issus in 333 BCE. Alexander, who had studied under Aristotle, one of the greatest philosophers the world has ever seen, took the opportunity to unite those he conquered by establishing Greek culture throughout his empire. The Greek philosopher and historian Plutarch wrote that Alexander 'believed that he had a mission from God to harmonize men generally and to be the reconciler of the world, bringing men from everywhere into a unity, and mixing their lives and customs, their marriages and social ways, as in a loving cup'. This policy of Hellenization, a process which had already begun through the activity of Greek traders, meant that people throughout the Mediterranean world came to share similar customs, beliefs and language, including at least token allegiance to Greek religious practices.

Palestine proved to be an exception in this latter aspect. The fiercely monotheistic Jews refused to countenance the worship of Greek gods like Zeus. But most of them were quite prepared to accept what they saw as the more innocuous features of Hellenism. Especially among the ruling classes, the use of the Greek language and enjoyment of its culture became commonplace. This, incidentally, was one of the factors which helped the Christian faith to spread so quickly throughout the Mediterranean world. There were exceptions, though, represented by a Jewish group called the Hasidim, who firmly opposed the changes brought about by Hellenization.

Following Alexander's death at the age of 32 (just 13 years after he had acceded to the Macedonian throne), the unity he had worked for was fatally undermined as his empire was divided between four of his generals. Ptolemy (323–285 BCE) and his successors (known as the 'Ptolemies') ruled Egypt and Palestine from Alexandria until the last of them, Cleopatra, died in 30 BCE. Seleucus (312–280 BCE) and his successors (the 'Seleucids') ruled Syria and Babylon from their capital in Syrian Antioch, named after Seleucus' father. But then in 198 BCE the Seleucid king Antiochus III defeated the Egyptians, and Palestine became part of his empire. To begin with, the Seleucids permitted the Jews to retain their distinctive religious practices. All this changed in 168 BCE, when the Seleucid king Antiochus IV (who rather immodestly chose to call himself 'Epiphanes', a word which means 'illustrious') was prevented by the Romans from conquering Egypt and so strengthening his empire further. Seeking to reassert his authority in Palestine and recover some of his financial losses, he tried to impose Greek religion on the reluctant Jews. He banned distinctive Jewish practices like sabbath observance and circumcision and even set up an altar to Zeus in the temple at Jerusalem. Here, in outright and very public contempt for the sensibilities of the native population, he sacrificed a pig, an animal regarded as 'unclean' in Jewish ceremonial law.

This was too much. In 166 BCE an armed resistance movement gathered round an elderly priest named Mattathias, who lived with his five sons in the village of Modein, 20 miles north-west of Jerusalem. Known as the 'Maccabees' after Mattathias's successor, his third son was Judas Maccabaeus (the 'Hammer'), they defeated Antiochus's troops, reoccupied Jerusalem and restored the temple. Jewish people celebrate this victory to this day in the annual Feast of Hanukkah. These events are set out in 1 Macabbees (part of the Apocrypha, a selection of writings that were not included in the Jewish canon of the Old Testament) and Book 12 of *The Antiquities of the Jews* by the Jewish historian Josephus (c.37–c.100 CE).

With the support of the Romans to keep the Syrians at bay, the Jews now in power (known as the Hasmonean dynasty, after Hasmon, the great-grandfather of Mattathias) were responsible, over the next 100 years, for enlarging the territory of the Jewish state beyond the borders of Judea. Its zenith was reached during the reign of Alexander Jannaeus, who came to the throne in 103 BCE. Eventually, though, squabbles among the leading families led to decreasing control and a loss of independence. Hyrcanus II succeeded to the throne in 67 BCE, but his brother Aristobulus led a revolt against him. Both sides appealed to Rome for help and the Roman general Pompey decided to back Hyrcanus, probably because, being weaker, he was likely to be easier to control. When Aristobulus reacted by seizing Jerusalem, Pompey and his army laid siege to the city in 63 BCE. They captured it after three months and Pompey established Roman rule in what was now an important frontier post for the whole empire. The empire inherited by Hyrcanus II was broken up and he was left to rule over a much-reduced territory.

The five Herods

With the Hasmoneans unable to maintain control, the Romans eventually replaced their dynasty with Herod the Great (c.74–3 BCE), who became ruler of Judea in 37 BCE. Herod's father, Antipater, had been the chief minister of Hyrcanus. Herod himself showed his mettle early on as ruler of the fiercely independent region of Galilee. Charged with the illegal execution of his opponents, he withdrew to Syria, where he stayed until being recalled to help Hyrcanus ward off an invasion inspired by his nephew Antigonus (the son of Aristobulus) and the Parthians, attacking from the north-west of Syria. Although the invaders were repelled, they tried again the following year in 40 BCE. This time they were successful. Herod's brother, Phasael, committed suicide and Herod himself fled to Egypt, leaving the surviving members of his family to take refuge in the desert fortress of Masada by the Dead Sea. From Egypt, where he was welcomed by Cleopatra, Herod went to Rome and succeeded in persuading the emperor that he alone could both govern Palestine successfully and keep the Parthians at bay. Returning to Judea, Herod eventually gained control of the whole country, finally taking Jerusalem and bringing the Hasmonean dynasty to an end by executing Antigonus in 37 BCE.

As 'King of the Jews', Herod was a loyal friend and ally of Rome but less appreciated by his Jewish subjects, despite the prosperity they enjoyed under his rule and the fact that he had forged an alliance with the Hasmonean royal family by marrying Hyrcanus' granddaughter, Miriam. The problem was that, as well as having supplanted the Hasmonean dynasty, he was only half Jewish, with ancestors from among the Edomites (also known as the Idumeans), ancient enemies of the Jews (e.g. Nu 20:14–21). His first act on being proclaimed king in Rome had been to offer sacrifice to the Roman god Jupiter, something that was hardly likely to endear him to his new subjects back at home. He also interfered with the senior religious appointment in Jerusalem. Traditionally, the high priest was a descendant of Zadok, the first holder of the office in the reign of King David. Following the Babylonian exile, the high priest also served as head of state. The custom whereby one individual held both offices was continued by the Hasmonean rulers, but Herod's non-Jewish origins meant that he himself could not possibly become high priest. Unwilling to undermine his position by appointing a member of the

Hasmonean family, Herod selected a priest called Hananel for the office instead. Before long, however, he was persuaded by his wife Miriam to replace him with her brother, Aristobulus. This Hasmonean victory was short lived. When the first public appearance by Aristobulus led to talk of rebellion against Herod, the king had him drowned, passing the tragedy off as an accident. Herod's ruthlessness and cruelty in the exercise of power are also reflected in the violent deaths he prescribed for two of his wives and three of his sons and the episode described in Matthew 2:1–16 highlighting his reaction to news of the birth of Jesus. His private life was one of great turmoil. He married ten times and many of his problems were caused by the competitive efforts of his wives and mothers-in-law to secure the interests of their children. Even so, Herod's commercial, military and political skills enabled him to consolidate his rule during a time of great upheaval in the Roman Empire. Indeed, the Romans trusted him sufficiently to extend his territory when neighbouring rulers proved less able.

After 35 years in power, Herod the Great died in 4 BCE. The Romans confirmed the wishes expressed in his final will that his kingdom be divided among three of his remaining sons:Archelaus (see Mt 2:21), Herod Antipas (see Lk 14:1–12) and Philip (see Lk 3:1). Archelaus was made 'ethnarch' (i.e. not quite 'king') of Judea, Samaria and Idumea. He ruled for ten years before the Romans stripped him of his title and banished him for incompetence. He was replaced by Coponius, the first of a series of regional governors, known as 'procurators', who were based in Caesarea and operated under the overall authority of the governor of Syria. The governor Quirinius is mentioned in the New Testament (see Lk 2:2) as undertaking a census of the area in order to assess the people for taxation purposes. This was bitterly resented by the Jews, despite the efforts of the then high priest to persuade them to go along with it. The opposition, which centred around Judas the Galilean and a Pharisee called Zadduk, led to the establishment of the Zealots as a movement (see below) and the replacement of the high priest with Annas (Lk 3:2, Jn 18:13, 24; Ac 4:6).

The best known of these Roman procurators is Pontius Pilate, who ruled from 26 to 36 CE. He was the Roman governor before whom Jesus was tried and sentenced to death. The ruling Jewish council in Jerusalem (known as the Sanhedrin) had the authority to try Jews for religious offences and could impose a sentence of up to 39 lashes. But when they judged Jesus guilty of a capital offence, they had to bring him before Pilate. Since Herod had curtailed the powers of the Sanhedrin, Pilate was the only one with the legal authority to pass the death sentence on those under his jurisdiction (see Mt 27:1–2).

Unlike his predecessors, Pilate was less than tolerant of Jewish sensitivities and caused great offence by, for example, bringing Roman standards (which incorporated a picture of the emperor) into Jerusalem in defiance of the Jewish law against such images. His incitement of the people frequently led to uprisings, which he was quick to put down with savage ferocity. It was this that led to his ultimate undoing. Following a massacre of Samaritans at Mount Gerizim in 36 CE, Vitellius, who was governor of Syria, relieved Pilate of his office and sent him back to Rome in disgrace.

Herod Antipas ruled as 'tetrarch' (i.e. ruler of a quarter of a nation) of Galilee and Perea. He was the Herod who had John the Baptist executed after he objected to the way Antipas had divorced his wife in order to marry Herodias, the wife of his half-brother, Herod Philip. Jesus had less than complementary things to say about him (see Mk 8:15 and Lk 13:31f.). Along with Pontius Pilate, Antipas was involved in the trials of Jesus (Lk 23:6–12).

Philip (not to be confused with Herod Philip mentioned above), whose territory was up in the north-east of Palestine, developed the town of Caesarea Philippi, to which he gave both his own name and that of the emperor. He ruled until 34 CE.

Back down south, the nation was not entirely done with the descendants of Herod. Alexander, one of Herod's sons, had been executed by his father in 7 BCE. His son was Herod Agrippa I, most of whose early life was spent amassing enormous debts in Rome. His only hope lay in the fact that he was a close friend of Caligula, who became emperor in 37 CE. Caligula made Agrippa king of Philip's old realm in the north-east of Palestine. Meanwhile, Antipas was still tetrarch of Judea. His wife, Herodias, was incensed that her husband was of lesser rank than his nephew and so persuaded him to go to Rome and ask Caligula to make him a king as well. Caligula's response was to depose Antipas altogether and give his territory to Agrippa. After the assassination of Caligula, Agrippa's role in helping Claudius claim the imperial throne led in 41 CE to his being given the whole of the territory ruled over by his grandfather. After 45 years of division, Herod the Great's kingdom was thus reunited. Agrippa managed to combine loyalty to Rome with devotion to Judaism, two features which were combined in his evident willingness to persecute the infant Christian church (see Ac 12:1–4). Luke also takes the trouble to record his sudden and gruesome death at the age of 54 (see Ac 12:19b–23).

His son, Herod Agrippa II, was only 16 years old at the time of his father's death, and so considered too young to inherit the whole of the kingdom. The result was that Roman procurators were reintroduced, beginning with Cuspius Fadus in 44 CE. Two of his successors appear in the New Testament – Antonius Felix (in power from about 52 to 60 CE) and Porcius Festus (60–62 CE). From Festus' point of view, Agrippa II's familiarity with Jewish customs made him the ideal arbiter in a case involving the apostle Paul. Luke describes the trial in Acts 25:13–26:32. By this time, Agrippa II was king of the realm formerly ruled over by his great-uncle Philip, together with other territory ceded to him by the emperor Nero, who succeeded Claudius in 54 CE.

Life under Rome

Like the Greeks before them, the Romans preferred, where they could, to leave local structures and customs in place. But those who caused trouble, as the Jews of Jerusalem discovered in 70 CE, were punished without mercy. Under the weak leadership of Festus' successor, Albinus, law and order had broken down as Jewish nationalism grew stronger in the early 60s. Nero replaced him with the much harsher Gessius Florus, but it was too late. The Zealots instituted a revolt which spread rapidly and led to the defeat of the Romans in Jerusalem. Such a challenge to Roman authority could not go unnoticed. In 67 CE, command of the war was given to the experienced general Vespasian. With his son, Titus, Vespasian began the systematic reconquest of the country, cutting Jerusalem off in preparation for a final assault. With Vespasian pursuing his imperial ambitions in Rome, it was left to Titus to lay siege to Jerusalem. Despite their fanatical devotion to their cause, the Zealots defending the city were no match for the might and persistence of Rome and Jerusalem finally fell in 70 CE. Its walls were flattened and Herod's magnificent temple – finally completed only six years earlier – was totally demolished.

Sixty years later, a further revolt took place against Roman rule, led by Simon Bar-Kokhba and provoked by plans to build a temple to Jupiter on the temple site in Jerusalem. When this uprising had been crushed, Jerusalem was rebuilt as Aelia Capitolina and Jews were banned from entering it on pain of death. They were not allowed to return until the fourth century.

Such Roman intolerance of dissent is reflected in the New Testament's account of the anxiety of the city clerk in Ephesus when his fellow citizens came close to rioting, an event which Luke describes at the end of Acts 19. Those who behaved were largely left alone, as long as they kept the peace and paid their taxes.

Roman taxation was one of the issues that caused particular resentment among the Jews. They had to pay poll taxes to Roman officials, assessed by means of regular censuses (see Luke 2:1–2) on the basis of their property and income. What irked them particularly was that Roman taxes had to be paid in Roman currency which, since it bore the stamp of the emperor's head, was seen to break Jewish prohibitions against the making of idols reflected in the second of the Ten Commandments (see Ex 20:4). As if this was not bad enough, they were also required to pay a variety of indirect taxes – import and export duties, road tolls and the Roman equivalent of a value added or sales tax. The right to collect these on Rome's behalf was auctioned every five years. Not surprisingly, those who took up this potentially lucrative business opportunity were hated and despised, both for collecting taxes in the first place and for their habit of taking more than was due in order to line their own pockets (see Lk 3:13; 19:8). This is why tax collectors, an entirely innocuous group of professionals in our own day, appear as the epitome of villainy in the New Testament (e.g. Mt 18:17; Lk 18:9–14).

But it wasn't all bad news. In return for this heavy burden of taxation, the subjects of the Roman Empire enjoyed a period of relative peace (the *Pax Romana*) and stability. This was due in no small part to Roman administrative ability, especially the efficiency of the army, a highly professional and well-organised force. Roman skills in building were – and still are – much in evidence, with roads a particular priority, both so that the army could move rapidly through potentially hostile territory and also so that trade could flourish. To be a Roman *citizen* (as opposed to a subject) conferred considerable privileges, as shown by the stir caused when the apostle Paul revealed his status on one occasion (see Ac 22:22–29). Top of the tree were those who, like the apostle Paul, were born as Roman citizens. But you could become a second-class Roman citizen by paying '*a big price*' (Ac 22:28) for it. A Roman citizen could not be subjected to the degradation of being whipped (let alone being crucified, which is why it is usually thought that Paul was executed by being beheaded) and also had the privilege of a personal appeal before Caesar, a right which Paul himself chose to exercise when on trial before Festus (Ac 25:11).

While the existence of the Roman Empire had many advantages for Christianity, there was also another side to the coin. One of the ways in which the Romans sought to hold their enormous empire together was through the cult (i.e. worship as God) of the Emperor. For most of the people they conquered, this presented no major problem. Adding another god to the list of those they already had by saying 'Caesar is Lord' and sprinkling some incense on an altar was neither here nor there. Under Roman law, Jews were regarded as a special case and allowed to get away without having to fulfil such tests of loyalty. To begin with, since most Christians came from a Jewish background, Christianity was viewed as a Jewish sect and so treated in the same way. But as more and more Gentiles became Christians, it became apparent that Christianity and Judaism were distinct. Many of those who became convinced that 'Jesus is Lord' and refused to compromise their allegiance to Christ suffered a great deal in consequence. Something of this tension is revealed in 1 Corinthians 12:3.

——— Questions to consider ———

1 What do you think life in Palestine would have been like in the first century?
2 In what ways was the Roman empire (a) a help and (b) a hindrance for the early Christians?

4

THE PEOPLE AND DAILY LIFE OF THE NEW TESTAMENT

Particular groups

The New Testament refers to a number of particular groups within Palestine during the time of Jesus and his apostles.

First, the **Pharisees**, of which there were about 6,000 in Jesus' day. While some were priests and others worked as professional scholars (the 'teachers of the law': see below), most, like the apostle Paul, had secular jobs. They were addressed as 'Rabbi' (derived from the Hebrew for 'great one', coming later to mean 'teacher'). The word 'Pharisee' means 'separated one' and comes from their desire to maintain the purity of the Jewish faith against the onslaught of hostile foreign influences represented by what they saw as the insidious influence of Hellenization. They began as a development of the Hasidim shortly after the Maccabean revolt and took the view that Jewish difficulties were ultimately caused by their failure to obey God's Law properly. They responded by trying meticulously to keep every one of the commandments and seeking to encourage others to do so as well. On top of the 613 commandments they counted in the Law itself, they built a complex structure of additional regulations designed as a hedge around it in order to keep people from accidentally breaking the rules.

Life could become very complicated under such a regime. For example, the law on tithing (giving to God a tenth of what you produced) was applied in minute detail, even to herbs grown in the garden! Despite this, they seem to have had the respect of ordinary people for generally practising what they preached. But they attracted the condemnation of Jesus for preaching the wrong things in the first place. According to him they were unable to see the wood for the trees. Matthew's Gospel records Jesus' verdict on one occasion: *'Woe to you, teachers of the law and Pharisees, you hypocrites! You give a tenth of your spices – mint, dill and cummin. But you have neglected the more important matters of the law – justice, mercy and faithfulness. You should have practised the latter, without neglecting the former...'* (Mt 23:23). Not surprisingly, the Pharisees were deeply suspicious of Jesus and what they saw as his attacks on much that they held dear. Although there were some Pharisees among his followers – notably Nicodemus (Jn 3:1; 7:50; 19:39; see also Ac 15:5) – most were opposed to him. Indeed, the Gospels report the Pharisees as prime movers in the conspiracy which led to Jesus' death (e.g. Mt 12:14).

Although there was overlap between the Pharisees and the **teachers of the law**, they were distinct groups. The teachers of the law (also referred to as the **scribes** in some older translations) were a professional class who could trace their history back to the time of Ezra at the end of the Babylonian exile in the middle of the sixth century BCE (see Ne 8:9). Their job was to preserve the written law and the oral traditions developed from it, to pass it on to groups of pupils and to administer it as judges in the Sanhedrin (see below). There were two main schools of thought within the teachers of the law. One followed the strict teaching of Rabbi Shammai, while the other, dominant in Jesus' day, followed the more liberal approach adopted by Rabbi Hillel. The apostle Paul was a pupil of Hillel's grandson, Gamaliel, who is referred to in Acts 5:34 and 22:3 as a Pharisee, teacher of the law and a member of the Sanhedrin.

Another major group were the **Sadducees**. They were much smaller in numbers than the Pharisees but wielded considerable influence. Their origin is disputed, though most of them were priests and many came from wealthy families and were used to being in positions of authority. They formed the dominant power block within the Sanhedrin. Whereas the Pharisees were keen on maintaining religious purity, the Sadducees were more interested in holding on to the political power and privilege delegated to them by the Romans. They exercised this through the 71-member council known as the **Sanhedrin**. Based in Jerusalem, this body was the supreme court and council of the Jews, responsible for interpreting the Law of Moses in the light of current concerns. When he came to power, Herod the Great executed 45 of its members for having previously opposed him, and reduced its role to that of a forum for the discussion of purely religious matters. The New Testament records appearances by Jesus before this group, as well as Peter, John, Stephen and Paul. The Sanhedrin members were anxious lest Jesus and his followers undermine the status quo. John's Gospel draws attention to the depth of their concern (see Jn 11:45–54).

When it came to religion, the Sadducees were conservatives who would only take what the Pentateuch (the first five books of the Old Testament) had to say as authoritative. This meant that they refused to accept the validity of all the additions to the law which the Pharisees taught. They also rejected any ideas that they did not think could be decisively demonstrated from the Pentateuch. Among these was belief in the coming of a Messiah, the existence of angels and the resurrection of the dead. This latter issue lay at the root of a discussion with Jesus on one occasion (see Mt 22:23–32 and parallels). Luke reports how Paul was able to exploit the differences between Pharisees and Sadducees on this same issue when he was on trial. When Paul claimed that he was being tried for his belief in the resurrection of the dead, furious arguments broke out between Pharisees and Sadducees and the proceedings had to be abandoned (see Ac 23:1–10). With the destruction of the temple in 70 CE and consequent loss of their power base, the Sadducees soon died out, leaving the Pharisees as the dominant group to set the direction of orthodox Judaism for future generations. The **Herodians** were a group consisting mainly of Sadducees who chose to support the Herodian dynasty. They are mentioned in the New Testament as enemies of Jesus – once in Galilee, and again at Jerusalem (Mk 3:6; 12:13; Mt 22:16).

Way back in Israel's history, members of the tribe of Levi had been selected to take a lead in the nation's worship, an honour which stemmed from their refusal to join their fellow Israelites in a particular instance of rebellion against God (see Ex 32:25–26). They were known as the **Levites**. They were originally set apart specifically for religious duties and had to be supported by contributions (tithes) from the members of the other tribes. Within the tribe of Levi, the **priests** and the **chief priests** came from the descendants of Aaron. Over all of them was the **high priest**, appointed year by year (e.g. Jn 11:49;

18:23). Only priests could offer sacrifices in the temple and only the high priest could enter the holiest part of the temple on just one day each year, the 'Day of Atonement'. John the Baptist's father, Zechariah, was a priest (Lk 1:5–25) who served on a rota which split his time between serving in the temple at Jerusalem and being at home with his family in the country. Levites were responsible for other aspects of worship, including the music.

The **Essenes**, numbering about 4,000 people, displayed an enthusiasm for strict religious purity which was even greater than that of the Pharisees – so much so that many of them withdrew from normal life altogether. Their headquarters was at Qumran, near the Dead Sea, where a monastic community of Essenes lived and worked. Like the Pharisees, their origins go back to the time of the Maccabees in the second century BCE. They are not mentioned in the New Testament but have come to prominence in recent years with the discovery in 1947 of the so-called Dead Sea Scrolls and the subsequent excavation of nearby ruins. The collection of scrolls includes manuscripts of the Old Testament and other Jewish writings, together with works by the Essenes themselves. These show their disdain for those of their fellow Jews who had sold out to secular influences and their expectation that God would break in to assert his sovereignty and install them, the Essenes, as his chosen people. Archaeological evidence from Qumran shows that the site was abandoned between around 40 BCE and 4 CE (perhaps as a consequence of the Parthian invasion). Resettlement was followed by a violent end during the war with Rome in 68 CE. It's been suggested that early Christianity was influenced by the Qumran community. Although it's true that they do have certain features in common, there are also many striking contrasts which make any direct connection unlikely.

Not everyone was prepared to wait so patiently for freedom from Rome. A group known as the **Zealots** was founded by Judas the Galilean (referred to in Ac 5:37) and Zadduk the Pharisee in 6 CE to protest against the payment of taxes to Rome, which they regarded as an act of treason against God. They were seen as the first-century counterparts of those who had opposed Antiochus IV Epiphanes a century and a half earlier. One of the disciples of Jesus is described as 'Simon the Zealot' (e.g. Mt 10:4), though this may be a reference to his temperament rather than his political affiliation! The Zealots were a splinter group of the Pharisees who sought to take direct guerilla action in order to secure their ends and, as we saw earlier, were especially active during the war with Rome which began in 66 CE.

Their stronghold was the fortress of Masada, which overlooks the Dead Sea at its narrowest point. After the fall of Jerusalem, the Romans laid siege to Masada and overcame it in 73 CE. Rome's usual technique was to blockade a fortress so that its defenders were kept in, cut off from outside help and eventually starved into submission. Battering rams and enormous catapaults would also be used in order to undermine defensive walls. But Masada's enormous supplies of food and water, together with its impressive natural defences, meant that it could not be overcome by this method. There was no way the surrounding cliffs could be stormed directly, and so the Romans had to resort to building an enormous ramp, a task which took seven months. When they finally broke through, they discovered that all but a handful of the occupants, nearly 1,000 people, had committed suicide. This defeat marked the end of the Jewish state until its revival in 1948.

Next we come to the **Samaritans**. John's Gospel includes the stark comment that '...*Jews do not associate with Samaritans*' (Jn 4:9). This is putting it mildly! The antipathy between them stemmed from the fact that after the exile of the northern kingdom of Israel by the Assyrians in 722 BCE, Samaria was recolonised largely by foreigners (see 2 Ki 27:24–41) who intermarried with the few native Israelites who remained and with those who returned from exile half a century later. This was too much for their southern Jewish neighbours, who branded them as heretics and refused to have anything to do with them. In time, the Samaritans developed their own distinctive brand of Judaism, which included the building of their own temple on Mount Gerizim (which they justified from their way of interpreting the text of Deuteronomy 27:4). This is the point of difference with mainstream Judaism which lies behind the discussion between Jesus and a local Samaritan woman in John 4:19–22.

As the years went by, the rift between Samaritans and Jews deepened as each in turn sought to do the other down. For example, Sanballat, the governor of Samaria, strongly opposed the rebuilding of Jerusalem in the time of Nehemiah (around 440 BCE). Later, during the Maccabean revolt, although the Jews sought to stand firm, the Samaritans came to a compromise with Antiochus IV Epiphanes and dedicated their temple to the Greek god Zeus. Forty years later, the

Jewish king Hyrcanus exploited Jewish ascendancy over Samaria by capturing Shechem and destroying the Gerizim temple. During Herod the Great's reign, relations seem to have improved somewhat, but the rapprochement came to a bitter end when a group of Samaritans scattered human bones in the grounds of the temple in Jerusalem.

Jesus' attitude to the Samaritans stands in marked contrast to most of his fellow Jews (see Jn 8:48 for example!), including some of his own disciples (see Lk 9:52–56). As well as the encounter with Samaritan villagers referred to in John 4, a Samaritan is the hero in one of the most famous of Jesus' parables (Lk 10:30–37). Samaria was specifically included in the ever-widening circle of those to whom the early church was told to preach the gospel (Ac 1:8) and Luke goes on to record how they actually did so (Ac 8:5–25). The descendants of the Samaritans continue to live in Israel to this day, still maintaining their distinctive forms of worship.

Daily life

Jesus' habit of telling stories or parables based on the ordinary incidents of life tells us a great deal about what it must have been like in his time. Like much of the world today, first-century Palestine was a land of contrasts. This is graphically illustrated by the parable of the rich man and Lazarus: *'There was a rich man who was dressed in purple and fine linen and lived in luxury every day. At his gate was laid a beggar named Lazarus, covered with sores and longing to eat what fell from the rich man's table. Even the dogs came and licked his sores...'* (Lk 16:19–21). It's no exaggeration. If you were wealthy, you would live in luxury, probably in a town, with servants to look after you. But if, like the majority of the population, you were poor, your income would be far from certain. The more fortunate would have been taught a trade by their father – as Jesus himself seems to have been. Many of those without a steady job would have been casual labourers whose day's wage depended on the whim of those who hired a group of workers each morning (Mt 20:1–16). Failing this, and in times of misfortune, you might well be reduced to a life of begging or even slavery (Mt 18:25).

Clothing in the first century was much simpler than it is today. Most garments were made from wool, though linen was also used (made from flax grown in the Jericho area or imported from Egypt). Both men and women would normally wear an ankle-length tunic next to the skin, often held at the waist by a belt (which could also be used as a purse). A cloak could be worn over this, especially at night or if the weather was cool during the day (see Mt 24:18). Jewish law required the cloak to have tassels attached to its four corners (Nu 15:37–41). Each tassel was to include a blue cord and was intended as a way of helping people to remember to keep God's Law.

In the account of Jesus' crucifixion in John's Gospel, the soldiers divided his cloak between them but because his tunic was 'seamless, woven in one piece from top to bottom' (Jn 19:23), they decided to gamble for it rather than tear it into pieces. For special occasions, a long flowing garment known as the 'stole' was worn. In the parable of the Prodigal Son, this would have been *the best robe* (Lk 15:22), brought out to celebrate the younger son's return home. If shoes were worn at all, they would generally have been leather (or perhaps wooden) sandals.

In the modern world, the ability to turn on a tap for a plentiful supply of water is something most people are able to take for granted. But for the ordinary citizens of Palestine in New Testament times, an adequate water supply was nothing like as straightforward. Rain was virtually unknown in the summer months and they had to rely on streams, wells and storage cisterns. It's little wonder that one of the central features of the picture of heaven presented in the book of Revelation is *the river of the water of life, as clear as crystal, flowing from the throne of God and of the Lamb down the middle of the great street of the city* (Rev 22:1–2). The local well would be a natural centre of village life, a fact implied in the way the Samaritan woman in John 4:6–7, perhaps ostracised by her community, had to come to fetch water at mid-day (*the sixth hour*), when no-one else would be around.

The lack of a secure water supply was one of the major weaknesses affecting the city of Jerusalem, especially when under siege. Part of the answer was provided by King Hezekiah in about 702 BCE. 2 Kings 20:20 records his achievement in excavating a tunnel 630 metres long from the spring of Gihon outside the city to the Pool of Siloam. By New Testament times this was supplemented by a series of overground aqueducts.

Though water and milk were drunk, there was always the danger of their being polluted. This problem, together with the answer to it, is reflected in a reference in Paul's first letter to his young friend Timothy: *'Stop drinking only water, and use a little wine because of your stomach and your frequent illnesses'* (1 Ti 5:23). Juice would have been extracted from the grapes by people trampling on them, a process which perhaps added a certain piquancy! It would then be stored in cool cellars in jars or leather bottles made, usually, from goatskins. A small hole allowed gases to escape while fermentation took place. Fresh juice was put into new skins rather than old ones which, having already stretched, would be liable to split under the pressure exerted by the wine as it matured. Jesus uses this observation to illustrate the impossibility of seeking to constrain the new wine of his teaching in the old wineskins of conventional Judaism (see Mt 9:14–17 and parallels).

The range of food was much more limited in New Testament times than it is today. Seasonal vegetables (e.g. beans, onions, lentils, leeks, cucumbers), flavoured with herbs and salt, and bread (made from wheat or barley flour) provided the basis of a staple diet. There would also have been fruit (though not the citrus fruits for which Palestine is known today), together with nuts, honey and cheese. Fish were plentiful, especially around Galilee, and could be preserved by drying and salting. Meat would have been something of a luxury. For the Jew, there were strict regulations about which animals could be eaten and which were regarded as 'unclean'. This raised problems in the mixed community of the early church whose Gentile believers did not share these views. Luke records how the apostle Peter was led to change his mind on this matter (see Ac 10:9–15) and how the church as a whole dealt with the problem (see Ac 15:1–33).

Although life was hard for the ordinary people of Jesus' day, it had its lighter moments. Feasting, singing, story-telling and dancing all had their place as recreational activities. Games, both indoor and outdoor, were also popular. Archaeologists have discovered a number of gaming boards with playing pieces, one particularly well-preserved example coming from what may well have been the Roman garrison in Jerusalem where Jesus was tried before Pilate.

Growing up

The arrival of a new child was a particular cause for rejoicing. As Psalm 127:3–5 puts it: *'Sons are a heritage from the Lord, children a reward from him. Like arrows in the hands of a warrior are sons born in one's youth. Blessed is the man whose quiver is full of them. They will not be put to shame when they contend with their enemies in the gate'*. By the same token, infertility was a serious social stigma, as shown by the reaction of John the Baptist's relatively old and previously childless mother Elizabeth to her surprise pregnancy: *'The Lord has done this for me,'* she said. *'In these days he has shown his favour and taken away my disgrace among the people'* (Lk 1:25; compare verse 7).

The Gospel accounts of the naming of John the Baptist (Lk 1:59–63) and Jesus (Mt 1:21; Lk 1:31– 33; 2:21) when they were eight days old show how names had special significance and were thought to represent the child's character. At the same time, boys would be circumcised. In addition, a first-born son would be presented in the temple to be offered to God and then redeemed by the sacrifice of two doves or pigeons. Luke records this event in the life of Jesus (Lk 2:22–40, cf Ex 13:1–16).

Circumcision was performed for its religious significance rather than for any other reason. Though not unique to the Jews, the Bible records this as an essential mark of the relationship between God and his people from the time of Abraham (Genesis 17:10–14). Because it was so deeply ingrained in their culture, some Jews who converted to Christianity found it very difficult to accept that it was not necessary for Gentile Christians also to be circumcised in order to become proper believers. The apostle Paul decisively rejects this view as totally contradicting what Christianity is all about. He deals with the subject quite heatedly in his letter to the Galatians (see especially 5:2–12 and 6:12–15).

Schooling for Jewish boys (girls were not thought worth the expense and trouble of a formal education) took place at the local synagogue from the age of five or six. During the reign of Herod the Great, the Pharisees instituted a nationwide programme of education. The main focus was on learning the religious and moral law contained in the Torah. Otherwise, as soon as they were able, children were occupied in the work of their parents on the farm, in the workshop or around the home. At the age of 13, boys were initiated into religious and legal maturity. Before this time, a father was responsible for the deeds of his son.

Most children would marry in their mid-teens, their partner being chosen for them by their parents, who would also negotiate an amount to be paid to the bride's father as compensation for the loss of the useful work his daughter would have continued to do as a member of his household. A year-long period of betrothal or engagement would follow while arrangements were made for the marriage itself. This would be made the excuse for lavish celebration, often going on for several days. An engagement was much more binding in Bible times than it is in modern Western society. The narrative of Matthew's Gospel begins with an account of how Joseph, about to break off his engagement to Mary because she had become pregnant, was told about the extraordinary circumstances of Jesus' conception and urged to go ahead and marry her (1:18–25). Several of Jesus' parables allude to the celebrations which accompanied the marriage ceremony (e.g. Mt 9:14–15; 22:2–14; 25:1–13; Lk 14:8–11) and John records that Jesus' first miracle was performed at a wedding feast (Jn 2:1–11; see also 3:26–30).

Old Testament law recognises the possibility of a husband divorcing his wife (thought not vice versa) and includes appropriate regulations for her protection (Dt 24:1–4). The schools of Rabbi Hillel and Rabbi Shammai (see p. 59) differed in their understanding of what Deuteronomy 24 means by a husband finding 'something indecent' about his wife and so being permitted to divorce her. The former saw it as anything at all which the husband found displeasing, while the latter restricted the grounds for divorce to unfaithfulness. In Matthew's Gospel, Jesus is recorded as supporting Shammai's interpretation (5:31–32; 19:3–12). Although the parallel passages (Mk 10:2–12; Lk 16:18) do not specifically mention *any* permitted grounds, this is probably because they would have been taken for granted in the case of infidelity. 1 Corinthians 11:6–15 reflects the concern of the early church to take sexual morality more seriously than their pagan contemporaries. Women in the church were to wear their hair long, probably because short hair was the mark of a woman found guilty of adultery.

In biblical times, women tended to be treated as possessions rather than people in their own right. Daughters could be sold into slavery without the prospect of release enjoyed by their brothers in the same position (see Ex 21:7). A woman was only able to inherit from her husband or father if there were no male heirs to whom the property could go. And unless a woman's husband or father gave permission, she could not make any legally-binding vows. In the light of this, the attitude of Jesus is refreshing. Luke's Gospel in particular brings out his refusal to go along with many of the discriminatory conventions of his time, but to welcome and accept those in society who were looked down on by others. In the early church, women clearly exercised a considerable degree of leadership and ministry (e.g. see Paul's list of greetings in Romans 16; also Ac 21:9). And although Paul is often castigated for his attitude to women, seeing what he wrote in context (both textually and culturally) very much reduces the evidence for the misogynist label that is applied to him. For example, his instruction that wives should submit to their husbands (Eph 5:22) needs to be seen in the context of what, in the first century, would have been the quite astonishing instruction that husbands should actually love their wives (Eph 5:25)!

Agriculture

Agriculture was a major source of employment in a culture whose people were heavily dependent on what they could produce for themselves. Palestine was noted for its rich and fertile soil and deserved its description as 'a good and spacious land, a land flowing with milk and honey' (e.g. Ex 3:8). Not that it was always easy. Pests, diseases, adverse weather (especially drought) and the risk of raiders combined to make life potentially hazardous for those whose livelihood depended on what they could grow.

So, as is still the case in many parts of the world today, it was hard and sometimes frustrating work. Animals might be harnessed for their ability to pull ploughs along, but apart from this, most of the work had to be done by hand, using the most basic implements.

They grew wheat and barley which, once the fields were cleared of stones, were sown from mid-November to mid-January. The procedure was either to sow first and then plough the seed into the ground or to plough first, scatter the seed into the furrows and then send the oxen back to trample the seed into the ground. The relative inefficiency of such methods is reflected in Jesus' famous parable of the sower (see Mt 13:3–9 and parallels). This story also indicates some of the continuing work that had to be done once the seed was sown: the hungry birds that had to be kept away from the seedlings and the weeds that had to be picked out (though see Mt 13:24–30 for another way of dealing with this particular problem).

The crops would be ready for harvesting around April and May. The whole family would be involved in this work and, if the fields were extensive, casual labourers would be hired on a daily basis. In Matthew 9:36–39, Jesus uses this as an illustration of the spiritual harvest of people that is ready to be gathered in and the need for his disciples to pray that more workers will join in.

Once harvested, the corn would be threshed to separate the grain from the stalks and husks. This was done by animals either trampling on the corn or pulling a threshing-sledge in circles while tethered to a central pole. The crop would now be ready for winnowing. In this process, the farmer would toss the chaff and grain into the air with a large wooden fork. The heavier grain would fall into a pile and be separated from the lighter chaff which would tend to blow away in the breeze. John the Baptist used this as a picture of the way Jesus would judge humanity and separate the good from the worthless: '*His winnowing fork is in his hand, and he will clear his threshing floor, gathering his wheat into the barn and burning up the chaff with unquenchable fire*' (Mt 3:12). The completion of the harvest was a time of great celebration (the Feast of Weeks or Pentecost) as the back-breaking work came to an end for another year and the people were able to celebrate the safe ingathering of enough food to see them through the coming months. Luke 12:16–21 records a parable of Jesus that warns against the danger of such celebrations being unduly self-centred and leading people to forget the ultimate source of their good crops. Grain could be roasted and eaten as required or it could be ground into flour and made into bread. It was stored domestically in large pottery jars or in stone-lined silos buried in the floor or in the ground outside the house. Archaeologists have also found large communal store houses which enabled the authorities to store and ration grain during times of famine or siege.

Once the wheat and barley harvests were over, landowners could focus on their vineyards and olive trees. These needed relatively little attention apart from care of the soil and, in the case of vines, regular pruning to ensure that they concentrated on producing fruit rather than wood. Jesus used this as a vivid illustration of how God deals with his followers in order to make their lives more fruitful (see Jn 15:1–8). Harvesting took place between August and October and was followed by another opportunity for celebration: the Feast of Ingathering. Some of the olives would be preserved in salt water, to be eaten later, but most were crushed to provide olive oil, useful both in cooking and as a source of fuel for lamps (e.g. Mt 25:1–13).

The Bible's frequent references to sheep reflect the significant part they played in the economy, so much so that they almost represented a unit of currency. Most families had at least a few of them as a source of meat, wool and milk. Caring for them was hard work. For one thing, they needed to be protected from wild animals such as the lion and the bear mentioned by David when referring to his shepherding days (1 Sa 17:34–35). The New Testament reflects their propensity for wandering off and getting lost and their consequent vulnerability to attack (e.g. Mt 9:36; 10:6, 16; Ac 20:28–29; 1Pe 2:25; Rev 7:17). They also needed to be provided with adequate pasture and water, something which often necessitated travel far from home. Sheep also play an important role in several of Jesus' parables (see Mt 12:9–14; 18:12–14; Lk 15:4–7; 17:7–10) and one of the most abiding pictures of the relationship between Jesus and his followers is that of the shepherd and his sheep (e.g. Jn 10:1–18; Heb 13:20). This reflects a similar Old Testament image of how God relates to his people, the most famous example of which is in Psalm 23.

Sheep were not the only animals to be put to good use. Herds of goats were kept for their milk, meat, hair and even skins which, when cleaned, served as useful containers. The fact that goats were often kept alongside flocks of sheep lies behind Jesus' description of the way he would, at the end of time, *separate the people one from another as a shepherd separates the sheep from the goats* (Mt 25:32). Oxen were also kept, not so much for food as for their ability to pull ploughs and carts.

Sickness and healing

A variety of illnesses is mentioned in the New Testament, often in connection with the healing ministry of Jesus. Skin diseases were common and are often referred to as 'leprosy' in the Bible. But although leprosy as we know it today was certainly prevalent in the first century, the term covers a much wider range of skin diseases than this.

To be able to restore sight to the blind and hearing to the deaf was seen as one of the signs associated with the coming of the Messiah (see Isa 29:18). Mental disturbance is also reported on several occasions in the New Testament. The concept of madness was clearly understood (e.g. Ac 26:24–25) and needs to be distinguished from cases of demon possession which, though they sometimes have parallels with psychiatric disorders, cannot be entirely accounted for in these terms.

Paul describes Luke as *our dear friend, the doctor* (Col 4:14) who accompanied him on some of his travels. Doctors in the ancient world were usually trained by being apprenticed to those with greater experience, though by New Testament times there were also medical schools. Surgery was performed, though the only operation mentioned in the Bible is the minor procedure of circumcision (see above).

Frankincense and myrrh, two of the gifts from the wise men to the infant Jesus (Mt 2:11), were used for a number of medicinal purposes. Modern science has discovered that myrrh helps to prevent the growth of some bacteria, thus confirming the wisdom of its use in ancient medicine. Potions to ease pain were also available and the Gospel writers record Jesus' refusal to take such a mixture while he was being crucified (Mt 27:34). In Jesus' parable, the Good Samaritan went to the victim '...and bandaged his wounds, pouring on oil and wine' (Lk 10:34). It may be that the reference to oil in James 5:14 has medicinal as well as religious significance.

Modern Western culture tends to try to protect us from the impact of death. But in biblical times death was very much an openly acknowledged 'fact of life'. Mourning was both public and demonstrative, with uninhibited expressions of grief (e.g. Lk 8:52). The hot climate demanded that burial take place as soon as possible – on the same day if death was a result of execution. Bodies would be embalmed with linen cloths and special spices. It was the impossibility of finishing this procedure before the Sabbath began that resulted in a group of women coming to the tomb of Jesus *very early on the first day of the week'* (Mk 16:2) to complete the job, only to discover that his tomb was empty. Cremation was almost unknown. Coffins were not used, though bones would sometimes be collected and stored in a special box known as an ossuary. Wealthy people (like Joseph of Arimathea, in whose tomb Jesus was buried – Mk 15:46) would have family burial chambers cut into the rock in which several corpses could be laid to rest.

Jewish worship

There are plenty of references to Jewish religious practice in the New Testament.

The first book in the Old Testament records the way God made an agreement or covenant with Abraham, the first of the patriarchs, who lived around 4,000 years ago. God calls him to leave his homeland with the promise that *'I will make you into a great nation'* (Ge 12:2). Although a childless old man aged 99 with a barren wife aged 90, God promises that he will have a son and become *'the father of many nations'* (Ge 17:4). In response, he and his male descendants are required to undergo circumcision as a physical sign of the covenant, to offer sacrifices and to give tithes (a tenth of their produce) to God. All these practices continued into New Testament times.

In Israel's hey-day, the **temple** in Jerusalem built by Solomon was the great centre for worship and a focus for nationalistic fervour, indicating the supremacy of the God of Israel. Its destruction by the Babylonians in 587 BCE was a great shock. Although it was rebuilt by the returning exiles under the direction of Nehemiah, it never achieved its former significance. Indeed, despite the fact that this second temple stood for almost 500 years, we know very little about it. It was dismantled and rebuilt by King Herod, primarily in order to try to win favour with his Jewish subjects. His aim was to recapture something of the splendour it had in Solomon's day. Beginning in 19 BCE, the main structure was completed within ten years, but the building was not fully completed until 64 CE. Even taking into account all his other construction activity, Herod's temple was his greatest building achievement.

Herod's Temple

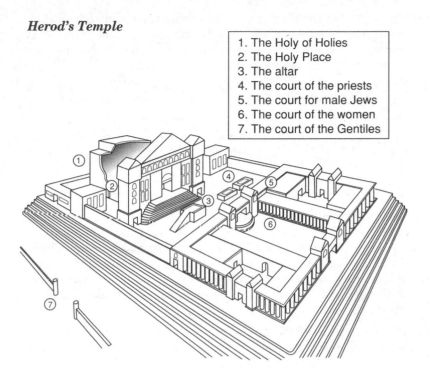

1. The Holy of Holies
2. The Holy Place
3. The altar
4. The court of the priests
5. The court for male Jews
6. The court of the women
7. The court of the Gentiles

Herod built his temple with its surrounding courts on a huge 30-acre site. To prevent the most holy parts of the site from being defiled, he even had 1,000 priests trained as carpenters and stonemasons. The whole area, known as the 'Court of the Gentiles', surrounded by colonnades and gateways, was open to all. Towards the centre of this area lay three other courts to which there was restricted access. Notices in Greek and Latin threatened death for any Gentiles who crossed the boundary. Acts 21:26–31 describes the uproar that resulted when some Jews thought Paul had taken a Gentile in with him. Inside this court, known as the Court of Women, were the Court of Israel (the normal limit for Jewish men) and the Court of the Priests (usually for priests only, except during the Feast of Tabernacles, when Jewish laymen were allowed in) where the altar was situated. Within this area was the temple proper, with its Holy Place and Holy of Holies, separated from each other by an enormous curtain. The Gospels record the tearing of this in two, from top to bottom, at the moment of Christ's death (e.g. Mt 27:50–51).

The temple was a busy area, with a regular routine of services and sacrifices. There were animals being bought and sold, together with the clamour of money-changers exchanging Roman money for shekels so that it could be paid as temple tax. All this distracting activity so provoked Jesus that he cleared the area on at least one occasion (Mt 21:12–13). It was also a popular meeting place. Teachers would gather with their disciples and, especially during the major Feasts, the area would attract pilgrims from all over the world (Ac 2:9–11).

Herod's temple must have been an impressive sight, faced in cream marble, overlaid with gold and 'adorned with beautiful stones and with gifts dedicated to God' (Lk 21:5). But, as Jesus predicted, it didn't last long. The capture of Jerusalem in 70 CE by the Romans under Titus, son of the emperor Vespasian, led to its complete destruction and the end of the Jewish nation as a separate state until the modern era.

The destruction of Solomon's temple and exile of Jews to Babylon 657 years earlier had far-reaching consequences, one of which was the development of the **synagogues**. These arose as places where Jews, unable to use the temple in Jerusalem, could still gather together (which is what the word 'synagogue' means) for worship. They would often be constructed on the model of the Jerusalem temple, though when it came to what went on in worship, the sacrificial rituals of the temple were replaced by prayer and the reading of Scripture. Teaching in the synagogue was one of the main ways in which both Jesus and Paul exercised their public ministry (e.g. Lk 4:15–30; Ac 13:13–43).

To set up a synagogue required just ten Jewish men. If there were any fewer than this or if a suitable building could not be found, then they would gather at a 'place of prayer', often by a river (so that they could perform ritual washings). Luke mentions a visit made by the apostle Paul to such a site in Philippi (Ac 16:12–14). Both in Palestine itself and wherever else in the world communities of Jews found themselves, the local synagogue became an important focus for their life and identity. The central focus of the building was the box (or 'ark') in which the Old Testament scrolls were kept. But as well as being the place for worship, the local synagogue also functioned as the school, the town hall and the aid centre for the poor. To be expelled from the synagogue was therefore to incur a severe penalty (see Jn 9:22; 12:42; 16:2). By the first century, synagogues were widespread – to the extent that there may have been as many as 400 in Jerusalem alone.

A Synagogue

1. The Holy Ark – a cupboard for the Scrolls of the Law.

2. The bimah – a raised platform with a desk from which the scrolls are read. In Jesus' day it would also have a seat from which the preacher gave his sermon.

3. Seats for the men – on the ground floor. In Jesus' day the seats probably ran along the walls, leaving more space for people to gather.

4. The balcony for the women and children. They were separated from the men.

Public worship was conducted weekly on the Sabbath and on special festival days. Services of prayers and readings would be held, with a sermon and concluding blessing. Luke's Gospel records an occasion near the beginning of the ministry of Jesus when he chose, read and expounded a passage from the book of the prophet Isaiah. The reaction to what he had to say on this occasion was quite dramatic (see Lk 4:16–30)! The presence of synagogues all over the Roman empire was one of the factors that helped the spread of Christianity. Acts 17:1–4 illustrates the way in which the Christian missionaries would usually begin with the Jewish community centred on the synagogue before moving on, where they could, to the Gentile population.

Pagan belief and thought

In some ways, the religious life of the first century was not dissimilar to that of today. Devotion to the traditional gods and goddesses of Greece and Rome was waning, although there was political pressure to maintain the cult of the emperor. Even in places like Ephesus, centre of the cult of Artemis (the Greek equivalent of the Roman goddess Diana), the commercial anxieties of those who made their living selling silver shrines seemed to be at least as important as concerns for the goddess's honour (see Ac 19:23–41). There were many alternative belief systems waiting to fill this spiritual vacuum. There was a growing interest in magic, astrology and the occult and ways of manipulating these forces through what we now call 'mystery religions', with their esoteric ceremonies.

For Greeks and Romans disillusioned by the moral decline in their own culture, Judaism had many attractions. It was fairly straightforward and easy to understand, its Scriptures were readily accessible (see below) and it promoted standards of ethical behaviour which many were ready to embrace. Those who converted fully to Judaism became '**proselytes**'. Others, enthusiastic for Judaism's moral code but not quite so keen on the ritual aspects of Jewish law (such as circumcision), became known as '**God-fearers**'. One of these, a Roman centurion called Cornelius, was one of the first Gentiles to become a Christian (see Ac 10).

Others were quick to follow and it was not long before every major centre in the Roman Empire had at least the beginnings of a group of

Christians. The process which began on the Day of Pentecost with representatives from all over the known world (Ac 2:5–11) spread with astonishing rapidity.

───────── **Away from home** ─────────

Despite years of seeking to consolidate their identity in Palestine, Jews in the first century of the Common Era were scattered all over the world. This process, sometimes known as the 'Diaspora' (from the Greek for 'dispersion'), had begun with the exile of Jews from Israel to Assyria in the eighth century BCE and from Judah to Babylon in the sixth century BCE. With the conquest of Babylon by Cyrus the Persian in 539 BCE, the Jews were allowed to return home. But many of them, having adapted successfully to life outside Palestine and to worship without the temple, chose to remain behind. Babylon was by no means unique in this. Jewish communities became established all over the Mediterranean world, so much so that by the first century of the Common Era there were an estimated 4,000,000 living in the Roman Empire, some 7 per cent of the entire population. Of these, only 700,000 were living in Palestine.

Not that they lost all their links with home. For one thing, all Jewish men between the ages of 20 and 50, no matter where they lived, were required to pay the temple tax of half a shekel once a year just before the Passover (see Ex 30:11–16; Mt 17:24–27). Those with the necessary resources would make regular pilgrimages to Jerusalem for the major feasts, a fact reflected in the presence of so many different nationalities in the capital on the Day of Pentecost (see Ac 2:5–11). Young Jewish boys would often be sent back to Jerusalem for their education – the apostle Paul being a prime example (see Ac 22:3). At the other end of the scale, then as now, pious Jews would return to die and be buried in Jerusalem in order to be among the first to greet the Messiah at the resurrection.

Outside Palestine, one of the most important centres was the Egyptian city of Alexandria, founded in 332 BCE by, as its name implies, Alexander the Great. Ptolemy I settled captives from Palestine there in 312 BCE. Egypt also served as a refuge for Jews wanting to escape from trouble back home – one famous example of this being Joseph, who took Mary and Jesus there when they were under threat from King Herod (Mt 2:13–15). A considerable Jewish community was based at Alexandria from the start. They occupied their own quarter in the north-east corner, but had places of worship all over the city. One of these synagogues was so vast that the congregation's responses in worship could only be kept together by the use of flags as signals! By the time of Jesus, there were probably more Jews living in Alexandria than there were in Jerusalem.

Alexandria is renowned as a leading centre of learning, with the most famous library in the ancient world. It is also the place where the Greek version of the Old Testament known as the Septuagint (usually abbreviated to 'LXX') was produced. Such a translation became necessary as, away from their homeland, many Jews forgot the Hebrew in which the Scriptures were written and the Aramaic which was spoken in Palestine. In fact, by the time of Jesus, Hebrew had more or less disappeared as a living language and even though the official language of the empire was Latin, everyone spoke Greek. The production of the Septuagint had the added benefit of opening up the Scriptures to their Greek-speaking neighbours, many of whom, as we have seen, decided to follow the Jewish way of life. In addition, the Targums (oral translations of the Old Testament into Aramaic) were beginning to be written down for the benefit of those who did not understand Hebrew.

Throughout history, Jews living outside their country have received a mixed response from those amongst whom they have settled. This was certainly true in New Testament times. Although, as we have seen, some chose to embrace Judaism, Jews were frequently the target of attack, not least because of the way they refused to blend in with the society around them. Their loyalty was suspect because they would not break their own law by offering official sacrifices. And they had to be excused from military service because they were unable to march (which they saw as a form of work) on the Sabbath.

As we have seen, many Gentiles were influenced by Jewish thought, especially as the Septuagint became available and they were able to read the Scriptures for themselves. But the traffic was far from being one way. Especially in Alexandria, Judaism and, later on, Christianity, were both profoundly affected by Greek patterns of thought. Among the most famous names in this connection is Philo, a Jewish philosopher from Alexandria who used allegory to interpret the Old Testament in a way which appealed to the Greek world.

Questions to consider

1 In what ways did the Pharisees and the Sadduccees differ from one another? How did this diversity affect Jesus and his disciples?
2 Compare and contrast your own lifestyle with that of people in New Testament times.

5

THE TRANSLATION
OF THE NEW TESTAMENT

Latin

Down the years, the New Testament has been translated into more languages than any other work of literature. Early on, it was translated into Latin, the official language of the Roman Empire. Many later copies of these so-called 'Old Latin' versions survive to this day, providing important evidence of how the text was passed on down the years. The need for a standardised Latin text led to the production of what we now call the Latin Vulgate (from the Latin *vulgata versio*, meaning 'common version'), compiled by St Jerome (*c.* 342–420) between 383 and 405 CE. Jerome, the finest scholar of his day in Western Christendom, was secretary to the Pope, St Damasus (*c.* 304–84), who commissioned him to undertake this new translation after promulgating a Canon of Scriptural Books at a Council in 382 CE. Of the many different Latin translations which were circulating in the fourth and fifth centuries, Jerome's became the one which, eventually, most people accepted and used. So much so that on 8 April 1546 the Roman Catholic Council of Trent pronounced an anathema (i.e. excommunication) on anyone who did not accept the Vulgate as *the* authentic version of the Bible.

– Syriac, Coptic, Gothic and Slavonic –

Back in the second century, translators had begun work on translating the Greek New Testament into Syriac, a precursor of Arabic and a dialect of the Aramaic language which Jesus himself spoke. Several different Syriac versions have survived. Indeed, the early fifth-century translation (known as the Peshitta, or Syriac Vulgate) is still used by some churches today in the Middle East and India. It is notable for having been transmitted with particular accuracy: no other ancient version has so few variant readings. Similar translation projects were undertaken elsewhere. For example, translations of the different Egyptian Coptic dialects were made from about the third century, and the Coptic Bible continues to be used in worship today.

The conversion of the Roman Emperor Constantine (d. 337) to the Christian faith in 312 CE led to the rapid spread of Christianity and to an increasing need for new translations of the Bible. A famous example of such work is that done by Ulphilas (c. 311–83). Although born as a Goth, he spent much of his life in Constantinople, becoming the city's bishop in 341. Later he returned as a missionary to his native country and was the first to translate the Bible into the Gothic language. However, he is recorded as having omitted the Old Testament Books of Kings – lest his rather belligerent fellow citizens be adversely influenced by all the wars which they describe!

The official version of the Russian Orthodox Church today dates from the time of St Cyril (826–69) in the ninth century. He and his brother, St Methodius (c. 815–85), known as the 'Apostles of the Slavs', were sent as missionaries to what is now Moravia, where St Cyril took a great interest in the language, developed what we now know as the Glagolitic alphabet and circulated a Slavonic version of the Bible.

English

In Britain, too, there were isolated examples of translation into the vernacular. The earliest known example dates from the beginning of the eighth century when St Aldhelm (d. 709), Abbot of Malmesbury and subsequently Bishop of Sherborne, translated the Psalms. At the other end of the country, St Bede (c. 673–735) undertook translation work into his native Anglo–Saxon in response to the fact that many of his priests could not read Latin. A letter written by his disciple Cuthbert reveals that he was engaged in the work of translating John's Gospel even while on his death bed on Ascension Day in 735. Another well-known figure from history, King Alfred (849–899), is famous not only as the founder of English law and a prominent burner of cakes, but also as a noted translator of various parts of the Bible, including the Ten Commandments, parts of Exodus 21–23, some of the Psalms and sections of the New Testament book of Acts.

Go into any religious bookshop today and the choice of versions available in English is bewildering! But there hasn't always been this enthusiasm for people to be able to read the Bible in their own language. Not until the days of John Wycliffe (c. 1330–84) were efforts made to provide a complete English translation. But there was stiff opposition from the church authorities (which were at this time Roman Catholic) and this became a key issue in the events of the Protestant Reformation. Church officials were afraid that uneducated common people might misinterpret the Bible and distort its teaching if they could read it for themselves. On the other hand, retorted the translators, having the Bible in their own language might enable people to understand its true message and so recognise the errors being perpetrated by the church's official teaching. The result of such conflict was that scholars who undertook translation work were condemned as heretics, imprisoned and even executed. But they pressed on, Wycliffe taking the view that 'Christ and his apostles taught the people in the tongue that was best known to the people. Why should not men do so now?' He published the first full English translation of the Bible, itself based on a translation of the Latin Vulgate, in 1382. Most of the actual work of translation was done by Nicholas of Hereford (d. c. 1420) and John Purvey (c. 1353–c. 1428), who revised the work in 1395. Since this was all before the invention of printing, each copy had to be painstakingly and expensively hand-produced. About 170 copies still exist today.

Printing

The famous Gutenberg Bible, a version of the Latin Vulgate, was the first major work to emerge from the presses of the inventor of printing, Johann Gutenberg (c. 1396–1468), in 1456. Versions in German, Italian, Dutch and Catalan followed during the next few years.

Even though there was a considerable influx of Greek manuscripts to the West after the fall of Constantinople in 1453 and consequent exile of Christian scholars, it took quite some time for the first Greek New

Testament to be printed. This was partly because of the large variety of type required. Although the Greek alphabet has only 24 letters, printers needed some 200 characters to cope with the varied forms of the individual letters and the different combinations of letters (like, in Old English, the character 'æ'). In addition, printers were unwilling to be seen to be undermining the prestige and authority of the Latin Vulgate. Eventually, though, the first printed Greek New Testament emerged from the presses in 1514–17. This was the conclusion of a project suggested by Pope Leo X and begun by the Spanish cardinal Francisco Ximénez de Cisneros (1436–1517) in 1502. It forms part of the Complutensian Polyglot Bible (owing to the Latin name of the town where it was printed, Complutum, and the several different languages it contains). Although this was the first Greek New Testament to be *printed*, it was not actually circulated until 1522.

The first *published* Greek edition of the New Testament to appear in print was by the Dutch scholar Erasmus (1469–1536). It was printed at Basel, Switzerland, by John Froben in 1516. Erasmus included his own translation into classical Latin. Here is his vivid affirmation of the value of such work: 'I wish that the Scriptures might be translated into all languages, so that not only the Scots and the Irish, but also the Turk and the Saracen might read and understand them. I long that the farm labourer might sing them as he follows the plough, the weaver hum them to the tune of his shuttle, the traveller beguile the weariness of his journey with their stories'.

Based in the German city of Cologne, Peter Quentel began to produce the first major printed English translation of the New Testament in 1525. It was based on a translation made by William Tyndale (c. 1494–1536). He too mentions farm workers in his defence of his work to a fellow clergyman: 'If God spare my life, 'ere many years I will cause a boy that driveth a plough to know more of the Scripture than thou dost'. The Bishop of London, Cuthbert Tunstall (1474–1559), had refused support for Tyndale and his translation project in England, so he had emigrated to Germany to continue his work there, moving from place to place in order to avoid discovery and disruption by his enemies. Tyndale's translation is from the Greek text of Erasmus rather than Latin. Only two copies of this first edition are known to be in existence today. One is in the British Museum, which bought it from the Bristol Baptist College for £1,000,000 in 1994. The other is in the library of St Paul's Cathedral in London. One reason why so few survive is that Bishop Tunstall bought up large quantities in order to burn them! But Tyndale could not be put off so easily and by 1566 his work had been revised twice and reprinted 40 times. The quality of Tyndale's work is reflected in the fact that about 90 per cent of his translation was subsequently reproduced in the King James Authorized Version.

Tyndale was betrayed, arrested and executed before he could complete his translation of the Old Testament, and so it was left to Miles Coverdale (1488–1568), building on Tyndale's work, to produce the first printed English translation of the whole Bible, a project which he completed at Zurich in 1535. His was the first Bible to include a summary of contents with each chapter. Four years later, with the benefit of other Hebrew and Greek texts then available, Coverdale produced what became known as the *Great Bible* because of its larger than usual pages. By this time, attitudes to the English Bible were very different. The king, Henry VIII (1491–1547), ordered that every parish church was to have 'a book of the whole Bible of the largest volume in English' which was to be set 'in some convenient place within the church, whither your parishioners may most conveniently resort to the same and read it... It is the very living Word of God that every Christian person is bound to embrace, believe and follow if he look to be saved'. Such official approval was not to last. Even before Henry's death, these English translations were forbidden and large numbers were destroyed. But so many were already in use that the *Great Bible* survived in the churches throughout the reign of Edward VI and even Mary, even though services went back to being said in Latin.

Meanwhile, the first English Bible actually to be printed in England had been produced in 1537, usually called *Matthew's Bible*, but actually published by John Rogers (c. 1500–55), who used the name 'Thomas Matthew' as an alias. Rogers, a colleague of Tyndale's, became the first Protestant to be martyred in the reign of Mary for his refusal to embrace Roman Catholic doctrine. *Matthew's Bible* was one of the first to be 'set forth with the King's most gracious licence', a privilege also granted to Coverdale's Bible.

The first printed New Testament to be divided into verses was produced in Geneva in 1557, intended particularly for Protestants exiled during the reign of Mary. The complete Bible, known as the *Geneva Bible* or, more popularly, the *Breeches Bible* (from its translation of Genesis 3:7 in which Adam and Eve are said to have '...*sewed figge leaves together, and made themselves breeches'*), was printed in 1560 and dedicated to Elizabeth I. As might be expected from its city of origin, its marginal notes reflect a markedly Protestant and Reformed theology. It was the first version to display each verse as a paragraph and to print in italics words which did not appear in the original text but were added to make the sense clearer. Its second edition dates from 1562 and is called the *Placemaker's Bible* owing to a misprint of Matthew 5:9 – *'Blessed are the placemakers'* instead of *'Blessed are the peacemakers'*. It certainly showed up the shortcomings of the *Great Bible*, however, and so, a few years later, Archbishop Matthew Parker (1504–75) began a revision of the *Great Bible* which incorporated some of the *Geneva Bible's* readings while omitting some of its more controversial marginal notes. This was published in 1568 and is known as the *Bishops' Bible*. It has the distinction of having certain passages marked as unedifying and so not to be read in public! The Roman Catholic Church, though not yet ready to acknowledge the right of lay people to read the Bible in their own language without special permission, allowed the production of the *Douai-Reims Bible* in 1609 (the New Testament having appeared in 1582). This began as the work of English scholar Gregory Martin (d. 1582) who, together with a number of colleagues, had moved to France at the beginning of the reign of Elizabeth I and established a college, first at Reims and then at Douai. As a translation of the Vulgate, his version is in places little more than an anglicisation of the Latin (e.g. Philippians 2:8 reads *'He exinanited himself'*) and so it was not ideally suited for use in public worship or private devotions. In response to this, Bishop Richard Challoner (1691–1781) issued two revisions of the Old Testament and five of the New up to 1772. His final revision replaced the original Douai as the official Roman Catholic version.

—— The Authorized Version ——

In 1611, James I (1566–1625) gave his approval to what we now call the *Authorized Version* (AV), though it was not in fact formally authorised at all. It is also known, especially in the United States, as the *King James Version* (KJV) because of the way it received, in the words of its dedication, 'approbation and patronage from so learned and judicious a Prince as Your Highness is...'. It had the advantage of having been produced by a committee of 47 scholars rather than an individual, a group whose work was partly organised by the king himself. Their work has remained, for well over 300 years, *the* English Bible. At the king's insistence, the AV was not to include any of the contentious marginal notes which prevented other versions from being widely accepted. Despite the claim on its title page that it was 'newly translated out of the original tongues', it was actually based on the *Bishops' Bible*. It also took other versions into account, including the *Geneva Bible* and the *Reims* New Testament. Its preface sets out the translators' purpose not 'to make a new translation, nor yet to make of a bad one a good one... but to make a good one better, or out of many good ones one principal good one, not justly to be excepted against'. The Anglican *Book of Common Prayer* of 1662 uses it for the text of the Epistles and Gospels in the lectionary (though not for the Psalms) and it retains a special place in the affections of English-speaking Christians throughout the world. Not that the AV today is exactly the same as that produced in 1611. Over the years, the spelling has been modernised and other changes, some deliberate, some accidental, have crept in. One of the most famous examples of a careless misprint occurs in what has become known as the *Wicked Bible*, where the 'not' is omitted from the seventh commandment in Exodus 20:14, leading to the reading *'Thou shalt commit adultery'*. For this mistake, the king's printers were fined £300, an enormous sum in those days, by Archbishop Laud.

Two factors have served to undermine the dominance of the AV in recent years. The first is the discovery of more reliable and accurate Greek and Hebrew manuscripts. This means that modern translators can improve on the work of their predecessors by providing a more accurate rendering of the likely original. The methods employed by textual critics in this work are examined more closely in Chapter 6. The second arises from the recognition that English has changed a great deal in the last 350 years. Many people today find it very difficult to make sense of the undoubtedly beautiful but sometimes rather quaint text of the AV.

This has led to a flood of new translations being produced over the last hundred years or so. Some are revisions of the AV, while others are completely new translations and paraphrases.

Revisions of the Authorized Version

In 1870, the Church of England's Upper House of Convocation in the Province of Canterbury initiated the process which resulted in the AV being revised in the light of recent manuscript evidence. The 54 translators, appointed from across the Protestant denominations, were to make as few alterations as possible in the language of the AV. Any changes in the Greek and Hebrew text were only to be adopted with the agreement of a two-thirds majority. This *Revised Version* (RV) of the New Testament was published in 1881, with about 36,000 changes to the text of the AV. The whole Bible appeared in 1885. Much of the improvement to the Greek text from which the translators worked was due to two Cambridge scholars, B.F. Westcott (1825–1901) and F.J.A. Hort (1828–1902). They decided that the readings in the newly available so-called Alexandrian texts were often to be preferred to the Byzantine (also called the Syrian) text from which the AV had been translated.

While the Old Testament received a largely favourable response, the reaction to the revision of the New Testament was rather more mixed. For one thing, the quality of the underlying textual criticism did not meet with universal approval. In particular, the Dean of Chichester, J.W. Burgon (1813–1888), could not accept that God would have allowed the text of Scripture to be corrupted, even in the relatively minor ways that Westcott and Hort sought to demonstrate, and argued strongly for the primacy of the Greek text on which the AV is based. Doubts were also cast on the RV's merits as a work of literature. Its quest for accuracy of translation (for example, unlike the AV, the RV seeks to translate each occurrence of every Hebrew or Greek word with the same English word) meant that stylistic elegance received a lower priority.

Some American scholars involved with the RV project produced the *American Standard Version* (ASV) in 1901. This was revised as the *New American Standard Version* (NASV) in 1971. More recently, the *New King James Version* (NKJV) of the New Testament was published in 1979 in the USA. The British edition is known as the *Revised Authorized Version* (RAV).

The *Revised Standard Version* (RSV) of the New Testament was produced in 1946, with the Old Testament following six years later. The RSV is a revision of the ASV (itself a revision of the AV) and so tends to adhere to the style of the old version. A 'Catholic edition' of the RSV was produced in 1965 (New Testament) and 1966 (Old Testament). The official acceptance of this version signalled a formal end to Roman Catholic insistence since the Council of Trent that the Vulgate text should be supremely authoritative. An ecumenical edition appeared in 1973 as the *Common Bible*, and the *New Revised Standard Version* (NRSV) was issued in 1989. Among other changes, it seeks to eliminate gender-specific language.

—— New translations into English ——

In 1946, the Church of Scotland took the lead in gathering together a joint committee of non-Roman Catholic scholars to produce a completely new translation. Adopting a much more contemporary idiom, the New Testament section of the *New English Bible* (NEB) was published in 1961, with the complete NEB being made available in 1970. In 1989 it was revised in the light of more recent textual scholarship and changes in English usage and issued as the *Revised English Bible* (REB).

Roman Catholic translations include the *Westminster Version of the Holy Scriptures*, the New Testament of which was published in 1935, and the version of R.A. Knox (1888–1957), the New Testament of which dates from 1945. In 1966 an English version of the 1955 Roman Catholic French *La Bible de Jérusalem* was brought out as the *Jerusalem Bible* (JB). Its lively and modern style has met with approval from many Protestants as well as Roman Catholics. A revision of this was published as the *New Jerusalem Bible* (NJB) in 1985.

The *New International Version* (NIV) was published in 1973 (New Testament) and 1978 (Old Testament). The NIV includes the principle of *dynamic equivalence* in translation. This means that, rather than translate the text literally, an attempt is made to convey the impact the original would have had on its first readers. For example, the phrase translated literally in James 5:4 as the *'Lord of sabaoth'* (AV) or *'Lord of hosts'* (RSV) is rendered as the *'Lord Almighty'* in the NIV. In recognition of continued changes in English usage, an inclusive language edition of the NIV New Testament, Psalms and Proverbs was published in 1995, with the complete Bible expected to follow in 1996. As with the NRSV, gender-specific references to people have been changed, though language relating to God remains masculine.

A translation which relies even more heavily on dynamic equivalence is *Today's English Version* (TEV), first published in 1966 and known also as the *Good News Bible* (GNB). Its translators aimed to provide a version which would be clear for people who have no Christian background, those without much formal education, and those who use English as a second language. Technical religious terms are avoided and, at the other end of the scale, so are all slang expressions.

Paraphrases

Obviously, Greek/Hebrew and English are very different, not only in vocabulary but also in structure and style. Translating from one to the other forces scholars to make choices. A translation which keeps very closely to the exact words and phrasing of the original may look stilted and not come across at all well in English prose. With this in mind, some scholars have opted to go for readability above everything else. Their primary aim is to communicate the *ideas* in the text as clearly as possible and so, where necessary, they opt to gloss over the *precise* meaning of the text and 'paraphrase' it instead. One such is J.B. Phillips' *New Testament in Modern English* which appeared as one volume in 1957. Another is Kenneth Taylor's *Living Bible* (LB), the New Testament of which was first published in 1966. More recently, a very lively and contemporary translation by Eugene H. Peterson entitled *The Message* has been published by the Navigators, a world-wide movement which emphasises the continuing relevance of Bible study. Translations like this are excellent for reading through and getting the general sense of the text, but are not recommended for more careful study.

As the above shows very clearly, readers of English have an embarrassment of riches when it comes to translations of the Bible. Not all language groups are so fortunate. According to the Ethnologue database in March 1995, there are currently 6,721 languages being spoken in the world. Of these, only 2,065 have some or all of the

Bible: 299 have the whole Bible, an additional 752 have the New Testament and another 1,014 have at least one book of the Bible. Groups such as Wycliffe Bible Translators are working all over the world to improve these statistics and make the Bible available to the millions of people who cannot yet read it in their own language.

Questions to consider

1 What is the origin of the Latin Vulgate translation of the Bible?
2 Why was there so much opposition to the production of English translations of the Bible during medieval times?
3 What lies behind the undermining of the dominance of the 'Authorized Version' of the Bible during the last hundred years or so?
4 Why is Bible translation such a difficult task?

6

THE TEXT
OF THE NEW TESTAMENT

We know a little from the New Testament documents themselves about how they were first written. Towards the end of Paul's Epistle to the Romans, Tertius, presumably writing at Paul's dictation, includes a personal greeting (Rom 16:22) while Paul writes the conclusion to his Epistle to the Galatians (Gal 6:11–18) and the whole of the Epistle to Philemon (Phm 19) in his own hand (see also 1 Co 16:21). But, apart from these tantalisingly brief references, the process of how the New Testament was first committed to writing remains largely unknown.

It would be wonderful if, tucked away in the world's museums and libraries, we had access to the originals of each New Testament book (known technically as the 'autographs'), all signed and dated by their authors! Unfortunately, as with all ancient literature, we have no such thing and have to rely instead on copies, translations and quotations in other writings, most of which date from hundreds of years after the originals were first written. A further factor to take into account is that many of the manuscripts to which we have access differ from one another to a greater or lesser degree. All of which begs the question: how do we know that the New Testament we have now bears any resemblance to what the authors originally wrote? The answer is that we can be reasonably sure that it does. In fact, the manuscript evidence for the New Testament far outweighs that of any other piece of classical literature. Even examples of other Christian literature have nothing like as many surviving manuscripts. For example, there is only one complete manuscript (dating from as late as the year 1056) of the *Didache* (from the Greek for 'teaching'), a manual on Christian behaviour and church practice dating from the first or second century.

———— Papyrus and parchment ————

Ancient manuscripts were written by hand (the word 'manuscript' derives from the Latin *manus*, meaning 'hand' and *scriptum*, meaning 'something written') using papyrus or parchment. Most papyrus came from Egypt, where the shallow waters of the Nile delta provided excellent conditions for its cultivation. In addition, Egypt's dry and warm climate has proved to be an ideal environment for the preservation of ancient papyri.

Papyrus was made by taking lengths of the papyrus plant's pith, cutting them into thin strips and laying them side by side. A second layer, with fibres running at right-angles to the first, would be placed on top and the two layers would then be pressed together to form a single sheet. About 20 of these would be cut to size and then glued together to make a roll. Although both sides would usually be used, it was easier to write on the side where the fibres ran vertically (known as the *recto* side) rather than the reverse where the pen would go against the grain (the *verso*). A roll was known in Greek as a *biblion* (from the name of the plant, *byblos*, itself related to the Greek name of a town in Phoenicia). Greek-speaking Christians called the collection of Old and New Testament books or rolls *ta biblia*, 'the books', from which comes the Latin word *biblia* and the English word 'Bible'.

Parchment is thought to derive from the Asian city of Pergamum (near Bergama in modern Turkey), mentioned in Revelation 2:12–17. It was developed as a result of a ban on the export of papyrus which was imposed by Egypt in order to try to undermine a growing challenge to the supremacy of the library at Alexandria by its rival at Pergamum. Parchment is a much stronger material which was made from the skins of animals (the younger the better). These were first soaked in a caustic solution in order to loosen the hair and remove any flesh. After being shaved, washed, dried and stretched, they were then smoothed down with pumice stone and finally dressed with chalk. Parchment was used by those who could afford it to preserve a permanent record of what was written. Not only is it stronger and more durable than papyrus, but it is also easier to write on using both sides (e.g. see Rev 5:1), though its edges are inclined to become ragged and uneven. It is also far superior to untreated leather, with which it should not be confused. Top-quality parchment, for which the hair and flesh sides were carefully prepared so that they became indistinguishable from one another, is known as vellum and was usually made from calfskin.

Sheets of papyrus or parchment were glued together to make scrolls about 10 metres in length. These were awkward to handle, a fact which hastened the development, late in the first century or early in the second, of the book form we use today. Such a volume is called a *codex* (from the Latin for 'block of wood', 'block split into leaves or tablets' and hence 'book'). Whereas the New Testament would take up several unwieldy scrolls, it could be fitted into a single codex and so prove much easier to handle and use.

Writing

Pens were made from reeds which were cut and specially sharpened or, later on, from quills. Text was written in columns about 6 to 9 cm wide. In the ancient world, a form of 'joined–up' writing (known as a 'cursive' or 'running' script) would be used for everyday items like shopping lists and receipts, while literary works were written in a style more like our capitals, with the individual letters separated from each other. This style is known as 'uncials' (from the Latin for 'a twelfth' since there were usually 12 characters per line) or 'majuscules'. Early in the ninth century, this was replaced by a new running script whose letters are known as 'cursives' or 'minuscules' (from the Latin for 'rather small'). The noun 'minuscule' must not, by the way, be confused with the adjective 'miniscule'! The earliest example known today is the Leningrad Gospels (MS. 219), dating from 835. Surviving cursives outnumber uncials by about ten to one. This script was indeed more compact, much quicker and so a significantly cheaper way of writing. Another means of saving space and time was to contract certain *nomina sacra* (a Latin expression meaning 'sacred names'). For example, Χριστος (Christos) would be written as ΧC, eliminating all but the first and the last letters. Such a contraction would be indicated by placing a horizontal bar above the letters. (The final 'C' in the above example is an early form of the capital letter sigma (equivalent to the English letter S), known as a 'lunate sigma' because of its crescent shape. The more familiar Σ form was a later development.)

Ordinary copies were written in black or brown ink with decorated headings, usually coloured red. Standard ink was made from charcoal, gum and water (references to ink appear in 2 Co 3:3, 2 Jn 12 and 3 Jn 13). De-luxe editions with complex ornamentation and the use of several different colours were also produced, much to the disgust of St Jerome (c. 342–420): 'Parchments are dyed purple, gold is melted into lettering, manuscripts are decked with jewels, while Christ lies at the door naked and dying' (Epistle 22.32). Colour plays an important part in the manuscript identified as Codex 16, a copy of the Gospels dating from the fourteenth century. Just as it's possible today to buy a special 'red-letter edition' of the Bible, in which the words of Jesus are printed in red, so Codex 16 has the words of Jesus, his genealogies and the words of angels in crimson. Quotations from the Old Testament and the words of what might be described as the 'goodies' are in blue, while the 'baddies' (who include, for some reason, the shepherds!) are in black. The rest of the text is in vermilion.

To begin with, copies would be produced individually as scribes sought to reproduce the text from the best available manuscript laid out in front of them (the 'exemplar'). Then, during the fourth century, multiple copies began to be made. Instead of looking at the 'exemplar', a group of scribes would listen to the manuscript being read out loud. Such transcription was arduous and exacting work, as shown by some of the colophons, or notes, which frequently appear at the end of books. One such comes across as a metaphorical sigh of relief: 'As travellers rejoice to see their home country, so also is the end of a book to those who toil in writing'.

Identifying manuscripts

Until the seventeenth century, the only widely available text of the Greek New Testament was one of Byzantine origin dating from some time after the sixth century. It was naturally accepted as *the* traditional text and called, after a comment in the Preface to the second Elzevir edition from 1633, the *Textus Receptus* (from the Latin for 'received text'). But then other manuscripts came to light (notably the

Codex Alexandrinus: see below) which differed significantly from this Byzantine-based text. Such discoveries convinced scholars that the Greek of the original must have been rather different. Not that this happened overnight. The strong attachment to the *Textus Receptus* proved difficult to break, partly because to suggest that it might contain errors was felt to undermine the authority of the Bible. Eventually, though, scholars such as the German Karl Lachmann (1793–1851) took the plunge, abandoned the *Textus Receptus* and prepared a text of the New Testament which was based completely on the older manuscripts.

The modern system of identifying manuscripts goes back to the work of the Swiss scholar Johann Jakob Wettstein (1693–1754). He used capital letters from the Latin and Greek alphabets (plus ℵ, the Hebrew letter aleph) to identify uncial manuscripts and Arabic numerals for cursive manuscripts. In the nineteenth century, Caspar René Gregory, originally from the United States, introduced some refinements to Wettstein's system. Under his system, papyrus manuscripts are designated by a capital 'P' followed by a superscript numeral (known as a 'siglum'). Nowadays, some authors identify papyri by using 'P' while others use the Old English letter 𝔓 or the abbreviation *pap.*

When the number of uncial manuscripts outgrew the number of capital letters available to describe them, the same letters came to be used to identify two or three different manuscripts. For example, Codex Bezae contains the text of the Gospels, Acts and the Catholic Epistles, while Codex Claromontanus contains the text of the Epistles of Paul. Since both manuscripts are known as D, their precise identity has to be worked out from their content. One drawback is that calling them both 'D' implies a closer relationship between them than is actually the case. In an effort to avoid confusion, Codex Claromontanus is sometimes known as D^p or D_2. But because of the potential for misunderstanding and the growing number of such manuscripts (there are at present more than 299), Gregory began the practice of assigning each uncial manuscript an Arabic numeral preceded by a zero. Under this system, Codex Bezae is 05 and Codex Claromontanus 06. The use of the older lettering has survived, though, and some scholars choose to use both systems, e.g. identifying Codex Bezae as D 05.

The official register of New Testament manuscripts is maintained at the Institute for New Testament Textual Research at the University of Münster in Germany. Its classification system is based on that adopted by Gregory and continued by Kurt Aland and his widow Barbara. The highest papyrus number to date is P^{99}, while the parchment uncials go up to 0306 and the cursives reach 2856. Over the years, some numbers have been deleted and so these figures do not reflect the precise number of manuscripts available. There are various reasons for such deletions, such as the discovery that the same manuscript has been registered more than once or that two separately registered fragments actually come from the same manuscript. After taking this into account, the present state of play is that there are 97 extant papyri, 270 uncials and 2,747 cursives.

It's important to realise that of these 3,000 or so manuscripts available to us, only about 50 are copies of the New Testament as a whole. Of the remainder, by far the majority (around 2,000) contain just the text of the Gospels. The Epistles are found, together with Acts, in about 400 copies, while the Pauline Epistles alone appear in about 300 copies. There are 250 or so surviving copies of the Book of Revelation.

As well as the manuscripts of all or part of the New Testament itself, scholars have also classified the manuscripts of ancient lectionaries, books of readings from the New Testament set out for use in public or private worship. There are 2,310 of these, designated by an italic letter *l* followed by an Arabic numeral, the highest of which is *l*2403. *l* by itself denotes a lectionary containing passages from the Gospels, while l^a refers to Acts and the Epistles and l^{+a} means that passages from the Gospels, Acts and the Epistles are present.

Although the vast majority of textual evidence comes from papyrus and parchment manuscripts, a few are in the form of ostraca, broken pieces of pottery which were used for writing purposes by poorer members of the community. These are identified by the prefix O or the Old English letter Ꝋ followed by a superscript numeral. And then, although their use was frowned on officially, a number of talismans or good luck charms have come to light which contain quotations from the New Testament. These are identified by T or the Old English letter Ꞇ followed by a superscript numeral.

Many manuscripts show evidence of later correction. Where appropriate, citations from such corrections are identified by a superscript ^{c}, while successive corrections are denoted by a superscript Arabic numeral. Readings of the original hand are shown by an asterisk, *.

—— Some important manuscripts ——

During the nineteenth century, the collapse of the Turkish Empire and the progress of archaeological discovery led to large numbers of manuscripts being discovered and brought to the West. Whereas only 481 Greek manuscripts were known of in 1806, this figure had grown to 4,079 by 1909. Some of the more significant manuscript volumes discovered so far are as follows.

Greek papyri

Notable among discoveries during the twentieth century are the papyri collected by Sir Chester Beatty and M. Martin Bodmer. The libraries built to house their discoveries are in Dublin and Cologny, a suburb of Geneva. The first Chester Beatty papyrus, identified as P^{45}, is made up of 30 out of the original 220 papyrus leaves, each measuring about 25 by 20 cm, containing part of the text of the Gospels and Acts. P^{46}, the second Chester Beatty papyrus, is made up of 86 of the original 104 leaves. Dating from the third century, it originally contained the text of ten of the epistles of Paul, and includes Hebrews but not the Pastoral Epistles. An interesting point is that the doxological conclusion to Romans (16:25–27 in our Bibles) appears at the end of Chapter 15 in this manuscript, suggesting either that the rest of Chapter 16 may not be original or that it may have been omitted from earlier copies not intended for the Roman church itself. The third Chester Beatty manuscript, P^{47}, is part of the Book of Revelation. Though it was discovered in Egypt in 1920, its significance was not realised until 1934. Ten of the original 32 or so leaves remain. Measuring less than the size of half a postcard, P^{52} contains the text of John 18:31–33, 37–38. It dates from around 130 CE, some 25 years after, in the opinion of most scholars, John's Gospel was written. For many years, this fragment held sway as the oldest copy of any part of the New Testament known to exist (see page 11).

Late in 1994, however, the German scholar Carsten Thiede suggested that three tiny fragments of Matthew's Gospel, preserved in the library of Magdalen College, Oxford, actually date from the middle of the first century, not, as previously thought, from the end of the second century. Thiede's expertise as a papyrologist led him to this conclusion from the style of the script preserved on these scraps of papyrus, a style which, though common in the century before Christ, was dying out by the middle of the first century. His suggestions have not yet been widely accepted, however, and other scholars have judged his conclusion to be mistaken.

P⁶⁶ is part of the Bodmer collection and consists of a substantial part of the Gospel of John (1:1–6:11 and 6:35–14:15) set out on 104 leaves. Bodmer was able to acquire a further 46 leaves of the same codex, though these are much less well preserved. The earliest known copy of the two epistles of Peter and the Epistle of Jude is found in P⁷², an assortment of various biblical and non-biblical documents. The earliest known copy of the Gospel of Luke and one of the earliest of John is found in P⁷⁵, a manuscript which contains 102 of 144 pages and dates from 200 CE.

Greek uncial manuscripts

Codex Sinaiticus (ℵ or 01)   Probably dating from the late fourth century, this Greek manuscript of the Bible was discovered in 1844 by Constantin Tischendorf (1815–74) in the monastery of St Catherine on Mount Sinai in Palestine. It was acquired by the Tsar of Russia and placed in the Imperial Library at St Petersburg before being sold by the Soviet Government to the British Museum for £100,000 in 1933. Although parts of the Old Testament have perished, the whole of the New Testament has survived, making this the only known complete copy of the Greek New Testament in uncial script. The manuscript has a number of amendments, dating from when it was first corrected (designated by ℵ ᵃ) and some centuries later (ℵ ᶜᵃ or ℵ ᶜᵇ). Together with Codex Vaticanus (see below), it was the basis for the Greek text of the New Testament prepared in the nineteenth century by B.F. Westcott and F.J.A. Hort. These two codices thus had a considerable influence on the translators of the 1881 *Revised Version* of the New Testament.

Codex Alexandrinus (A or 02)   Probably from the fifth century, this Greek manuscript of the whole Bible (together with two Epistles of St Clement) was presented to the English King Charles I by the Patriarch of Constantinople and reached England in 1627. It was placed in the British Museum in 1757, where it has remained ever since. Its discovery was among the first which led scholars to question the accuracy of the Byzantine text. Much of the content of Matthew's Gospel has been lost, together with parts of John and 2 Corinthians.

Codex Vaticanus (B or 03) This fourth-century manuscript of most of the Greek Bible (all after Hebrews 9:14 having been lost, including the Pastoral Epistles and Philemon) has been in the Vatican Library since at least the fifteenth century, apart from a period during which Napoleon brought it to Paris, when it came to the attention of scholars. Of its 820 pages, 759 have survived. It provides the best example of what is known as the Alexandrian form of the New Testament text.

Codex Ephraemi (C or 04) This is one of the best-known examples of a *palimpsest* (from the Greek for 'rescrape'), a manuscript in which the original writing has been obliterated and the papyrus or vellum re-used. In this case, a French scholar, Pierre Allix, discovered what turned out to be a fifth-century Greek Bible which had been covered over in the twelfth century with some of the writings of St Ephraem Syrus. The manuscript is now in the Bibliothèque Nationale, Paris, where it was brought by Catherine de Medici. The use of special chemicals and ultraviolet light has enabled scholars to decipher the earlier writing. It contains 64 leaves from the Old Testament and 145 (about 60 per cent) of the New, including at least part of every book except 2 Thessalonians and 2 John. Amendments have been made by two correctors, one from the sixth century and one from the ninth. Their work is identified as C^2 or C^b and C^3 or C^c.

Codex Bezae Cantabrigiensis (D or 05) Dating from the fourth or fifth century, this manuscript has the Greek and Latin text on facing pages. It contains the four Gospels, Acts and a small fragment of 3 John. Its name comes from the fact that it was discovered in Lyons by Theodore Beza (1519–1605), a French scholar who succeeded John Calvin as leader of the church at Geneva. He presented the codex to the University of Cambridge in 1581. This manuscript is the main representative of what is known as the Western text. Codex Bezae displays many variations from what is usually deemed as the norm, especially in the Acts of the Apostles, which is nearly a tenth longer than in other manuscripts. Although most scholars consider it to be a result of scribal rewriting, a significant case can be made for the suggestion that its variants are much earlier and, given their characteristically Lukan phraseology, may even be a rewriting of Acts by Luke himself.

Codex Purpureus Petropolitanus (N or 022)   This is an example of a particularly luxurious manuscript. Dating from the sixth century, it contains the four Gospels written in silver on vellum which was first dyed purple. Gold ink has been used for the contractions of the names of God and Jesus. Originally consisting of 462 leaves, it was taken apart in about the twelfth century. Its surviving pages are scattered in museums and libraries throughout the world.

Greek cursive manuscripts

These are identified by Arabic numerals without a prefixed zero. Several show such striking similarities that scholars have grouped them together as 'families'. Family 1, for example, contains manuscripts 1, 118, 131 and 209, all of which date from the twelfth to fourteenth centuries. Most of the cursives available to us represent the Byzantine text.

Ancient translations

In addition to all these early Greek manuscripts, there are also about 10,000 early Latin translations for textual critics to work on.

Old Latin manuscripts (designated by lower-case letters of the Latin alphabet) are divided into those coming from Africa (e.g. e, h and k) and those coming from Europe (e.g. a, b, c, d, ff², gig and m); 'gig' refers to Codex Gigas (the 'giant') whose pages measure some 50 by 90 cm. Now preserved in the Royal Library in Stockholm, it originates from Bohemia in the thirteenth century and contains the whole Bible in Latin, together with a good deal of other material. A large coloured picture of the devil on folio 290 lies behind its description as the 'Devil's Bible' (*Djävulsbibeln*).

As described in Chapter 5, St Jerome was commissioned to undertake a complete revision of the Latin Bible. The fruit of his labours is evident in the manuscripts of the Vulgate which exist today, of which there are well over 8,000. The major ones are described by capital letters (or sometimes by the first syllable of their name). The following are examples of the more important.

Codex Amiatinus (A)   This is the oldest known manuscript of the Jerome's Latin Vulgate and dates from the end of the eighth century when, as one of three copies, it was written under the direction of Abbot Ceolfrith in England. He intended to present it personally to Pope Gregory II but died before he could reach Rome. Until the eighteenth century it remained in the monastery at Monte Amiata (hence its name), at which time it was moved to the Laurentian Library at Florence.

Codex Fuldensis (F)   This sixth-century Latin manuscript of the New Testament largely agrees with the Vulgate. It is in Fulda, Germany, where it has been since the death of its one-time owner, St Boniface (680–754), the 'Apostle of Germany'.

Preserved in the British Museum, the beautifully decorated 'Lindisfarne Gospels' (Y) date from around the beginning of the eighth century. The text is very similar to A and includes an interlinear gloss in Anglo-Saxon added by Aldred, provost of Lindisfarne, in 970.

As if all these were not enough, there are some 9,300 early manuscripts in other languages, notably Syriac, Coptic (Egyptian), Gothic, Armenian, Georgian, Ethiopic and Old Slavonic. Discovering the nature of the Greek text from which many of these were translated is not always easy. For a start, there may have been imperfections in the work of translation, especially if translators were not completely familiar with the languages they were dealing with. St Augustine complains that 'No sooner did anyone gain possession of a Greek manuscript, and imagine himself to have any facility in both languages (however slight that may be) than he made himself bold to translate it' (*On Christian Doctrine* 2.11.16). In addition, there are certain features of Greek which simply cannot be translated directly into some other languages. It's well known, for example, that, unlike Greek, Latin has no definite article, thus making the word 'the' impossible to translate.

As well as these manuscripts of the New Testament itself, numerous quotations from the New Testament survive in the lectionaries, commentaries and sermons of early church writers. It would in fact be possible to reconstruct the text of practically the whole of the New Testament from such citations alone. Because these documents can be fairly accurately localised and dated, they can be useful in confirming the likely place and time of manuscripts whose textual similarities suggest they have been quoted from. Such calculations are complicated by the fact that authors may allude to passages rather than quote them directly. And, of course, even if they intend to quote, it's always possible that they may do so inaccurately. Nevertheless, studying such citations can yield valuable information about the history of how particular texts have been transmitted.

The conclusion from this wealth of evidence must surely be, as New Testament scholar Professor F.F. Bruce put it:'There is no body of ancient literature in the world which enjoys such a wealth of good textual attestation as the New Testament'. Nothing else even approaches it. Coming a distant second is Homer's *Iliad*, with less than 650 surviving manuscripts. The earliest fragment dates from 500 years after it was written. Compare this with the thousands of New Testament fragments we have, the earliest from just 25 years after the original was written.

Working with all these different pieces of a complex jigsaw (together with the new discoveries that are made from time to time) is the stuff of the science of textual criticism. Scholars engaged in this work seek to try to reconstruct the most likely form of the original. Although we today have access to the most accurate text since the sixth century, it's still unlikely that we have exactly what the New Testament writers wrote. Scholars await further discoveries so that the text can be further refined and uncertain readings clarified. The unearthing of the Dead Sea Scrolls in 1947 made available manuscripts of the Old Testament that were 1,000 years older than those known previously. Who knows what parallel discoveries of New Testament manuscripts there may be in the future?

——— Variations in the text ———

What sort of problems do textual critics seek to solve and how do they go about it? We begin with a consideration of how variants might have arisen as texts have been copied.

First, there are errors which have arisen unintentionally. Letters which are very similar in appearance, like λ and δ, can easily be confused. For example, although most manuscripts include the word ἐπιλεξάμενος (epilexamenos, meaning 'having chosen') in Acts 15:40, Codex Bezae has the almost identical ἐπιδεξάμενος (epidexamenos, meaning 'having received'). Another sort of error can occur where lines which are near to one another end in the same way (a phenomenon known as *homoeoteleuton*, from the Greek for 'similar ending'). If a scribe's eye moves back to the wrong place (*parablepsis*), he may accidentally omit part of the text (*lipography*). For example, because the last five words in Luke 14:26 and 27 are identical, it is hardly surprising that several manuscripts accidentally omit verse 27 altogether. Writing only once what should be included twice is known as *haplography,* while the opposite error, of writing twice what should only be included once, is called *dittography*. A probable example of this is in Acts 19:34, where Codex Vaticanus repeats the crowd's reply, 'Great is Artemis of the Ephesians'.

Another sort of unintentional error arises from the practice of making copies from dictation. Here, words that sound the same can easily be confused. For example, should Romans 5:1 read 'Therefore, since we have been justified through faith, we have (*echomen*) peace with God through our Lord Jesus Christ' as the main text of the NIV renders it? Or should we follow the variant set out in the NIV footnote and translate it as '...let us have (*echōmen*) peace with God...'? The difference depends on the pronunciation of a single letter, which can be easily confused. Manuscripts such as ℵ *, A, B* C and D contain the long 'o', omega, whereas ℵ ᵃ and B³ contain the short 'o', omicron. Translators have usually followed the ancient correctors and opted for the short 'o', assuming that this was misheard at some stage in transmission. This certainly makes better sense in the context of the passage, but the conclusion is not so overwhelming that the variant can be ignored altogether. Another example is in 1 Corinthians 15:54. 'Death is swallowed up in victory (*nikos*)' appears in most manuscripts while the rather peculiar reading 'Death is swallowed up in conflict (*neikos*)' is found in P⁴⁶ and B. Such confusion of vowels because of their similar 'i' sound is known as *itacism*. A similar confusion in pronunciation leads to 'from you' (*ek sou*) becoming 'from whom' (*ex ou*) in the ℵ ᶜ version of Matthew 2:6.

A third type of unintentional error occurs in the mental process that co-ordinates what the eye sees (or the ear hears) with what the hand writes. For example, 'they took' (*elabon*) in Mark 14:65 becomes 'they threw' (*ebalon*) in some manuscripts (an example of *metathesis*).

A number of other errors are sometimes seen, such as the incorporation into the main text of a note in the margin. This is the most likely explanation for the inclusion of John 5:4 in many manuscripts (such as A and C³), its omission in others (such as P⁶⁶, P⁷⁵, B C* and D) and its inclusion with asterisks or obeli to indicate the possibility of its being an addition in others (such as S, Λ and Π).

There is also evidence to show that deliberate changes were sometimes made by copyists, either seeking to improve on the spelling and grammar of the exemplar or in an attempt to reconstruct the original text from which they presume the exemplar had departed. This is a particular feature of copies of the Book of Revelation, where the original Greek is not always of a particularly high standard. But it doesn't stop there. Scribes who knew their New Testament well would sometimes attempt to harmonise passages with one another. For example, in many manuscripts the shorter version of the Lord's Prayer in Luke 11:2–4 is amended so that it agrees with the longer version in Matthew 6:9–13. Others sought to clarify and enhance the text with their own additions. An example of this occurs at Galatians 6:17. In the earliest manuscripts this verse concludes '...*I bear on my body the marks of Jesus*'. This straightforward reference to 'Jesus' has clearly been embellished by later copyists, with 'the Lord Jesus', 'the Lord Jesus Christ' or 'our Lord Jesus Christ' being found in different manuscripts. A copyist working from two or more manuscripts who came across different readings for a particular passage would sometimes try to select the original. More often, though, he would simply include both readings, a process known as *conflation*. For example, in Acts 20:28, some early manuscripts (e.g. ℵ and B) refer to the 'church of God' whereas others (e.g. A and C*) refer to the 'church of [the] Lord'. Several later manuscripts (e.g. C³ and P) have the conflated reading 'church of [the] Lord and God'. Some alterations seem to have been made in order to safeguard particular doctrinal positions which were perhaps felt to be a matter of doubt in the original. For example, although the original text of Luke 2:41 and 43 refers to 'the parents' of Jesus, some copyists, presumably intending to avoid any potential confusion about the virgin birth of Jesus, substitute the names 'Joseph and Mary' for 'the parents'.

While admitting that there are differences in the texts we have, these must not be overstated. The variations are comparatively minor and for most of the New Testament there is no problem. Certainly, no fundamental New Testament Christian doctrine would unravel, even if disputed readings went the 'wrong' way. Details of such alterations must be balanced against the many cases where copyists have *not* made corrections but faithfully copied what are sometimes glaring grammatical errors. For example, the natural sense of Galatians 2:12 requires the plural reading '...But when *they* arrived...' (hote de ēlthon) whereas most manuscripts faithfully transmit the phrase as '...But when *he* arrived...' (hote de ēlthen), a phrase that, incidentally, appears quite correctly in the singular at the beginning of verse 11. Comparison with other ancient works is helpful. For the New Testament, only 40 of its 20,000 lines are in doubt (0.2 per cent). But of the *Iliad's* 15,600 lines, as many as 764 are textual variants (4.89 per cent).

— Working out the likely original —

A number of criteria have been developed to enable scholars working with a variety of different texts to work out which is more likely to be a more accurate reflection of the original. Textual critics ask two sorts of questions. First, is there anything about a reading which could explain how another reading came into existence as a variant of it? Secondly, is there anything about a reading which could explain how it came about as a development of another reading?

To help in this task, the textual critic has a number of lines of evidence to consider. Clearly, the likely date of the manuscripts under consideration, the age of the type of text and the geographical distribution of variant readings are factors to take into account. This must, however, be done with care. We might expect an earlier manuscript to be closer to the original. But it would be quite possible for a manuscript to be early *and* a very poor copy. Similarly, just because a manuscript is late does not necessarily mean that it is inaccurate. For example, faced with two manuscripts, one of which comes from the tenth century and the other from the thirteenth, we would naturally expect the earlier one to be a more accurate reflection of the original text. But suppose that the tenth-century manuscript was copied from a ninth-century exemplar while the thirteenth-century one was copied directly from a sixth-century exemplar. In this case, despite being much younger, the later thirteenth-century copy is likely to have fewer variants which can be put down to errors in copying. Because of the uncertainties in this area, some textual critics choose to concentrate on internal factors such as language, style and usage in assessing the likelihood of a particular reading being original and pay little attention to the external criteria of age and provenance.

On the basis of the similarities between them, it's been possible to sort many of the texts available into four different families.

The first, the **Alexandrian** family, associated with the Egyptian city of Alexandria, goes back to the early part of the second century. Until earlier this century, this family was chiefly represented by codices ℵ and B, dating from the fourth century. However, from work on the discovery of the Chester Beatty and Bodmer papyri, notably P⁶⁶ and P⁷⁵, it's become clear that this family goes back to the second century and most scholars now view the Alexandrian text as the one which is closest to the original.

The second is the **Western** family (mainly from Rome), so-called because the chief pointers to it are Codex Bezae (D), Latin translations and quotations in the writings of the early church Fathers from around 150 CE, including Marcion, Irenaeus, Tertullian and Cyprian.

Thirdly there is the **Caesarean** family, sometimes known as 'Family Theta', thought to have originated in Egypt. This early form is represented by P⁴⁵, W, family 1, family 13, 28 and many Greek lectionaries. Brought to Caesarea by Origen, it was then taken to Jerusalem, where it found its way to the Armenians and then the Georgians. This later Caesarean text is represented by Θ, 565 and 700, quotations in Origen and Eusebius, and the Old Armenian and Old Georgian versions.

The fourth family goes by a number of names, including **Byzantine**, Syrian or 'Koine', and comes from Antioch or Constantinople towards the end of the third century. This is the one from which the *Textus Receptus* was circulated until discovery of the others led scholars to produce a new and more accurate text.

We have considered a number of different ways in which variants could have arisen in the process of copying, either accidentally or deliberately. There is an important judgement to be made here. On the one hand, given a choice between, for example, two variants with good Greek and bad Greek, the bad Greek is usually to be preferred as the more likely original. This is because we can see how the good Greek version could have arisen as the result of a copyist's *deliberate* amendment. But on the other hand, the bad Greek version could have come about as the result of a copyist's *accidental* amendment. Sorting out which is which keeps textual critics busy and shows the way in which their work is often a matter of artistic judgement rather than scientific precision. Another useful criterion is that shorter readings are to be preferred, on the grounds that scribes were more likely to *add* to the text than *omit* from it. Once again, this is far from absolute since copyists could have accidentally or, for various reasons, deliberately omitted material from a longer original. And then, since we know that copyists had a tendency to harmonise parallel passages so that they conform with one another, variants which maintain any differences are more likely to be original.

Doing such work on a manuscript as a whole allows textual critics to decide where it is likely to be on the spectrum of reliability. Any points of remaining uncertainty between readings can then be at least provisionally resolved by taking into account the general trustworthiness of the manuscripts under consideration.

A further source of evidence comes from considering what the author was more likely to have written in the first place. Some estimate of this can sometimes be made from the style and vocabulary he uses in the rest of his writing. In the case of the Gospels, it's often useful to compare parallel passages.

At the end of the day, there are places where it may be that *all* the manuscripts that survive record a deviation from the original. In this case, scholars try to deduce what the original form might have been. Such a reading is known as a *conjectural emendation*. An example of this is found in the approach some scholars have taken to 1 Peter 3:19, which the NIV translates as '*...through whom also he went and preached to the spirits in prison...*'. This is a notoriously difficult passage to interpret and a great number of not entirely satisfactory suggestions have been made. The difficulties are somewhat eased by the suggestion that we have here an example of haplography in which an early scribe copied ENΩKAI (the uncials for 'through whom [he] also') but then omitted a reference to Enoch, the uncial characters for which are ENΩX. The New Testament scholar and Bible translator James Moffatt (1870–1944) was so persuaded by this proposal that he translated the verse like this: '(It was in the Spirit that Enoch also went and preached to the imprisoned spirits...)'. Such an emendation has not received widespread approval, however. Even though the reference to preaching to spirits in prison accords with a passage in the Jewish pseudepigraphical work known as 1 Enoch, it's also true that mentioning Enoch at this point disturbs the flow of the argument of 1 Peter. In other words, while appearing to solve some difficulties, this particular emendation creates others. For this reason it should probably be rejected.

A modern New Testament Greek text usually includes a number of footnotes in addition to the main text. These footnotes, known as the *critical apparatus*, give variant readings from other manuscripts and are intended to show how the editors arrived at their conclusions about the likely shape of the original text. A page from such a text is shown on page 109, together with a sample of uncial text. Although it looks complex enough as it is, such texts actually contain only a small sample (about 5 per cent) of all the variant readings which exist. Part of the editors' task is to select the ones which are thought to be most significant.

Codex Sinaiticus.

24.39–49   Κατα Λουκαν

καὶ ἴδετε, ὅτι πνεῦμα σάρκα καὶ ὀστέα οὐκ ἔχει
41 καθὼς ἐμὲ θεωρεῖτε ἔχοντα. ἔτι δὲ ἀπιστούντων 341.9
αὐτῶν ἀπὸ τῆς χαρᾶς καὶ θαυμαζόντων, εἶπεν
Jn. 21. 5, 10   42 αὐτοῖς, Ἔχετέ τι βρώσιμον ἐνθάδε; οἱ δὲ ἐπέδω-
43 καν αὐτῷ ἰχθύος ὀπτοῦ μέρος· καὶ λαβὼν ἐνώπιον
44 αὐτῶν ἔφαγεν. Εἶπεν δὲ πρὸς αὐτούς, Οὗτοι οἱ 342.10
27; 9. 22, 45;   λόγοι μου οὓς ἐλάλησα πρὸς ὑμᾶς ἔτι ὢν σὺν ὑμῖν,
18. 31–33   ὅτι δεῖ πληρωθῆναι πάντα τὰ γεγραμμένα ἐν τῷ
νόμῳ Μωϋσέως καὶ τοῖς προφήταις καὶ ψαλμοῖς
45 περὶ ἐμοῦ. τότε διήνοιξεν αὐτῶν τὸν νοῦν τοῦ
46 συνιέναι τὰς γραφάς· καὶ εἶπεν αὐτοῖς ὅτι Οὕτως
1 Ti. 3.16   γέγραπται παθεῖν τὸν Χριστὸν καὶ ἀναστῆναι ἐκ
47 νεκρῶν τῇ τρίτῃ ἡμέρᾳ, καὶ κηρυχθῆναι ἐπὶ τῷ
ὀνόματι αὐτοῦ μετάνοιαν εἰς ἄφεσιν ἁμαρτιῶν εἰς
πάντα τὰ ἔθνη,—ἀρξάμενοι ἀπὸ Ιερουσαλημ.
Jn. 15. 26;   48 ὑμεῖς μάρτυρες τούτων. καὶ ἰδοὺ ἐγὼ ἐξαπο-
16. 7   49
Ac. 1. 4

---

39 (και B) σαρκα και οστεα ουκ εχει] σαρκας κ. ο. ουκ ε.
ℵ*: ο. ουκ ε. Mcion Tert: οστα ουκ ε. κ. σαρκας **D** (Ir) |
fin. **D** a b d e ff² j l r¹ sy^sc Mcion; R^m] *add* (Jn. 20.
20) (40) και τουτο ειπων εδειξεν (επεδ- **WΘ** *al* ϛ) αυτοις
τας χειρας και τους ποδας *rell* c f q vg sy^p ϛ; R^t   42
μερος ℵ**ABDW** *pc* d e sy^s Cl Or; R^t] *add* και απο μελισ-
σιου κηριον **MNΘ** fr₁₃^pt *157 pl*: *add* κ. α. μ. κηριου fr
al sy^c, P ϛ; R^m   43 και λαβ. εν. α. εφαγεν ℵ**ABDW**
fr *pm* it sy^s ϛ; R] φαγων εν. α. (*et om* δε *in* vs. 44)
it: φαγ. εν. α. λαβων τα επιλοιπα εδωκεν αυτοις **Θ** vg:
λαβ. εν. α. εφαγεν και (*add* λαβων 713 sy^c) τα επιλ. εδ.
αυτοις fr₁₃ 713 sy^c   44 και ψαλμοις] *om* **F** 1 22
1582   46 Ουτως γεγρ. ℵ**BD** *pc* it; R] Ουτ. εδει 72
pc (sy^s): Ουτ. γεγρ. και ουτως εδει **AWΘ** fr fr₁₃ *pm* f q
z vg ϛ | εκ νεκρων] *om* **D** *pc* d sa | τη τρ. ημερα] *om* b ff²
l Ir   47 εις αφ. ℵ**B** co sy^p.; R^m] και αφ. *rell* ϛ; R^t |
αρξαμενοι ℵ**B** *pc*; R] -νον **AW** (fr) fr₁₃ *pm* it ϛ: -νων **D**:
-νος **ΘΨ** *al*

274

———— Questions to consider ————

1 How do we know that the New Testament text we have today is an accurate reflection of what the authors wrote?
2 What different reasons are there to account for the variant readings we find in New Testament manuscripts?
3 What does 'conjectural emendation' mean?

7

THE FOCUS OF THE NEW TESTAMENT

The New Testament focuses on one man, arguably the most remarkable person who has ever lived. Mind you, for those living in first-century Palestine, there wouldn't have been all that much about Jesus of Nazareth to write home about, at least at first sight. Wandering preachers were two a penny, each with their own little band of disciples, people who dedicated their lives to learning from their master as he travelled from place to place with his message.

But Jesus stands head and shoulders above them all. For a start, within 20 years of his death, every major centre of population in the Roman world had a group of his followers. Had that been that, the study of the New Testament would simply be an interesting exercise in historical enquiry. But it didn't stop there. Far from fading, his influence has continued to grow during the last 2,000 years. All over our planet today, millions of people claim an allegiance to him as the Son of God and Saviour of the world. For them the New Testament is not only an account of the past but a guidebook for the present and a manifesto for the future. And many others, even if sceptical about the religious claims made about Jesus, still look to his ethical teaching as a valuable framework for living.

The fact that the New Testament functions as part of the Scriptures or holy book of one of the world's major religions is not without its problems for the student. Many Christians, hearing the sometimes radical conclusions reached by modern biblical scholars, fear that the academic study of the New Testament will undermine their otherwise simple and straightforward faith. And on the other hand, some scholars complain that to look at the New Testament through the lens of committed Christian faith is to introduce a built-in distortion which refuses to deal properly with what can sometimes be embarrassing questions. Of course, the reverse may also be the case. No-one can be neutral about the claims Christians make concerning Jesus: distortions can also result from the prior conviction that the Christian message *isn't* true.

We shall look at some of the different approaches to the historical reliability of the Gospels later in this chapter. First though, we shall examine some of what the New Testament actually has to say about Jesus and the movement which sprang up in his name.

——————— The beginning ———————

The birth of Jesus, recorded in the Gospels of Matthew and Luke, marks the pivotal point in history. Even those who don't subscribe to this view by describing years as BC ('Before Christ') or AD ('Anno Domini', i.e. 'the year of our Lord') use the same system but, as in this book, employ different labels – BCE ('Before Common Era') and CE ('Common Era'). Unfortunately perhaps, Jesus certainly did *not* come into the world on 25 December in the year 0 CE! Matthew tells us that he was born in the reign of Herod the king (Mt 2:1) and we know that Herod died in 4 BCE. Luke indicates that Jesus was baptised at the age of about 30 in the 'fifteenth year of the reign of Tiberius Caesar' (3:1). Although Tiberius came to the throne in 14 CE, he had shared power with his predecessor from 11 CE, allowing us to match what Matthew's Gospel says and date the year of Jesus' birth as 5 or 4 BCE. The fly in the ointment is Luke's statement that Quirinius was governor of Syria at the time (Lk. 2:2). The problem is that the Jewish historian Josephus says that Quirinius was brought in to conduct his census after the end of the reign of Archelaus, i.e. in 6 or 7 CE. One possibility is that Luke has been misunderstood and that Luke 2:2 should be translated 'This was *before* the first census that took place while Quirinius was governor of Syria'. Although many scholars support this suggestion, it's by no means universally agreed. Another possibility is that Luke simply made a mistake. The problem here is that he has been shown elsewhere in his writing to be such a reliable and trustworthy historian and it seems unlikely that he would have set out two such contradictory means of dating the events of Jesus' birth within such a short space in his Gospel. A suggestion which reconciles the information we have is that Quirinius *completed* a census in 6 or 7 CE which had actually *begun* several years earlier. We know that such exercises in information gathering by the Romans were often resisted by the local population. Add to that the difficulties and delays in communicating between different parts of the empire, and an interval of a dozen or so years between the start and finish of a census does not seem all that improbable.

In public

The Gospel accounts are content to skate over the early life of Jesus very briefly. Luke 2:40–52 does, however, give a hint of the consciousness that Jesus had as a boy of the special nature of his relationship with God, an observation to which we will return later. We read very little more about him until he emerged into the public arena at the age of 30. His cousin, known as John the Baptist, had begun to preach in the region round the Jordan. Part of his message was that people should turn from their sins (i.e. repent) and receive forgiveness from God. As a sign that his hearers were serious about this, John invited them to come and be ritually dipped (i.e. baptised, hence his title) in the river. Baptism in itself was nothing new and was, for example, used later as a means of formally admitting Gentile converts into Judaism. Similarly, in Christianity, baptism became the way individuals expressed publicly their new allegiance to Jesus Christ. The Essene sect (see page 61) also practised a complex system of religious washing which some think may have influenced John.

Another aspect of John's message was that he was simply preparing the way for someone else, whom he was later to identify as Jesus. While Jesus came to the fore, John himself was to fade into the background. What gave his message its sense of urgency was his conviction that this coming of Jesus marked God's decisive intervention in his world to bring evil to an end and usher in a golden age of righteousness and peace.

The public ministry of Jesus began after his own baptism, described in all four Gospels. In this way he showed his willingness to be identified with those he came to be with, setting a pattern for his life which he would follow through right to the end. The New Testament writers often use the image of identification and exchange to describe the relationship of Jesus with the rest of humanity. For example, here's how 1 Peter 2:24 describes one of the consequences of the death of Jesus: *'He himself bore our sins in his body on the tree, so that we might die to sins and live for righteousness; by his wounds you have been healed'.*

The Gospels also record the baptism of Jesus as the occasion when he was equipped for the task that lay ahead of him as the Holy Spirit supplied him with a sharpened sense of his identity as the Son of God. Then comes a time of solitude in the desert, concluding with a series of tests or temptations designed to subvert him from God's prescribed way of fulfilling his mission.

After successfully resisting the three-fold ordeal of temptation, Jesus was ready for his public ministry of *'proclaiming the good news of God'* (Mk 1:14). His teaching was certainly popular. People were excited by the fact that he seemed to know what he was talking about. He didn't just pass on the dry crusts of what other people said but *'he taught as one who had authority'* (Mt. 7:29), unlike the religious teachers they were used to.

A particular theme of the good news which Jesus proclaimed was the kingdom of God. *'The time has come,'* he said. *'The kingdom of God is near. Repent and believe the good news!'* (Mk 1:15). One of the main reasons why popular opinion seems to have turned against Jesus is that people's idea of what the kingdom was all about differed from his. They saw it as something external and immediate which would, for example, result in their freedom from domination by the Romans. But the view taken by Jesus had a rather different focus. For him, the kingdom was about deliverance from the spiritual realities of sin, evil, Satan and death – dealing with the roots of the human problem instead of concentrating simply on its different branches.

Parables

One particular feature of Jesus' teaching was his use of parables. 'Parable' is a word whose root suggests the idea of making an abstract truth easier to understand by setting it alongside and likening it to something more concrete and down to earth. Even though we tend to connect parables particularly with Jesus, this isn't a form of teaching that he invented. Indeed, the Old Testament book we call 'Proverbs' could equally well be translated 'Parables': the Hebrew word is the same. But whereas other teachers would use a parable just to *illustrate* something they were trying to get across, Jesus used the parables *themselves* to convey the whole of what he wanted to say, especially when talking to the crowds. They would be left with memorable stories to think about. This is what marks out Jesus as such a skilled communicator to ordinary people.

We also tend to think of the parables as 'stories'. But this isn't quite right. Even the Gospels themselves apply the label 'parable' to other sorts of picture language as well. Here are two examples from Luke. *He told them this parable: 'No one tears a patch from a new garment and sews it on an old one. If he does, he will have torn the new garment, and the patch from the new will not match the old'* (Lk. 5:36). *He also told them this parable: 'Can a blind man lead a blind man? Will they not both fall into a pit?'* (Lk 6:39).

Whereas Matthew concentrates on stories that illustrate the nature of the kingdom of God, Luke's tend to be about the activities of ordinary people in day-to-day situations. They bring out what Jesus had to say about money and possessions, pride and humility, the need to count the cost before beginning to follow him. Others give a unique insight into God's character as the one who delights to seek out the lost and welcome in the outsider.

We should also note that as well as *telling* parables, the Gospels also record the way Jesus *did* them as well. Many of his actions, especially his miracles of healing, had symbolic significance and communicated his message of salvation powerfully. Perhaps the most moving of these is his action in giving the broken bread and the wine to his disciples on the night before his body would be broken and his blood shed on the cross.

Although Jesus used parables to *reveal* truth and bring it home to his listeners, the Gospels also record how Jesus taught in this way in order to *conceal* the truth of what he was saying. Before responding to his disciples' request to tell them what the parable of the sower meant, Jesus said that *'The knowledge of the secrets of the kingdom of God has been given to you, but to others I speak in parables, so that, though seeing, they may not see; though hearing, they may not understand*' (Lk 8:10). Parables have a dual function. They communicate truth about God only to those who have been given the spiritual ability to understand their deeper meaning. These are those who, like the disciples, are serious about trusting and obeying Jesus. On the other hand, parables serve to obscure the truth to those who refuse to believe and apply what Jesus says to their own lives. Such people are satisfied with the surface impact of a good story.

Although much of what the parables contain is timeless, it can sometimes be helpful to 'translate' the details into our own culture in order to experience more of the impact they would have had when Jesus first told them. For example, when looking at the 'parable of the good Samaritan' in Luke 10:25–37, try reading it through as the 'parable of the good terrorist'.

——————— Who was Jesus? ———————

Jesus may have been popular with the ordinary people of his day. But the Gospels indicate that this enthusiasm was not shared by most of the religious authorities. It wasn't just that they were jealous of his success, but that they were deeply disturbed by certain features of his message, in particular what he had to say about himself.

We saw earlier the way in which John the Baptist saw Jesus as having been sent by God to deliver his people. This fitted in with Jewish longings for a return to the golden age enjoyed by Israel under King David. Such expectations were focused in the desire for the coming of the 'Messiah', the 'Son of David'. Messiah is a Hebrew word (whose Greek equivalent is 'Christ') which means 'anointed one', signalling an individual specially chosen by God and empowered for the task of rescuing God's people and exercising judgement on their enemies.

Running through the Old Testament are passages which, as well as having direct application at the time when they were written, can also be applied to this future hope of a Messiah which developed towards the end of Old Testament times. By the time of Jesus, the occupation of Palestine by the Romans had given even greater impetus to messianic aspirations. It seemed to many that Jesus, with his strong public following and ability to perform mighty miracles, fitted the bill nicely.

Jesus' own approach to this comes across in the Gospels as distinctly ambiguous. Although he does accept the term, he encourages his disciples to keep quiet about it. Here, for example, is how Luke's Gospel expresses the implicit and explicit claims of Jesus the Messiah. To begin with, the prophecies around Jesus' birth point to his special identity. Mary's song focuses on the way that Jesus will be the fulfilment of God's promise of mercy to the descendants of Abraham (Lk 1:54–55). Zechariah makes the same point (Lk 1:72–73) as he looks forward to the promised salvation of God's people through a descendant of David (Lk 1:68–69). One strand of messianic expectation was that the Messiah would be preceded by the arrival of the prophet Elijah. This explains why John the Baptist is described as operating *'in the spirit and power of Elijah'* (1:17; see also 9:8). His task is *'to make ready a people prepared for the Lord'*, an aspect which Zechariah repeats in Luke 1:76. Luke stresses this again by quoting the relevant prophecy from Isaiah 40 when commenting on John the Baptist's ministry (Lk 3:4–6; see also 7:27). Luke goes on to underline the fact that Jesus is a direct descendant of King David and so qualified to sit on his throne. The angel Gabriel announces to Mary that *'The Lord God will give him the throne of his father David, and he will reign over the house of Jacob forever; his kingdom will never end'* (Lk 1:32–33; see also 1:27,69; 2:4,11; 3:31; 18:38–39; 20:41–44). Towards the end of his public ministry, Jesus clearly illustrates this claim as he rides into Jerusalem on a donkey. Such an action recalls the messianic prophecy of Zechariah 9:9: *'Rejoice greatly, O Daughter of Zion! Shout, Daughter of Jerusalem! See, your king comes to you, righteous and having salvation, gentle and riding on a donkey, on a colt, the foal of a donkey.'*

Furthermore, Jesus is specifically identified as the Messiah or Christ on several occasions (see 2:11, 26; 4:41; 9:20; 22:67; 23:2, 35, 39; 24:26, 46). As he begins his public ministry, he quotes directly from the messianic prophecy in Isaiah 61 and applies it to himself (Lk 4:16–21). Later, when John the Baptist expresses uncertainty about whether or not Jesus is really *'the one who was to come'*, Jesus replies by quoting another messianic prophecy, this time from Isaiah 35 (Lk 7:18–23).

Perhaps a better way of approaching the subject is to suggest that Jesus did indeed think of himself as the Messiah – but that what it meant for him to be Messiah was rather different from what his fellow Jews were expecting. He kept quiet about it in order to try to scotch popular misconceptions. His mission runs far deeper than simply rescuing Israel from the grip of Rome: his goal is to release the whole world from the grip of Satan! And so, as soon as the penny has dropped for Peter and his fellow disciples, Jesus goes on to enjoin secrecy and to explain that *'The Son of Man must suffer many things and be rejected by the elders, chief priests and teachers of the law, and he must be killed and on the third day be raised to life'* (Lk 9:22).

In fact, as in this passage, Jesus usually avoided the term 'Messiah' altogether and used the term 'son of man' instead. What does this mean – and, in particular, what did it mean to people at the time? In the Old Testament, the phrase has two meanings. At one level, 'son of man' is simply a roundabout way of referring to a human being as distinct from God (e.g. Ps 8:4). 'son of man' is especially common as God's way of addressing the prophet Ezekiel in the book that bears his name. In the Gospels, Jesus sometimes refers to himself as the 'Son of man' instead of using the personal pronoun (e.g. compare Mark 8:27 and Matthew 16:13). But the term also appears in Daniel 7:13–14. Here it refers to a supernatural, heavenly figure who shares in God's power and glory, a connotation which it also has in other Jewish literature which may have been circulating in Jesus' day. This is how Jesus himself uses it in passages such as Matthew 24. Finally, Jesus seems to have introduced a new significance to the term as he links his being the 'son of man' with the fact of his anticipated suffering and death. For example, of the 14 uses of the term in Mark's Gospel, nine of them are in the context of his coming crucifixion.

It was not until after Jesus' resurrection that his disciples understood more fully how these threads come together. Talking with two disciples on the road to Emmaus, Jesus chides them: *'...How foolish you are, and how slow of heart to believe all that the prophets have spoken! Did not the Christ have to suffer these things and then enter his glory?' And beginning with Moses and all the Prophets, he explained to them what was said in all the Scriptures concerning himself'* (Lk 24:25– 27). Later, all the disciples have the benefit of the same Bible study: *He said to them, 'This is what I told you while I was still with you: Everything must be fulfilled that is written about me in the Law of Moses, the Prophets and the Psalms.' Then he opened their minds so they could understand the Scriptures. He told them, 'This is what is written: The Christ will suffer and rise from the dead on the third day, and repentance and forgiveness of sins will be preached in his name to all nations, beginning at Jerusalem'* (Lk 24:44–47). Once they have caught on, there's no stopping them. As Luke reports in the Acts of the Apostles, they come back again and again to the way in which Jesus, through his fulfilment of Old Testament prophecy, can clearly be identified as the Messiah (e.g. 2:25–28, 34; 3:18–26; 4:11, 25–27; 8:32–35; 10:43; 13:16–41; 17:2–3; 18:28; 26:22–27; 28:23). One set of Old Testament prophecies that Christians have often seen fulfilled in Jesus are the so-called 'Servant Songs' in Isaiah, especially in Isaiah 52:13–53:12.

As well as 'Messiah' and 'son of man', another term applied to Jesus is 'son of God'. It's true that this also carried a degree of ambiguity, certainly for those familiar with Greek and Roman culture, for whom the title 'son of God' was one way of describing a particularly heroic figure. It's also used in the Old Testament, where God refers to his people as 'my son' in Hosea 11:1. But the term seems to have meant more than this for Jesus. Even as a child, he referred to the temple as *'my Father's house'* (Lk 2:49). The claim to enjoy such a special relationship with God was characteristic of him. One passage from John's Gospel draws this out, together with its consequence for how Jesus was viewed by the authorities: *Jesus said to them, 'My Father is always at his work to this very day, and I, too, am working.' For this reason the Jews tried all the harder to kill him; not only was he breaking the Sabbath, but he was even calling God his own Father, making himself equal with God'* (Jn 5:17–18). Exactly what Jesus meant by calling God his Father is at the heart of much theological discussion.

The death of Jesus

It's clear from the differences between them that the Gospel writers have not chosen to organise their material in strict chronological order. Even so, there's a clear progression in Jesus' life from a time when he enjoyed widespread popularity to the events which resulted in his death.

The New Testament writers use a number of different pictures to describe the significance of this, one of the most common being that of sacrifice. After describing Jesus as the *'Word of God'*, John's Gospel goes on to talk about him as '*the Lamb of God, who takes away the sin of the world*' (Jn 1:29). Peter writes about '*the precious blood of Christ, a lamb without blemish or defect*' (1 Pet 1:19) and Paul takes up the theme by saying that '*Christ, our Passover lamb, has been sacrificed*' (1 Cor 5:7). Close parallels are being drawn here with the Jewish system of ritual sacrifice for sin, a symbolic means through which those who had sinned could be put right with God. Sin was thought of as being transferred to the sacrificial victim whose subsequent death in place of the worshippers would, as it were, 'clear their account' of guilt. In fact, the New Testament letter to the Hebrews goes so far as to say that the whole Old Testament system of sacrifice for sin serves simply as a sort of visual aid for what Jesus would achieve in reality, once and for all, through his death on the cross (e.g. Heb 10:1–18).

The idea of Jesus 'paying the price' for human sin can sometimes present a rather unattractive picture of the God who demands such hideous payment before being prepared to forgive sin. Some reject this altogether, while others draw attention to the significance of the *identity* of Jesus (from the point of view of orthodox Christianity) in responding to this question. If he were simply an innocent third party involved in putting right the relationship between God and humanity, then the picture of a harsh and stern God would be justified. But it can be argued that this is a distortion and that because Jesus is himself divine, then God himself ('*God... in Christ*' as Paul puts it in 2 Co 5:19) was personally involved in bearing the punishment (thus revealing his love and compassion) as well as passing the sentence (thus demonstrating his passion for justice and righteousness).

It's at this point that an important question arises. What was it that convinced the followers of Jesus that he had been successful? How did they know that his death really had achieved what they came to believe about it? The consistent answer in the New Testament is that this is one of the consequences of the resurrection of Jesus, his coming back to life on the third day after his death and burial.

Miracles

This introduces us to the whole concept of miracles. Start reading a Gospel and it isn't long before you come across an event which cannot easily be explained by the natural laws which usually seem to govern what happens. We usually associate the Gospels with the miracles performed by Jesus, though it's important to note that they happened in other circumstances too (e.g. Lk 1:19–20, 62–64; 9:1–6) and that their occurrence in the life of the early church is documented as well (e.g. Ac 3:1–9; 1 Co 12:28). Most are miracles of healing, where Jesus makes a sick person well or casts out an evil spirit. There are also three occasions in the Gospels where Jesus raises someone from the dead and a number of instances where he exercises power over the forces of nature.

Why did Jesus do these things? The New Testament's perspective is that his actions stem from, and so point back to, who he is as the son of God. In the first place, his miracles are an expression of the *love* of God as Jesus expresses his concern for those in need. For example, Matthew 14:14 tells us that *'When Jesus landed and saw a large crowd, he had compassion on them and healed their sick'*. Secondly, the miracles are an expression of the *power* of God. As we've seen, the coming of Jesus is seen as heralding the arrival of God's kingdom, the ushering in of the rule of God in a new way. Since sickness and death are hallmarks of the rule of Satan, they were bound to come in for a hammering in the ministry of Jesus. An especially clear example of this is where Jesus healed a woman *'whom Satan has kept bound for eighteen long years'* (Lk 13:16). The miracles signify the loosening of Satan's stranglehold on the world.

Miracles, then, are signposts which point to the identity of the one who does them and back up what he has to say. As Jesus reminds John the Baptist in Luke 7:18–23, the miracles he has been performing are simply what the Old Testament prophecies about the Messiah (in this case Isaiah 35:5–6 and 61:1–3) said he would do.

The people in the synagogue at Capernaum were impressed when they heard what Jesus had to say: *'They were amazed at his teaching, because his message had authority'* (Lk 4:32). But they were even more impressed when he went on to cast out an evil spirit. For what he *did* added significantly to the authority of what he *said*: *'All the people were amazed and said to each other, 'What is this teaching? With authority and power he gives orders to evil spirits and they come out!'* (Luke 4:36, my emphasis).

Another example where a healing miracle backs up the claims of Jesus is Mark 2:1–12, where Jesus was questioned about his authority to forgive the sins of a man who was brought to him. His answer was to prove it by healing the man's paralysis.

Notice that the miracles do not *compel* people to believe. Plenty of Pharisees remained unconvinced! Miracles are not absolute proofs of who Jesus is. Those who would prefer another explanation can usually find one (see Luke 11:15, for example). But they do serve as helpful pointers for those who are prepared for the consequences of believing that Jesus is who he himself and the miracles say he is. Miracles may be outside people's normal experience, but to argue that they cannot therefore have happened is foolish. The point is that they are entirely consistent with the claims Jesus made about his identity as God's son. Given who he was, the remarkable thing would be if he had *not* performed miracles, not if he had!

The resurrection of Jesus comes as the most striking miracle of the New Testament. Without it, the Christian faith falls apart. As the apostle Paul puts it, *'if Christ has not been raised, our preaching is useless and so is your faith'* (1 Co 15:14), a point he underlines a couple of verses later: *'if Christ has not been raised, your faith is futile; you are still in your sins'* (1 Co 15:17). But if it did happen, the consequences are momentous. It demonstrates that Jesus was right about himself all along and confirms the effectiveness of his death in dealing with overcoming sin and death.

It's often been noted that the stories about the resurrection in the four Gospels are very different and even seem to contradict one another. But this may be going too far. Although it's not yet proved possible to harmonise the accounts in a way which is universally acceptable, they are agreed on the main points. In fact, the minor discrepancies between the Gospels actually support the assertion that they are reporting reliable traditions. Agreement which was too close would be suspicious!

The early Christians

Clearly, something made a massive impact on the followers of Jesus, leading them to devote their lives to spreading what they saw as the good news about their Lord. The New Testament presents a picture of the disciples being given new hope by the resurrection of Jesus from the dead and new strength to continue the work he had begun as they received the power of the Holy Spirit (Ac 1:1–8). Their conviction was that the good news of who Jesus was and the significance of what he had achieved needed to be spread throughout the world (Mt 28:19). Acts 2 sets out an address given by the apostle Peter on the Day of Pentecost in which he seeks not only to convey information about Jesus but also to bring about a change of attitude in his hearers with the encouragement to 'repent and be baptized' (Ac 2:38). Much of the rest of the New Testament is concerned with the development of the Christian church – communities of individuals who, having repented and been baptised, seek to live as faithful followers of Christ in an alien world.

The Jesus of history

One of the major questions which scholars have asked concerns the relationship between the Christ that people believe in today and the Jesus who actually existed 2,000 years ago. Until the eighteenth century, the general assumption was that because the Gospels form part of sacred Scripture and were divinely inspired, they must therefore be reliable accounts of the life of Jesus. In other words, the Christ of faith and the Jesus of history were seen as identical. Not that contradictions and differences between the different Gospel accounts were ignored. But the response was to try to harmonise the accounts and show that any discrepancies were only apparent rather than real. One of the most famous surviving early harmonisations of the Gospels is by the second-century Christian apologist Tatian, a native of Assyria who studied in Rome. His influential *Diatessaron* (from the Greek for 'through four accounts') weaves the Gospel accounts of the life of Jesus into a single narrative, based on the framework of events set out in John's Gospel.

One of the consequences of what we call the Enlightenment in the eighteenth century was that people came to reject special pleading in the name of religion and began to ask potentially uncomfortable questions about the historicity of the Gospels. Doubts were cast on the extent to which the Christ people believe in today bears any relation to the Jesus who actually existed 2,000 years ago. Such questions are usually said to go back to the German scholar Hermann Samuel Reimarus (1694–1768), who was Professor of Hebrew and Oriental languages in Hamburg. His work on the subject, edited and published anonymously after his death by Gotthold Ephraim Lessing (1729–81), proposed that Jesus believed himself to have been chosen by God to establish a new regime on earth, a message that was summed up in his use of the phrase *'kingdom of God'* (or, as in Matthew, *'kingdom of heaven'*). In support of this, Reimarus notes the way Jesus applied an Old Testament royal prophecy (Zec 9:9) to himself by riding into Jerusalem on a donkey and also highlights the inscription above the cross which publicised the charge on which he was executed: *'This is Jesus, the king of the Jews'* (Mt 27:37). For Reimarus, Jesus was very much a child of his time who derived his understanding of himself and his mission from the beliefs held by many of his contemporaries about God's intention to deliver his people from Roman occupation and re-establish Israel as a world power. Events frustrated his ambitions, however, and so Jesus died a disappointed man, crying out *'My God, my God, why have you forsaken me?'* (Mk 15:34). The beliefs that his death resulted in the forgiveness of sins, that he was raised from the dead and that he will return in glory were, according to Reimarus, fabricated by his disciples. It was certainly never Jesus' intention to do away with the Jewish religion and substitute another. And if he could see now the religious system that bears his name, he would be horrified. In Reimarus' own words, '...the new system of a suffering spiritual saviour, which no-one had ever known or thought before, was invented only because the first hopes had failed'. Even though Reimarus' precise conclusions were not widely accepted, his underlying rejection of the *necessary* historicity of the Gospel accounts was. Jesus had thought himself to be a political messiah; the church had made him out to be something very different.

For Reimarus, nothing in history could be demonstrated beyond doubt. In other words, as Lessing put it, 'accidental truths of history can never become the proof of necessary truths of reason'. What he called 'an ugly great ditch which I cannot get across, however often and however earnestly I have tried to make the leap' was opening up between the Christ of religious faith and the Jesus who actually existed in history. What was later to be called 'the quest for the historical Jesus' was on! Modern faith had to be more authentically earthed in who Jesus actually was rather than relying on what were seen as the distortions introduced by the Gospel writers.

During the nineteenth century, literally hundreds of different writers undertook to sift out what they saw as biased and faith-inspired accretions from the Gospel accounts in order to get back to what Jesus 'must' really have been like, an ordinary man whose life can be explained in purely human terms. Such new biographies of Jesus were intended to provide a more adequate foundation for the faith of modern believers so that they would be able to share in the profound impression that he had made on his first followers. One benefit of such work was that it began to take more seriously the historical context of first-century Palestinian Judaism in which Jesus lived. But this approach was open to criticism on a number of fronts.

The first stemmed from scholars who questioned the efforts of their colleagues to remove the supernatural elements from Jesus' teaching about the kingdom of God. The German scholar Johannes Weiss (1863–1914) concluded that Jesus' understanding of the kingdom was not simply the rule of God worked out in the behaviour of those who followed him, but that it clearly included his belief in the supernatural intervention of God to bring about his rule at the end of history. As we shall see, this view was taken up and developed by the great musician, medical missionary and religious thinker Albert Schweitzer (1875–1965).

Secondly, there were those who denied that true history could be disentangled from the theological fabric of the Gospels at all. Another German New Testament scholar, William Wrede (1859–1906), sought to show that Mark's Gospel in particular cannot be relied on to give an accurate historical picture of the life of Jesus, pointing out that liberal scholars were illogical in their selection of what they were prepared to accept and what they felt the need to reject in the Gospel portraits. Wrede went on to suggest that Jesus himself had never made any claims to be the Messiah. Only after his resurrection did the disciples come to the conclusion that this is who he must have been all along. In order to explain why no-one had realised this during his lifetime, Wrede thought that Mark had distorted history in the interests of theology by inventing the idea that Jesus had told them to keep it a secret. The biggest problem with this supposition is that Jesus' claims to messiahship seem to have been very far from secret and, even according to Mark, were actually the very reason he was brought to trial and executed for blasphemy. It simply does not seem to be the case that no-one knew about the messianic claims of Jesus until well after his death.

Thirdly, Martin Kähler (1835–1912), who became Professor of Systematic Theology at Halle in Germany, sought to undermine the significance of the quest to discover the Jesus of history on what we call 'dogmatic' grounds. In other words, he viewed the whole approach as fundamentally misguided and unnecessary. For him, faith has to be based simply on Christ as he is presented in the Bible, not on some artificial reconstruction of the 'historical Jesus'. He argues that Jesus was a 'supra-historical' rather than an 'historical' figure. The historical method, then, which depends on the assumption that the object of its study is, basically, an ordinary human being much like everyone else, is bound to lead to a distorted view of who he is because it cannot deal adequately with his 'supra-historical' features. For Kähler, the important thing is not so much who Jesus was back then, but the impact he makes now.

In 1906, Albert Schweitzer wrote a famous book called *The Quest of the Historical Jesus* in which he surveyed the work the previous century had produced. Its original German title was *Von Reimarus zu Wrede* (i.e. 'From Reimarus to Wrede'). Based on his own careful study of Mark's Gospel in particular, Schweitzer agreed with Weiss that Jesus expected the imminent end of the world and coming of the kingdom of God in his own lifetime (a view known as 'thoroughgoing' or 'consistent' eschatology). For Schweitzer, the words of Jesus to his disciples in Matthew 10:23 before sending them on a preaching tour were crucial: '*When you are persecuted in one place, flee to another. I tell you the truth, you will not finish going through the cities of Israel before the Son of Man comes*'. The problem for Jesus was that his followers were *not* then persecuted in the way that he had been expecting and Jesus was *not* revealed as the supernatural 'son of man'. According to Schweitzer, Jesus then concluded that the kingdom of God would only come about as a result of his own suffering. He told his disciples this (e.g. Mk 8:31) and then deliberately went on to provoke the confrontation with the authorities in Jerusalem that led to his death (e.g. Mk 10:32–34). Of course, if this *is* what Jesus thought, then he was wrong. His demise did not lead to the coming of the kingdom which Schweitzer thought he was expecting and had taught his disciples to expect. And yet, even so, his disciples concluded that the kingdom *had* come and went on to proclaim the fact all over the ancient world.

The effect of Schweitzer's work was to bring what we now call the 'old quest' to an end. He dismissed the Jesus portrayed by his predecessors as a figure who 'never had any existence. He is a figure designed by rationalism, endowed with life by liberalism, and clothed by modern theology in a historical garb'. As the British Roman Catholic scholar George Tyrell (1861–1909) commented, the Jesus whose biography so many scholars had tried to write was simply Jesus as they liked to think of him and so 'only the reflection of the Liberal Protestant face, seen at the bottom of a deep well'. Archbishop William Temple (1881–1944) made the point even more trenchantly: 'Why anyone should have troubled to crucify the Christ of Liberal Protestantism has always been a mystery'. For Schweitzer, the Jesus of history is irrelevant: what matters is the Christ of faith. As he put it, 'it is not Jesus as historically known, but as spiritually risen within men, who is significant for our time and can help it'. The focus shifts from what actually happened to Jesus to the effect he had on his followers. In other words, according to this view, (a) modern Christian faith does not depend on our knowing what took place in the first century, and (b) we cannot know what happened in the first century anyway. The period of Gospel study identified as 'no quest' had begun. One of its principal exponents was one of Weiss's pupils, Rudolf Karl Bultmann (1884–1976). As we shall see in Chapter 9, he came to see much of the material in the Gospels as having been shaped by a concern to promote faith rather than to transmit history. His conclusion was that the Jesus of history is simply inaccessible and that all we have of historical value is a few of his sayings. Not only that, but the very nature of faith itself would be compromised by any certainty arrived at through historical investigation. Bultmann held to an existentialist view of reality which emphasises the need to make choices in order to be authentically human. For him, faith is simply a matter of personal response to the *kerygma* (from the Greek for 'proclamation'), by which he meant the Christ of faith proclaimed by the church. Historical enquiry into the life of Jesus, far from supporting faith, actually denies it by seeking artificial props. Christianity is about taking a leap of faith and there's no point in trying to shine a torch across the gap!

But although it is vital to stress the need for personal response in Christian faith, there is no need to deny completely the ability of the Gospels to provide us with reliable historical data about Jesus. We can freely admit that they were written as Christian 'propaganda' to bring about and strengthen faith. Certainly, their writers were biased in favour of Jesus. But this does not mean that what they write *cannot* be historically accurate, simply that we must be careful to take their bias into account when assessing their evidence. Neither can we entirely dismiss the *need* for such historical data, a point made by, among others, Gerhard Ebeling (b.1912): 'If Jesus had never lived, or if faith in him were shown to be a misunderstanding of the significance of the historical Jesus, then clearly the ground would be taken from under Christian faith'. We need to be able to offer an opinion about whether Christianity is founded on historical facts about the human Jesus or based on pure invention. What connections are there between the church's faith and proclamation on the one hand and what Jesus himself believed and preached on the other?

In 1953, Ernst Käsemann (b. 1906) took the opportunity of a lecture at a reunion of Bultmann's former students (of which he was one) to introduce what subsequently became known as the 'new quest'. He saw no possibility of using the Gospels to write any sort of biography of Jesus. But he concluded that to ignore the Jesus of history altogether is mistaken because it fails to take account of what the early church actually did. The very existence of the Gospels shows that the first followers of Jesus were indeed concerned to earth their proclamation of the Christ of faith in what they knew of him as an historical figure. Käsemann questions the assumptions made by earlier scholars that the Christ of faith was a fictional distortion who bears no relation to the Jesus of history. As he wrote later, 'My concern is to show that, out of the obscurity of the life story of Jesus, certain characteristic traits in his preaching stand out in relatively sharp relief, and that primitive Christianity united its own message with these'. Käsemann's own work focused on the continuity between what Jesus had to say about the coming of the kingdom of God and what the early church took up in its preaching on the subject.

Following Käsemann's challenge, the new quest was taken up by many scholars, among them Günther Bornkamm (1905–90), Ernst Fuchs (1903–83) and James McConkey Robinson (b. 1924), who first coined the term 'new quest'. Whereas the aim of the 'old quest' had been to show the ways in which the New Testament accounts were a distortion of what had actually happened in history, the 'new quest' was concerned to stress the threads of continuity between what Jesus said about himself and what the early church said about him. Such threads are rather thin, however, and tend to isolate Jesus from the culture of his day.

More recently, a number of scholars, notably Joachim Jeremias (1900–79), Ed Parish Sanders (b. 1937) and Geza Vermes (b. 1924), have sought to be more rigorous in understanding Jesus against the social, cultural and political background of first-century Palestine, an approach sometimes identified as the 'third quest'. Jeremias, for example, concluded from his study of the Judaism of the time that the main themes of the preaching of the early church were present in the teaching of Jesus. He has also traced certain distinctive Aramaic forms of expression which are only found in the Gospel accounts of the teaching of Jesus, and concluded that these can be reliably attributed to Jesus himself.

———— Questions to consider ————

1 Who do you think Jesus was, and why?
2 What do we really know about Jesus and his life on earth?
3 Is it important that the Jesus people believe in today is the same as the Jesus who actually existed 2,000 years ago? Why?

8

THE CRITICAL STUDY OF THE NEW TESTAMENT: 1

Christians who believe the Bible to be the word of God are sometimes inclined to be impatient with the sort of discussion with which we shall be concerned in the next two chapters. For them, a prayerful encounter with the text results in what they experience as communication with God. What more would anyone want? There's no need to belittle claims that God speaks to people as they simply read the text in front of them. But we do need to make the gentle but firm suggestion that there is rather more to studying the Bible than this. For, apart from anything else, equally sincere Christians often come up with contradictory views about what they think God is saying. Claims to private and personal illumination all too often reflect the ideas and preconceptions of the reader instead of allowing the Bible to communicate on its own terms.

It's entirely appropriate to ask 'What might God be saying to me now?' and in recent years, as we shall see, this sort of question has received increasing attention from scholars. But to ask *only* this question is to fail to take seriously the fact that the Old and New Testaments are collections of books written in a setting very different from our own. They don't only need to be translated from the original Hebrew, Aramaic and Greek. Even when printed in English, the Bible still doesn't necessarily 'speak our language'. Assuming that it does is one of the traps into which those seeking to interpret the New Testament can all too easily fall. There are all sorts of other questions we need to ask if we are to understand it properly. Asking such questions is what we mean by the word 'criticism' in biblical studies.

In what follows we shall examine some of the tools which scholars have used to prise open and examine the New Testament and come to conclusions about what it means. One helpful way of classifying the range of available methods is to ask about where each strategy locates the *meaning* of a text.

For most of the last 200 years or so, most approaches to the New Testament have concentrated on discovering meaning *behind the text*. Rather than focus on the text itself, the aim is to use what the authors have written as a window through which their intentions may be discerned and discoveries may be made about the historical nature of what they describe. Such historical criticism helps us to be more sensitive to the New Testament as a series of documents from the distant past so that we recognise and learn to compensate for the distance between our world and that of the first century. Perspectives from the social sciences are also vital as we recognise that the New Testament is not only the product of a particular historical context but comes from a definite cultural and social setting too. An example of this is the way in which theories about social dissonance have been used to explain how early Christianity survived the apparent failure of its founder to return in the way that his followers were expecting.

In more recent years, interest has grown in ways of reading the New Testament which focus on the text rather than the author. Such literary approaches to the study of the New Testament emphasise the contribution made by *the text itself* in the process of communication. We shall look at some of these at the end of Chapter 9.

Thirdly, interest has shifted to the different ways the text can be approached by its readers. Strategies which locate meaning *in front of the text* highlight the role of the audience in the process of communication. Rather than using the text as a window to see back into history, such methods focus on the text as a mirror in which readers are invited to bring their own insights and so contribute to its meaning.

Towards the end of the eighteenth century there was a radical change in the approach taken towards the Bible by scholars. Before this time (in what is known as the pre-critical period), thinking about the Bible tended to be governed by the teaching of the church. But a growing discontent with the way the Bible was manipulated by those in ecclesiastical power, together with the rise of deism and the onset of the Enlightenment, led to the beginnings of the critical period. Scholars sought to throw off the constraints of the past and treat the Bible

(a) as a work of human literature and (b) as the product of a particular period in human history. In other words, even though it may well be appropriate to treat the Bible as the 'word of God', it was also felt right to study it as though it were just like any other ancient piece of literature. Instead of treating it and its ecclesiastical interpreters with the unquestioning reverence which previous generations tended to adopt, scholars began to subject it to the sort of scrutiny which was prepared to allow uncomfortable conclusions to be reached.

Although such an approach might seem to commend itself more to scholars who are not themselves practising Christians, it must not be thought that critical scholarship and religious faith are incompatible. On the contrary, many of the early critical scholars were in fact deeply committed Christian believers who were seeking to face up to the unavoidable questions about the Bible which arose from this new way of thinking. Such an approach continues today. People of faith have nothing to fear from a rigorous quest for the truth and there is nothing to be gained by retreating into unquestioning dogmatism and obscurantism.

One of the first series of questions to be asked concerned the sources that lie behind the Gospels. In this chapter we will concentrate on looking at what is known as 'source criticism' and how it has been used to pursue the solution to the 'Synoptic Problem'.

Source criticism

It's possible, of course, to imagine the New Testament writers sitting down after breakfast one day, taking a deep breath and then completing their literary creations in one go, with brief pauses for elevenses and lunch! Closer study makes it clear that the composition of the New Testament must have been a much more complex business. For the most part, what the authors wrote did not come straight out of their heads, nor does it appear to have been dictated to them from heaven. Instead, it arose from a number of different sources. For example, Paul is quite explicit in his citation of the traditions which he is handing on in 1 Corinthians 11:23–25 and 15:3–8. In addition, it is highly likely that hymn-like passages such as Philippians 2:5–11 are quotations from earlier traditions.

Careful observation of the Acts of the Apostles reveals that the writer, having described events in the third person, suddenly slips into the first person at various points (16:10–17; 20:5–21:18; 27:1–28:16) before resuming his narrative in the third person. Look these passages up. How do they strike you? Although it's possible that this is simply a literary device, many scholars conclude that the author is apparently able to rely on his personal recollection for these sections, going back to the reports he has gathered from others for the rest of his account. The beginning of Luke's Gospel draws attention to three of the stages which the work has been through.

Many have undertaken to draw up an account of the things that have been fulfilled among us, just as they were handed down to us by those who from the first were eye-witnesses and servants of the word. Therefore, since I myself have carefully investigated everything from the beginning, it seemed good also to me to write an orderly account for you, most excellent Theophilus, so that you may know the certainty of the things you have been taught. (Lk 1:1–4)

First, the truth about Jesus was 'handed down' by 'eye-witnesses and servants of the word'. Secondly, many had already 'drawn up' accounts of the life and work of Jesus and the early church. And thirdly, Luke himself, having 'carefully investigated' his sources, sets out to 'write an orderly account' for his readership.

Source criticism is the study of the different oral and/or written sources which lie behind the works as we now have them. A modern parallel is the way that teachers sometimes notice remarkable similarities between pieces of work submitted by their students and have to try to work out which is original and who has copied what from whom!

With the Synoptic Gospels, such sources may sometimes be available to us. An example is the way most scholars think that the authors of Matthew and Luke used Mark as a source for their own Gospels. In other cases, the existence and content of sources are a matter for conjecture. An example of this is the entirely hypothetical source known as Q, thought by many scholars to have been used by Matthew and Luke. One day, archaeologists may dig up a copy of Q and provide the answer to a whole series of questions – as well as raising quite a few more, no doubt! Until then, the nature of Q remains a useful but unproven theory.

Matthew 14:13–21

When Jesus heard what had happened, he withdrew by boat privately to a solitary place. Hearing of this, the crowds followed him on foot from the towns. When Jesus landed and saw a large crowd, he had compassion on them and healed their sick. As evening approached, the disciples came to him and said, 'This is a remote place, and it's already getting late. Send the crowds away, so that they can go to the villages and buy themselves some food.' Jesus replied, 'They do not need to go away. You give them something to eat.' 'We have here only five loaves of bread and two fish,' they answered. 'Bring them here to me,' he said. And he directed the people to sit down on the grass. Taking the five loaves and the two fish and looking up to heaven, he gave thanks and broke the loaves. Then he gave them to the disciples, and the disciples gave them to the people. They all ate and were satisfied, and the disciples picked up twelve basketfuls of broken pieces that were left over. The number of those who ate was about five thousand men, besides women and children.

Mark 6:32–44

So they went away by themselves in a boat to a solitary place. But many who saw them leaving recognised them and ran on foot from all the towns and got there ahead of them. When Jesus landed and saw a large crowd, he had compassion on them, because they were like sheep without a shepherd. So he began teaching them many things. By this time it was late in the day, so his disciples came to him. 'This is a remote place,' they said, 'and it's already very late. Send the people away so that they can go to the surrounding countryside and villages and buy themselves something to eat.' But he answered, 'You give them something to eat.' They said to him, 'That would take eight months of a man's wages! Are we to go and spend that much on bread and give it to them to eat?' 'How many loaves do you have?' he asked. 'Go and see.' When they found out, they said, 'Five – and two fish.' Then Jesus directed them to have all the people sit down in groups on the green grass. So they sat down in groups of hundreds and fifties. Taking the five loaves and the two fish and looking up to heaven, he gave thanks and broke the loaves. Then he gave them to his disciples to set before the people. He also divided the two fish among them all. They all ate and were satisfied, and the disciples picked up twelve basketfuls of broken pieces of bread and fish. The number of the men who had eaten was five thousand.

Luke 9:10–17

When the apostles returned, they reported to Jesus what they had done. Then he took them with him and they withdrew by themselves to a town called Bethsaida, but the crowds learned about it and followed him. He welcomed them and spoke to them about the kingdom of God, and healed those who needed healing. Late in the afternoon the Twelve came to him and said, 'Send the crowd away so they can go to the surrounding villages and country-side and find food and lodging, because we are in a remote place here.' He replied, 'You give them something to eat.' They answered, 'We have only five loaves of bread and two fish – unless we go and buy food for all this crowd.' (About five thousand men were there.) But he said to his disciples, 'Make them sit down in groups of about fifty each.' The disciples did so, and everybody sat down. Taking the five loaves and the two fish and looking up to heaven, he gave thanks and broke them. Then he gave them to the disciples to set before the people. They all ate and were satisfied, and the disciples picked up twelve basketfuls of broken pieces that were left over.

John 6:1–15

Some time after this, Jesus crossed to the far shore of the Sea of Galilee (that is, the Sea of Tiberias), and a great crowd of people followed him because they saw the miraculous signs he had performed on the sick. Then Jesus went up on a mountain-side and sat down with his disci-ples. The Jewish Passover Feast was near. When Jesus looked up and saw a great crowd coming towards him, he said to Philip, 'Where shall we buy bread for these people to eat?' He asked this only to test him, for he already had in mind what he was going to do. Philip answered him, 'Eight months' wages would not buy enough bread for each one to have a bite!' Another of his disciples, Andrew, Simon Peter's brother, spoke up, 'Here is a boy with five small barley loaves and two small fish, but how far will they go among so many?' Jesus said, 'Make the people sit down.' There was plenty of grass in that place, and the men sat down, about five thousand of them. Jesus then took the loaves, gave thanks, and distrib-uted to those who were seated as much as they wanted. He did the same with the fish. When they had all had enough to eat, he said to his disciples, 'Gather the pieces that are left over. Let nothing be wasted.' So they gathered them and filled twelve baskets with the pieces of the five barley loaves left over by those who had eaten. After the people saw the miraculous sign that Jesus did, they began to say, 'Surely this is the Prophet who is to come into the world.' Jesus, knowing that they intended to come and make him king by force, withdrew again to a mountain by himself.

Over the years, source criticism has been developed and applied particularly to the study of the Gospels. Because Matthew, Mark and Luke have so much in common in their accounts of the life of Jesus, they are known as the 'Synoptic Gospels', a term first coined by the German textual critic Johann Jacob Griesbach (1745–1812). This observation gives rise to the 'Synoptic Problem' – just *why* are they so similar in structure, tone and content to one another in some places? And why are they so very different from John? Similar issues arise in the study of other New Testament books. There are striking parallels and contrasts between Ephesians and Colossians and also between 2 Peter and Jude, observations which suggest that the author of one text may have used the other as a source. The value of source criticism is that it gives us an insight into the earlier history of the traditions which were drawn together to form the New Testament and enables us to see how those which are extant (i.e. have survived) have been changed by those who chose to shape and order them in particular ways.

The Synoptic Problem

To begin with, even a superficial look at the Synoptic Gospels shows that the **wording** is often very similar. To pursue this subject in detail you must look at the Greek text with the aid of a synopsis, a book which prints parallel passages alongside each other. For our present purposes, we shall simply compare the text of the NIV in the different Gospels. Here is an example of a so-called 'triple tradition' where all three of the Synoptic Gospels describe the same events in a remarkably similar way. For the sake of comparison, the way John describes what seems to be the same incident is also set out.

In fact, around 90 per cent of the 661 verses in Mark are also found in Matthew and about half of them are also found in Luke. But it isn't only the wording. A further similarity between the three is in the order of the events they describe. For an example of this, compare Matthew 12:46–13:58, Mark 3:31–6:6a and Luke 8:1–56. Then there is the idiosyncratic way in which they sometimes **quote from the Old Testament**, using a version which corresponds to neither of the two versions of the Old Testament commonly available at the time. For example, compare Mark 1:2, Matthew 3:3 and Luke 3:4.

For many centuries, the Synoptic Problem wasn't really seen as a 'problem' at all. The similarities were just there: this happens to be how the Holy Spirit chose to guide the authors of the first three Gospels. Another way of approaching the question is to assert that Matthew, Mark and Luke are similar because they are all reporting what actually happened. But even if they are historically accurate, this doesn't solve the Synoptic Problem. For one thing, the similarities are simply too close. Think back to the teacher marking his students' essays and finding passages which are identical. After all, it's almost always possible to write about a subject or to describe an event in several different ways – so why do the Gospel writers so often use exactly the *same* wording?

Back in the fifth century, Augustine (354–430), who laid the foundations of Christian theology for at least a millenium, dealt with the observation that Matthew, Mark and Luke are so similar to one another and so different from John like this:

> ...Matthew is understood to have taken it in hand to construct the record of the incarnation of the Lord according to the royal lineage, and to give an account of most part of his deeds and words as they stood in relation to this present life of men. Mark follows him closely, and looks like his attendant and epitomizer. For in his narrative he gives nothing in concert with John apart from the others; by himself separately, he has little to record; in conjunction with Luke, as distinguished from the rest, he has still less; but in concord with Matthew, he has a very large number of passages. Much, too, he narrates in words almost numerically and identically the same as those used by Matthew, where the agreement is either with that evangelist alone, or with himself in connection with the rest... (On the Consensus of the Evangelists, ii)

Clearly, Augustine observes the similarities but does not feel the need to go further and explain them. Not until the rise of biblical criticism were they seen as a problem to be solved. Four main proposals for solving the Synoptic Problem were put forward.

1 In 1771, Lessing proposed that there must have been an earlier Gospel (called a proto-Gospel, pre-Gospel or, in German, an *Ur-Gospel*), written in Hebrew or Aramaic, which was drawn on independently by each of the authors of the Synoptic Gospels. This **common dependence on one original Gospel** theory was modified by Johann Gottfried Eichhorn (1752–1827), who argued that there were several such 'original' Gospels, all of which have now been lost. This line of thinking has not received much support in the twentieth century. Its major weakness is its inability to account for the striking degree of agreement in the *Greek* text of the Gospels.

2 In 1796, Johann Gottfried Herder (1744–1803) suggested instead that the similarities between the Synoptic Gospels were due to their authors each making use of a **common oral tradition**. In a culture where writing was much less common than it is today, what Jesus said and did would have been passed round by word of mouth, initially in Aramaic and then in Greek, and only committed to the ancient equivalent of paper when the original witnesses were beginning to die out. Herder argued that the authors of Matthew, Mark and Luke drew from this oral tradition when they came to write their Gospels. This view, however, is unlikely to be right, though it is not without its supporters today. For one thing, it's very noticeable that, as we saw earlier, the Gospel writers preserve a similar *order* of events. Even when Matthew or Luke go off on an individual diversion, they always return to the sequence set out in Mark. Another point to be noticed is the similarity in the writer's editorial comments to his readers that cannot have been part of the oral tradition. For example, here is a parallel passage in Matthew and Mark which contains the identical aside 'let the reader understand'.

Matthew 24:15–16
So when you see standing in the holy place 'the abomination that causes desolation', spoken of through the prophet Daniel – let the reader understand – then let those who are in Judea flee to the mountains...

Mark 13:14

When you see 'the abomination that causes desolation' standing where it does not belong – let the reader understand – then let those who are in Judea flee to the mountains...

3 Friedrich Daniel Ernst Schleiermacher (1768–1834) took the view that earlier written sources existed, not as complete Gospels, but as fragments of tradition which grew to form the basis for our present Gospels. The idea that the Synoptic Gospels demonstrate **common dependence based on written fragments** is no longer thought of as an adequate solution to the Synoptic Problem as a whole, though the possible existence of one such fragment, known as Q, is widely acknowledged (see below).

4 Most scholars today argue that there must be some sort of a **literary interdependence** between the Synoptic Gospels, a relationship in which one or more of the Gospel writers have copied from what the others have written. With thoughts of students reproducing each other's essays in mind, we tend to regard copying as a form of cheating and rather look down on those who practise it. But in the ancient world, this sort of plagiarism was viewed rather differently. Indeed, to go to the trouble of copying someone was seen as a compliment rather than an affront.

This, then, is the essence of the Synoptic Problem as scholars approach it today: who is copying what from whom?

—— The Griesbach hypothesis ——

The solution which has come to bear the name of the eighteenth-century scholar J.J. Griesbach was that Matthew wrote first, then Luke (who used Matthew) and then Mark (who used both Matthew and Luke). In its favour is the fact that commentators from the time of the early church are unanimous in the view that Matthew was indeed the first Gospel to be written. Indeed, as we saw above, Augustine saw Mark as little more than an abridgement of Matthew. It is also able to account quite easily for something which the other main solution (the two-source hypothesis, which has Mark first with both Matthew and Luke using him independently: see below) finds difficult. This is the fact that when Matthew and Luke apparently reword something in Mark they often do so identically. This suggests that either Matthew knew Luke, or Luke knew Matthew. For example, here is Mark 9:2–4, together with the parallels in Matthew and Luke.

Mark 9:2–4
After six days Jesus took Peter, James and John with him and led them up a high mountain, where they were all alone. There he was transfigured before them. His clothes became dazzling white, whiter than anyone in the world could bleach them. And there appeared before them Elijah and Moses, who were talking with Jesus.

Matthew 17:1–3
After six days Jesus took with him Peter, James and John the brother of James, and led them up a high mountain by themselves. There he was transfigured before them. His face shone like the sun, and his clothes became as white as the light. Just then there appeared before them Moses and Elijah, talking with Jesus.

Luke 9:28–31a
About eight days after Jesus said this, he took Peter, John and James with him and went up onto a mountain to pray. As he was praying, the appearance of his face changed, and his clothes became as bright as a flash of lightning. Two men, Moses and Elijah, appeared in glorious splendour, talking with Jesus.

If Matthew and Luke are independent of each other, why do they *both* choose to remove Mark's comment about Jesus' clothes being 'whiter than anyone in the world could bleach them'?

Another strength of the Griesbach hypothesis is that, in making Mark dependent on Matthew and Luke, it can explain one of Mark's rather curious features, namely the many redundancies in his writing. For example, here is Mark 1:32: '*That evening after sunset the people brought to Jesus all the sick and demon-possessed*'. Why does Mark say both 'That evening' *and* 'after sunset' when either phrase would have been sufficient by itself? Add to this the observation that Matthew 8:16 has '*When evening came...*' and Luke 4:40 has '*When the sun was setting...*'. The suggestion is that where Matthew and Luke differ, then Mark, with both of them in front of him, has sometimes chosen to conflate them by including both readings.

However, most scholars consider that there is more to said against the Griesbach hypothesis than for it. For one thing, although early church tradition is unanimous in asserting that Matthew was written first, Papias (c. 60–130), Bishop of Hierapolis in Asia Minor, states that Mark was written *independently* of Matthew, and writers such as Origen (a great biblical scholar who lived from c. 185 to c. 254) and Augustine suggest that Luke was written after Mark, not before him. Then again, although the hypothesis can usefully explain agreements of Matthew and Luke against Mark, it has problems with Matthew and Mark against Luke on the one hand and Mark and Luke against Matthew on the other. A further point is that although there are as many as 213 examples of redundancy in Mark, in only 17 of these does one half of the redundancy come only from Matthew and the other half only from Luke. In fact, given Mark's relatively poor and unpolished Greek, it seems much more likely that Matthew and Luke have *eliminated* Mark's redundancies in compiling their own Gospels rather than that Mark has *created* them by combining Matthew and Luke.

The two-source hypothesis

We come then to the alternative view which is generally accepted by scholars today, though with certain exceptions (notably the American scholar William R. Farmer (b. 1921), who has written in support of the Griesbach hypothesis). The 'two-source hypothesis' was popularised by the German scholar Heinrich Julius Holtzmann (1832–1910) back in 1863. It states that Mark was written first and was then used independently by Matthew and Luke. In addition, Matthew and Luke are said to have drawn from a hypothetical source called Q (the initial probably derives from the German *Quelle*, meaning source), consisting mainly of a collection of the teachings of Jesus. Why has this view found such favour?

The priority of Mark

1 In the first place, there is the observation about the **length** of the Gospels. It is much easier to think of Matthew (18,293 words) and Luke (19,376 words) *adding* to Mark (11,025 words) than to imagine Mark *abbreviating* Matthew and Luke and omitting so much material. This isn't conclusive, of course. Mark may have had reasons which we know nothing about – though it is worth noting

that the argument that he simply wanted to produce a shorter Gospel falls down with the observation that some of his stories are *longer* than they are in Matthew and Luke! Here is an example of this.

Matthew 19:13–15
Then little children were brought to Jesus for him to place his hands on them and pray for them. But the disciples rebuked those who brought them. Jesus said, 'Let the little children come to me, and do not hinder them, for the kingdom of heaven belongs to such as these.' When he had placed his hands on them, he went on from there.

Mark 10:13–16
People were bringing little children to Jesus to have him touch them, but the disciples rebuked them. When Jesus saw this, he was indignant. He said to them, 'Let the little children come to me, and do not hinder them, for the kingdom of God belongs to such as these. I tell you the truth, anyone who will not receive the kingdom of God like a little child will never enter it.' And he took the children in his arms, put his hands on them and blessed them.

Luke 18:15–17
People were also bringing babies to Jesus to have him touch them. When the disciples saw this, they rebuked them. But Jesus called the children to him and said, 'Let the little children come to me, and do not hinder them, for the kingdom of God belongs to such as these. I tell you the truth, anyone who will not receive the kingdom of God like a little child will never enter it.'

It's also difficult to account for the wholesale changes (e.g. in the infancy and resurrection narratives at the beginning and end of the Gospel story) that Luke must have made to Matthew if the Griesbach hypothesis is true.

2 Secondly, the **order** of events in Matthew and Luke suggests that they have both independently followed Mark. For example, Mark reports the list of the 12 disciples (3:13–19) before the raising of Jairus' daughter (5:21–43), whereas Matthew puts these events the other way round (9:18–26; 10:1–4). What does Luke do? If, as the Griesbach hypothesis argues, he was following Matthew, we would expect the raising of Jairus' daughter to be followed by the list of the 12 disciples. But in fact he follows Mark's order by putting the list of the 12 disciples first (6:12–16; 8:40–56).

3 Then there are examples of where Matthew or Luke appear to have **softened passages** in Mark which might create theological difficulties by placing Jesus or his disciples in a less favourable light. For example:

Mark 10:35–37
Then James and John, the sons of Zebedee, came to him. 'Teacher,' they said, 'we want you to do for us whatever we ask.' 'What do you want me to do for you?' he asked. They replied, 'Let one of us sit at your right and the other at your left in your glory.'

Matthew 20:20–21
Then the mother of Zebedee's sons came to Jesus with her sons and, kneeling down, asked a favour of him. 'What is it you want?' he asked. She said, 'Grant that one of these two sons of mine may sit at your right and the other at your left in your kingdom.'

It's easier to imagine Matthew wanting to change Mark by reporting a mother's request on behalf of her sons than to think of Mark wanting to change Matthew's account for the unflattering portrait of the selfishness of James and John which his own Gospel contains.

An example relating to Jesus himself emerges from a comparison of two other passages.

Mark 6:5
He could not do any miracles there, except lay his hands on a few sick people and heal them.

Matthew 13:58
And he did not do many miracles there because of their lack of faith.

Can you see why scholars have suggested that Matthew has changed Mark? The answer is that Mark's rather unflattering portrayal of Jesus being *unable* to perform miracles on this occasion seems to have been toned down by Matthew's assertion that he simply *didn't* do many of them.

4 More than this, it seems that Mark's **theology is less developed** than that of Matthew and Luke. For example, Mark uses the title 'Lord' (*kyrios*) for Jesus just six times, whereas Matthew has five times as many instances and Luke even more. Again, although it's by no means impossible to think of Mark deciding to eliminate references to Jesus as Lord from Matthew and Luke, it's easier to think of Matthew and Luke adding them to what they found in Mark.

5 As noted earlier, Mark's **Greek is not as good** as that produced by Matthew and Luke. He also includes Aramaic expressions which Matthew and Luke omit. Here, for example, in the account of the healing by Jesus of Jairus' daughter.

Mark 5:41–42
He took her by the hand and said to her, 'Talitha koum!' (which means, 'Little girl, I say to you, get up!'). Immediately the girl stood up and walked around (she was twelve years old). At this they were completely astonished.

Matthew 9:25
After the crowd had been put outside, he went in and took the girl by the hand, and she got up.

Luke 8:54–55
But he took her by the hand and said, 'My child, get up!' Her spirit returned, and at once she stood up. Then Jesus told them to give her something to eat.

There's no problem with the idea that Matthew and Luke sought to improve what they found in Mark, but it's difficult to think of Mark taking Matthew and Luke and deliberately making their Greek worse.

6 A number of **stylistic features** suggest that Mark came first. For instance, Mark has a habit of using a characteristic 'for...' clause to explain things to his readers. An example is at the end of Mark 1:16: '*As Jesus walked beside the Sea of Galilee, he saw Simon and his brother Andrew casting a net into the lake, for they were fishermen.*' He does this 34 times, whereas in Matthew we find just ten such clauses. The point is that all ten are in material he shares with Mark. This is understandable if Matthew used Mark. But if Mark used Matthew, why are Matthew's 'for...' clauses only found in the material he shares with Mark?

None of these arguments is completely watertight and conclusive. But, taken together, their combined weight has led to a consensus among New Testament scholars that the best way to explain the Synoptic Problem is to assume that Matthew and Luke used Mark when they wrote their Gospels.

Q

Given that Matthew and Luke used Mark, how are we to explain material in both Matthew and Luke which is not found in Mark? Such material, known as the double tradition, consists of about 250 verses comprised mainly of the sayings of Jesus. The obvious alternative possibility, of course, is that either Matthew or Luke had each other as an additional source from which to work. However, there are good reasons for thinking that Matthew and Luke are independent of each other and that the non-Markan material they have in common comes from another source.

First, look at this example as Jesus replies to those who accuse his disciples of breaking Sabbath law.

Matthew 12:3–8
He answered, 'Haven't you read what David did when he and his companions were hungry? He entered the house of God, and he and his companions ate the consecrated bread – which was not lawful for them to do, but only for the priests. Or haven't you read in the Law that on the Sabbath the priests in the temple desecrate the day and yet are innocent? I tell you that one greater than the temple is here. If you had known what these words mean, 'I desire mercy, not sacrifice,' you would not have condemned the innocent. For the Son of Man is Lord of the Sabbath.'

Mark 2:25–28
He answered, 'Have you never read what David did when he and his companions were hungry and in need? In the days of Abiathar the high priest, he entered the house of God and ate the consecrated bread, which is lawful only for priests to eat. And he also gave some to his companions.' Then he said to them, 'The Sabbath was made for man, not man for the Sabbath. So the Son of Man is Lord even of the Sabbath.'

Luke 6:3–5
Jesus answered them, 'Have you never read what David did when he and his companions were hungry? He entered the house of God, and taking the consecrated bread, he ate what is lawful only for priests to eat. And he also gave some to his companions.' Then Jesus said to them, 'The Son of Man is Lord of the Sabbath.'

In what we may presume to be his revision of Mark, Matthew adds a comment about priests and the temple, whereas Luke limits himself to what Mark says. But if Luke used Matthew as well as Mark, we would expect him to follow Matthew in his revision of Mark, at least occasionally. The point is that he never does. And when the boot is on the other foot, Matthew never follows Luke in *his* revisions of Mark either. The obvious conclusion is that Matthew and Luke are independent of each other and that at least some of the material they have in common comes from the hypothetical source Q.

The way Matthew and Luke use Q is also significant. Matthew arranges his Q material in five blocks of teaching (Chapters 5–7, 10, 13, 18, 23–25) surrounded by six blocks of narrative. Luke, on the other hand, arranges his Q material in a completely different pattern – scattered throughout the Gospel with most of it in just two blocks: 6:20–8:3 and 9:51–18:14.

Despite this difference, there is still significant agreement in the *order* of the material. This, together with the close verbal agreements between the Q material in Matthew and Luke suggest that Q was a written rather than an oral source. For example, all 24 words in Matthew 7:7–8 and its parallel in Luke 11:9–10 are identical. On the other hand, this is true of only about half of the non-Markan material which Matthew and Luke have in common. The rest, though sharing similar themes, does not show the same verbal agreement. It may be then that Q as a written source accounts for just this half, while the remaining hundred verses or so came to Matthew and Luke independently.

In discussing the Griesbach hypothesis, we noted the advantage that it has in being able to account for the agreements between Matthew and Luke against Mark. But there are other ways of explaining this which allow the two-source hypothesis to stand. For example, many of these agreements may simply be coincidental decisions to improve Mark's grammar or syntax. In addition, it may be that there is a degree of overlap between Mark and Q (or another independent oral or written tradition) and that, when faced with a choice about which to use, both Matthew and Luke chose independently to follow this other source rather than Mark. Another proposal is that Matthew and Luke used a different version of Mark from the one which has survived, either an earlier one known to scholars as Proto-Mark (or, in German, *Ur-Markus*) or else a later one known as Deutero-

Mark. (The prefixes proto- and deutero- come from the Greek for first and second.)

Finally, we should note that it has been suggested more recently by scholars such as Austin M. Farrer (1904–1968) and Michael D. Goulder (b. 1927) that Mark wrote first, then Matthew, and that Luke then used them both. This has the advantage of doing away with the need for Q, but adds a whole series of difficult questions about why Luke should have omitted or revised so much of Matthew.

At the end of the day, the two-document hypothesis with the priority of Mark and the one-time existence of Q seems to account for the evidence better than any other theory. But it must be emphasised that the evidence is far from conclusive.

From two to four

In 1924, the Oxford scholar Burnet Hillmann Streeter (1874–1937) went a stage further with his 'four-source hypothesis' in which teaching material unique to Matthew or Luke was identified as M or L. On the basis of the present structure of Luke's Gospel, Streeter suggested that a writer (thought by Streeter to be Luke himself) had first combined Q with L to produce a single document identified as Proto-Luke and then, at a later date, the same or possibly another writer added parts of Mark to this work to produce what we now know as Luke's Gospel. Streeter's work on Matthew led him to conclude that the author of Matthew's Gospel had taken Mark as his basic framework and incorporated sections of Q and a document identified as M, material which has a markedly Jewish flavour. Since Streeter's time, M and L have been to used to identify, not so much specific sources, but all the material, both written and oral, narrative and didactic (i.e. teaching), which is unique to Matthew and Luke.

Finally, several scholars have sought to integrate some of the evidence from the early church into their view of the Synoptic Problem. This is the widespread tradition that Matthew was the first Gospel to be written, together with the reported remark by the second-century bishop Papias (quoted by Eusebius, who was Bishop of Caesarea in the fourth century) that 'Matthew collected the oracles in the Hebrew language, and each interpreted them as best he could'. From this, it's

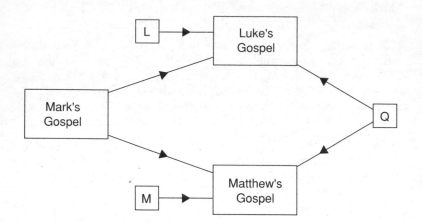

been suggested (a) that Matthew wrote first, (b) that he did so in Aramaic or Hebrew, (c) that Mark used this edition in composing his Greek Gospel, and (d) that Matthew revised his Gospel in Greek using Mark. Although this view has its attractions, it's by no means certain that Papias' statement about Matthew refers to an actual Gospel. As is so often the way with questions like this, the case remains unproven.

───── Questions to consider ─────

1 How would you answer someone who suggested that to study the Bible critically was irreverent?
2 What is the 'Synoptic Problem'? Which solution do you favour? Why?

9

THE CRITICAL STUDY
OF THE
NEW TESTAMENT: 2

Form criticism

The next major development in the critical study of the New Testament is form criticism. By 1920, a trio of German scholars, Karl Ludwig Schmidt (1891–1956), Martin Franz Dibelius (1883–1947) and Rudolf Bultmann, were busy investigating the way in which stories and sayings were transmitted before being written down in the Gospels. It's very striking how the Synoptic Gospels in particular consist of events and stories, more or less complete in themselves, which are simply linked like beads on a string and separated by brief link passages. Each individual unit, or 'bead', is known as a *pericope* (from the Greek for 'cut around'). (Incidentally, the final 'e' is pronounced as in 'anemone' rather than as in 'periscope'.) The possibility that the surrounding narrative framework may not be historical was proposed by William Wrede in 1901. Schmidt took this view further and argued that the links between the pericopae were only added to the tradition as and when the Gospels were written down.

The British scholar Charles Harold Dodd (1884–1973) challenged this view, pointing to the close parallels between Mark's narrative framework and the outline of Jesus' life and ministry set out in the sermons of Peter and Paul in the Acts of the Apostles (particularly Acts 10:37–41; 13:23–31). He suggested that the account of the life of Jesus in Mark's Gospel is therefore both early and accurate.

Form criticism is also sometimes referred to as *Formgeschichte* (the German for 'form history'), a term first used by Franz Overbeck

(1837–1905) in 1882. As a critical tool, it was first used by scholars such as Hermann Gunkel (1862–1932) in his work on the Old Testament. In Gospel criticism it seeks to discover more about how the individual pericopae were passed on by word of mouth, perhaps for several years, before being written down. Form criticism is closely related to the discipline of tradition criticism (*Traditionsgeschichte* or, sometimes, *Überlieferungsgeschichte*). Strictly speaking, form criticism seeks to *classify* pericopae into their different types, while tradition criticism examines their *history* and how they have changed over time. In practice though, there is considerable overlap between the two fields of study and so, for our purposes, we will use the umbrella term 'form criticism'.

Studying the Gospels in this way suggests that their writers are not so much *authors* of new material as *assemblers* of material they have collected together. Form criticism assumes that, with the exception of the extended narratives describing the passion and death of Jesus (see below), the Gospel pericopae circulated as individual units. It has not been possible to demonstrate that this is an accurate picture, however, and it may be better to think in terms of groups or *cycles* of pericopae associated with particular leaders in the early church. These would have been used as needed by teachers and preachers and only brought together when the Gospels were compiled. To help in their analysis, form critics have sought out parallels in the oral traditions of other ancient European cultures. Their conclusions suggest that what we now have in the Gospels was considerably amended during the stage of oral transmission, so that each of the individual pericopae conforms to one of a number of different patterns. This raises doubts about their ability to reflect accurately what Jesus actually did and said. Instead they are said to be a much more accurate reflection of the early church situation in which they were created – the *Sitz im Leben* (i.e. life setting), as it's usually called. Indeed, this is what Bultmann in particular saw as the purpose of form criticism – not so much to find out about Jesus but to discover more about the early church.

However, just because preachers and teachers in the early church found value in telling stories about Jesus does not necessarily mean that they invented them in the first place or that their reshaping of them was so radical that they no longer reflect what Jesus said or did. In fact it's very noticeable that the Gospels singularly fail to address many of the problems which arise in the rest of the New Testament. For example, we know from Acts 15 and Paul's letter to the Galatians that the early church was in danger of deep division over the question of following the Jewish custom of circumcising converts. If the early church really did feel free to invent sayings of Jesus to fit in with their needs, why do the Gospels say nothing at all about circumcision (apart from recording the fact that Jesus himself was circumcised)? This argument also works the other way round – for it's equally clear that some of what the Gospels *do* take care to preserve was not, as far as we can tell, especially relevant to the early church.

The task of the form critic is threefold:

a) to classify each individual self-contained unit according to its form.
b) to ask about the situation in the early church (i.e. the *Sitz im Leben*) which the pericope would have been used to address, perhaps in preaching, or in arguing the case for Christianity against its opponents, or in settling disputes within the Christian community, or simply in telling a story.
c) to try to chip away any accretions and restore any deletions in order to reconstruct the original shape of each pericope.

It's been impossible for scholars to agree on a precise way of classifying the different forms, but here is one list, based on the original work by Dibelius, which classifies them according to their presumed function in the early church. (Bultmann's terms classify pericopae in line with similar forms in other ancient literature.)

1 Paradigms (also known as apophthegms or pronouncement stories). These are stories which lead up to an especially striking conclusion. A typical example is Mark 3:31–35.

Then Jesus' mother and brothers arrived. Standing outside, they sent someone in to call him. A crowd was sitting around him, and they told him, 'Your mother and brothers are outside looking for you.' 'Who are my mother and my brothers?' he asked. Then he looked at those seated in a circle around him and said, 'Here are my mother and my brothers! Whoever does God's will is my brother and sister and mother.'

Dibelius called these pericopae 'paradigms' (from the Greek for 'example') because of the way he thought they would have been used in early Christian preaching. Paradigms are typically brief, lack any unnecessary detail and lead up to a saying of Jesus which stands out rather like the punch-line in a joke. Bultmann preferred the term 'apophthegm' for this type of pericope, believing Dibelius' limitation of them to preaching to be too narrow, while the British scholar Vincent Taylor opted for the term 'pronouncement story'.

2 Tales (also known as novellen or miracle stories). These are accounts of the miracles of Jesus which, rather than abandoning detail in the lead up to a striking saying, include points of interest and colour throughout. For this reason, Dibelius thought that they were the province of a distinct group of story-tellers in the early church. He further classified them into three types – exorcisms (e.g. Mark 5:1–20), other healing miracles (e.g. Mark 5:21–43) and nature miracles (e.g. Mark 4:35–41).

Typically, pericopae in this form begin by stating the disease or problem that needs putting right (in this case, the storm). They continue with an account of how Jesus remedies the situation and then conclude with a statement about the effect on the person healed and/or the onlookers (in this case, the calming of the storm and the terror and amazement of the disciples). Dibelius concluded that the purpose of such stories was to demonstrate the superiority of Jesus over rival gods and miracle-workers. In other words, they were used as a means of persuading non-Christians rather than for teaching Christians.

3 Legends (also known as historical stories or stories about Jesus). Dibelius held that the purpose of these stories (which are not necessarily unhistorical, as the word 'legend' might be thought to imply) was to satisfy the curiosity of Christians and others about Jesus and those who were with him. For example, the story of the fate of Judas in Matthew 27:3–8 is simply a piece of information about him – it isn't used as a way of getting any other message across:

When Judas, who had betrayed him, saw that Jesus was condemned, he was seized with remorse and returned the thirty silver coins to the chief priests and the elders. 'I have sinned,' he said, 'for I have betrayed innocent blood.' 'What is that to us?' they replied. 'That's your responsibility.' So Judas threw the money into the temple and left. Then he went away and hanged himself. The chief priests picked up the coins and said, 'It is against the law to put this into the treasury, since it is blood money.' So they decided to use the money to buy the potter's field as a burial place for foreigners. That is why it has been called the Field of Blood to this day.

4 Myths In general speech, to describe something as a 'myth' is to cast doubt on whether or not it is true. But that's not primarily what Dibelius meant. In his thinking, a myth is a narrative in which the supernatural breaks in on the normal course of events. There are only three: the events surrounding the baptism of Jesus (Mark 1:9–11 and parallels), the temptation of Jesus in the wilderness (Matthew 4:1–11 and parallels), and the transfiguration of Jesus (Mark 9:2–8 and parallels). Here is Mark 1:9–11.

At that time Jesus came from Nazareth in Galilee and was baptised by John in the Jordan. As Jesus was coming up out of the water, he saw heaven being torn open and the Spirit descending on him like a dove. And a voice came from heaven: 'You are my Son, whom I love; with you I am well pleased.'

5 Exhortations The purpose of this category is to gather together the teaching material in the Gospels, including the parables, commandments and wise sayings of Jesus. Bultmann preferred to divide this category into just two – the 'I-sayings' of Jesus and his parables.

6 Passion narrative Although content to divide most of the Gospels up into their constituent units, Dibelius saw the passion narratives like an unbreakable string of beads, in which all the pericopae were kept together and recounted as a whole.

Scholars have subsequently cast doubt on the wisdom of using this system of classification too rigidly – as is clear from the fact that there are so many different versions of it! It's been argued that though form criticism can be useful, many pericopae display characteristics of more than one type or are at best ambiguous. The attempt to force every Gospel pericope into such a structure is therefore unhelpful. Robert Henry Lightfoot (1883–1953), one of the British scholars who did much to bring form criticism across from Germany, concluded that pronouncement stories and miracle stories were the only useful categories which have emerged.

How does all this work out in practice? As an example, let's take Luke 16:19–31, a passage which has often been used by Christian preachers in the past as a source of information about life after death. In fact, this story has several parallels in Jewish and Egyptian folk stories and it seems much more likely that it's a parable in which Jesus adapts popular and well-known imagery to make his point about the need for repentance in this life. To draw deductions from this passage about what Jesus thought about life after death is therefore quite unwarranted. Further evidence that the passage is indeed a parable (even though Luke does not specifically identify it as such) comes from the style of its introduction. 'There was a man...' is an introductory formula (see also, for example, Luke 14:16, 15:11 and 16:1), rather like our 'Once upon a time...' which alerts us to the fact that what follows will be a story rather than a factual account.

Although the insights of form criticism can be useful, applying them too rigidly is bound to lead to conclusions which are, at best, dubious. For example, considerations of form have led scholars to assert that the parables of Jesus were designed to make only one point. An example of one which doesn't is set out in Luke 16:1–9.

Jesus told his disciples: 'There was a rich man whose manager was accused of wasting his possessions. So he called him in and asked him, 'What is this I hear about you? Give an account of your management, because you cannot be manager any longer.' 'The manager said to himself, 'What shall I do now? My master is taking away my job. I'm not strong enough to dig, and I'm ashamed to beg – I know what I'll do so that, when I lose my job here, people will welcome me into their houses.' So he called in each one of his master's debtors. He asked the first, 'How much do you owe my master?' 'Eight hundred gallons of olive oil,' he replied. The manager told him, 'Take your bill, sit down quickly, and make it four hundred.' Then he asked the second, 'And how much do you owe?' 'A thousand bushels of wheat,' he replied. He told him, 'Take your bill and make it eight hundred.' The master commended the dishonest manager because he had acted shrewdly. For the people of this world are more shrewd in dealing with their own kind than are the people of the light. I tell you, use worldly wealth to gain friends for yourselves, so that when it is gone, you will be welcomed into eternal dwellings.

Scholars have sometimes unwisely gone on to conclude that any parable which makes more than one point must therefore have been tampered with during transmission. In this case, form critical insights suggests that verse 9, in drawing out a second moral, is a later addition. But this isn't *necessarily* so at all. Why should Jesus be forced into the strait-jacket of being allowed to tell only parables with one point?

Other assumptions which form critics work with are also open to question. For example, even if it is allowed that significant distortion occurs in the oral transmission of traditions in other ancient cultures, the parallels with the Gospels are far from exact. For one thing, the timescale is very different, with the time between the events the Gospels purport to describe and their compilation into written documents being measured in four or so decades rather than the several centuries which other examples took to shape.

Form critical suppositions have been further challenged by Scandinavian scholars such as Harald Riesenfeld and his student Birger Gerhardsson. They have suggested that, far from exhibiting a story-teller's sense of creative freedom in the way they transmitted the traditions about Jesus, the early church followed the pattern of careful memorisation and accurate transmission laid down by Jewish rabbis for their teaching. The problem with this line of thought is the difficulty in demonstrating that Jesus *did* in fact teach like a Jewish rabbi. If he did, would we not expect the parallels between the Gospels to be even more exact than they are? And anyway, did rabbis in the first century necessarily follow the same practices as their second- and third-century equivalents, from whom Riesenfeld and Gerhardsson draw most of their evidence? More recently, the German scholar Rainer Riesner has broadened the net beyond rabbinic practice and sought to show, from educational methods used generally in the ancient world, that the followers of Jesus would have been careful to preserve accurate information about Jesus, even if they did not necessarily memorise it word for word.

In encouraging us to think about the *Sitz im Leben* a given Gospel story would have addressed in the first century, form criticism is a valuable tool which helps us to apply the Gospels more effectively in our own situation. An example is the interpretation of the so-called Beatitudes in Matthew 5:3–12. Klaus Koch has shown that, in terms of their *form*, these have more in common with Old Testament apocalyptic blessings (i.e. blessings which focus on the world to come) than with Old Testament wisdom sayings (i.e. blessings which focus on this life). It's more likely, therefore, that Jesus is referring to the future rather than to the present in this list of blessings.

As we've seen, one of the assumptions made by form critics is that the final shape of the Gospel pericopae has been influenced by the *Sitz im Leben* in which they were used. If this is true, then it's likely that some have been reworked more than others. To help work out which are more likely to have been transmitted without significant amendment, a number of 'criteria of authenticity' have been proposed. None can make the case by itself but, used together, they can give us greater confidence that a particular story or saying goes back to Jesus himself rather than originating with the early church.

There are three main such criteria. The first is the criterion of *multiple attestation*. This states that if a particular event or saying is found in more than one truly independent strand of the Gospel tradition, then it is more likely to be genuine. Secondly, there is the criterion of *coherence*. If there are good grounds for considering a particular tradition to be genuine, then traditions which cohere with or are similar to it are also likely to be genuine. Thirdly, there is the even more controversial criterion of *dissimilarity*. This suggests that a tradition is more likely to be genuine if it does *not* chime in with what one might expect from Jesus' Jewish background or the life of the early church. The problem is, of course, that rigid application of this criterion leads those who do not understand its limitations to throw the baby out with the bathwater! It's highly unlikely that Jesus' teaching would not have been influenced by his Jewish background to some extent or show a degree of continuity with that of the early church. A fourth criterion of authenticity is *unintended evidence of historicity*. These are incidental details which suggest an eye-witness report such as the 'green grass' of Mark 6:39. Fifthly, we have the criterion of *Aramaic* or *Palestinian features* which are presumed to be early. Finally, material which is short and lacking in detail is said to be more likely to be historical.

Although, as we have seen, form criticism can be a constructive tool in the study of the Gospels in particular, it must be used with caution. The scepticism with which form critics tend to view the possibility of material about Jesus being accurately transmitted should not be allowed to go unchallenged. It remains to be demonstrated, for example, that the early church really did feel free to place on the lips of the earthly Jesus the sayings of early Christian prophets who were presumed to be speaking in the name of their risen Lord.

Redaction criticism

If the work of form criticism is to focus on the 'bricks' that have been brought together to make up the Gospels, redaction critics work more on the 'wall' as a whole and ask about the Gospel writer's contribution to his work. How has he shaped the bricks he has chosen? What order has he decided to place them in? What sort of cement has he used? The focus is on the writer's role as editor (i.e. redactor) of the material before him, so that the question is not so much what the Gospels tell us about *Jesus* or the *early church* in which the stories about him were first told, but what they reveal about their *authors* and the particular perspectives which each has. The church's decision to recognise all four Gospels underlines a desire to take seriously the distinctive emphases which each provides.

Form criticism traces its origins back to the work of three German scholars (Schmidt, Dibelius and Bultmann) after the First World War. Redaction criticism began in earnest shortly after the Second World War, again with three German scholars, this time Günther Bornkamm (1905–90), Hans Conzelmann (1915–89) and Willi Marxsen (b. 1919). Each is noted for his contribution to the redaction criticism of specific Gospels – Bornkamm with Matthew, Conzelmann with Luke and Marxsen (who first coined the term *Redaktionsgeschichte*) with Mark.

Bornkamm's approach can be seen from his classic analysis (first published in 1948) of what Matthew has done with Mark in the account of the stilling of the storm.

Mark 4:35–41
That day when evening came, he said to his disciples, 'Let us go over to the other side.' Leaving the crowd behind, they took him along, just as he was, in the boat. There were also other boats with him. A furious squall came up, and the waves broke over the boat, so that it was nearly swamped. Jesus was in the stern, sleeping on a cushion. The disciples woke him and said to him, 'Teacher, don't you care if we drown?' He got up, rebuked the wind and said to the waves, 'Quiet! Be still!' Then the wind died down and it was completely calm. He said to his disciples, 'Why are you so afraid? Do you still have no faith?' They were terrified and asked each other, 'Who is this? Even the wind and the waves obey him!'

Matthew 8:23–27
Then he got into the boat and his disciples followed him. Without warning, a furious storm came up on the lake, so that the waves swept over the boat. But Jesus was sleeping. The disciples went and woke

him, saying, 'Lord, save us! We're going to drown!' He replied, 'You of little faith, why are you so afraid?' Then he got up and rebuked the winds and the waves, and it was completely calm. The men were amazed and asked, 'What kind of man is this? Even the winds and the waves obey him!'

Bornkamm seeks to show that Matthew takes what Mark sets out as a straightforward example of the power of Jesus over the forces of nature and adapts it so that it also functions as a lesson for disciples about the ability of Jesus to save his followers from the storms of life. He arrives at this conclusion from a number of observations. Mark (and Luke) includes this particular story as one in a series of miracles stories, whereas in Matthew it comes after a brief pericope on the cost of discipleship (8:18–22). Further, Matthew specifies the way the disciples 'followed' Jesus into the boat (verse 23). Bornkamm suggests that this picks up the 'follow' theme from the previous pericope and sets the scene for this story as an illustration of what is involved in faithful discipleship. Matthew records the cry of the disciples in the form of a prayer which is addressed to Jesus as 'Lord'. Notice too that in Matthew the actual stilling of the storm comes *after* Jesus' chiding of his disciples, whereas in Mark Jesus speaks to the wind and the waves first. The disciples themselves appear in a rather better light: in Mark they have 'no faith' at all, while Matthew presents them at least as being 'of little faith'. Bornkamm concludes that this is a story which has deliberately been shaped so that it encourages the followers of Jesus to have faith in his ability to save them as they face the storms of life.

Whether each of Bornkamm's often rather subtle observations were intended by the author of the Gospel to mean what he suggests they mean is open to question. For example, did Matthew really intend his use of the word 'follow' in verse 23 to have the significance that Bornkamm gives it? The changes made by an author may simply be a reflection of his distinctive *style* rather than the setting out of a significant *theological* point. In addition, to focus simply on the *changes* to a tradition may result in a distorted picture. The parts of a tradition which are passed on *without* being modified aren't necessarily any less central to the author's concerns than those which he has chosen to amend. Furthermore, redaction critics sometimes make the unwarrantable assumption that the changes made by a Gospel writer have no basis in the historical tradition they are seeking to pass on. It is, however, entirely possible to imagine the authors of Matthew or Luke having access to other evidence which they are able to include in their revision of Mark.

Conzelmann's work, mainly with Luke's Gospel and the Acts of the Apostles, was first published in 1954. As Bornkamm had done with Matthew, Conzelmann sought to show that the author of Luke was a theologian in his own right rather than simply an assembler of stories (which is how form criticism tends to regard the Gospel writers). He argues that Luke's central concern was to deal with the problem of why Jesus had not fulfilled the widely held expectation among his followers that he would return (an event known as the 'second coming' or Parousia). Whereas Mark seems to view the Parousia as imminent, the way Luke handles him as a source is said to show that he has adapted his material to cope with the fact that such expectations were not being met. One of the ways he does this is to give more emphasis to the significance of the period of time after Jesus' resurrection and ascension – not as a time for Christians just to sit around waiting but to get on with their God-given mission. This focus on the history of the church finds particular expression in Luke's second volume, the Acts of the Apostles. According to Conzelmann, Luke regards the Parousia as sudden rather than soon: the return of Christ is not to be expected at a particular point in history but is something that will take place in the indefinite future. This is the perspective from which he sets about revising Mark. Here is one example where Luke is said to soften the impact of a statement in Mark that implies an early Parousia.

Mark 9:1
And he said to them, 'I tell you the truth, some who are standing here will not taste death before they see the kingdom of God come with power.'

Luke 9:27
'...I tell you the truth, some who are standing here will not taste death before they see the kingdom of God.'

Whether this is an accurate interpretation of what Luke has done with Mark is open to question. It seems at least equally plausible that the reference to the coming of the kingdom of God applies not to the end of the world but to the transfiguration of Jesus which both Gospels go on to describe in the next pericope. It's also necessary to question Conzelmann's portrayal of Mark as someone for whom the Parousia was to be expected as an imminent event. Mark 13:10, for example, sets out Jesus' statement that '...*the gospel must first be preached to all nations*' before he returns. In other words, Luke's theological outlook does not seem to be quite as distinctive as Conzelmann claims.

The third pioneer in this field was Marxsen, whose work on Mark's Gospel was published in 1959. Once again, he goes beyond form-critical analysis of the Gospel to ask questions about Mark's own contribution and outlook.

Redaction criticism proceeds by looking particularly at the changes made by the writer to his presumed sources. Seven such types of change have been identified.

First, as mentioned above, he could have made no changes at all and reproduced his source exactly. Like the dog that didn't bark in Sir Arthur Conan Doyle's famous Sherlock Holmes story *The Hound of the Baskervilles*, this is often significant but easily ignored. Secondly, sources can be *conflated*, something which both Matthew and Luke seem to have done with Mark and Q in the temptation story (Mt 4:1–11; Mk 2:12–13; Lk 4:1–13). Thirdly, a source can be *expanded*. An example of this is Matthew's expansion of Mark's account of the story in which Jesus walks on the water (Mt 14:22–33; Mk 6:45–52). Fourthly, the *setting* of a story can be changed, as when Matthew and Luke give different locations for where Jesus expresses compassion for Jerusalem (Mt 23:37–39; Lk 13:34–35). Fifthly, parts of the source can be *omitted*, as when Matthew leaves out the details of demonic activity which Mark includes in his account of the exorcism of a child (Mt 17:14–21; Mk 9:14–29). Sixthly, a writer can decide to *explain* details which a source takes for granted. An example of this is Mark's explanation of the significance of hand-washing (Mt 15:1–9; Mk 7:1–8). Finally, a source can be altered in order to *avoid possible misunderstanding*, as when Matthew changes Mark's '*Why do you call me good?*' (Mk 10:18) to '*Why do you ask me about what is good?*' (Mt 19:17).

Observing the patterns of such changes enables the student to come to tentative conclusions about their theological significance. As an example of this, here is the way Matthew and Mark end their accounts of when Jesus walks on the water.

Mark 6:51–52
Then he climbed into the boat with them [i.e. the disciples], *and the wind died down. They were completely amazed, for they had not understood about the loaves; their hearts were hardened.*

Matthew 14:32–33
And when they climbed into the boat, the wind died down. Then those who were in the boat worshipped him, saying, 'Truly you are the Son of God.'

It is apparent from this that Matthew has changed the focus of the story. What appears in Mark as an event which underlines the failure of the disciples is now one which highlights the way the presence of Jesus overcomes failure. That this might be significant is borne out by another example. This time, Jesus is warning his disciples against the 'yeast of the Pharisees', an image that they take literally.

Mark 8:20–21
'And when I broke the seven loaves for the four thousand, how many basketfuls of pieces did you pick up?' They answered, 'Seven.' He said to them, 'Do you still not understand?'

Matthew 16:11–12
'How is it you don't understand that I was not talking to you about bread? But be on your guard against the yeast of the Pharisees and Sadducees.' Then they understood that he was not telling them to guard against the yeast used in bread, but against the teaching of the Pharisees and Sadducees.

Once again, Matthew focuses on Jesus' success in helping the disciples to understand whereas Mark concentrates more on their failure to understand in the first place. In fact, it turns out that this theme of 'disciple failure' is one of Mark's primary concerns – he even ends the Gospel with an example of it (Mk 16:8). Tracing theological emphases like this in each Gospel as a whole is sometimes called 'motif analysis'.

As well as looking at individual pericopae, the redaction critic also examines the overall structure and content of the Gospel in order to identify the theological outlook of its writer. It's particularly important to look at the 'seams' in a Gospel – the introductions, conclusions and transition passages. For example, here is how Matthew introduces two episodes of teaching in the ministry of Jesus.

Matthew 4:23
Jesus went throughout Galilee, teaching in their synagogues, preaching the good news of the kingdom, and healing every disease and sickness among the people.

Matthew 9:35
Jesus went through all the towns and villages, teaching in their synagogues, preaching the good news of the kingdom and healing every disease and sickness.

Such repetition underlines Matthew's emphasis on the three main activities of teaching, preaching and healing in the ministry of Jesus.

A further way of identifying a writer's theological perspective is to examine the insertions and asides he makes to the narrative. This is particularly valuable in redactional analysis of John's Gospel, the most famous example of which is in Chapter 3, where verses 16–21 comment on the universal significance of the dialogue Jesus has with Nicodemus in verses 1–15.

Another aspect of the redaction critic's work, sometimes referred to as 'composition criticism', is to look not only at how the Gospel writers *change* the traditions they received, but also to examine the way they choose to *arrange* them.

For example, what significance is there in the fact that, in their accounts of the temptations of Jesus, Matthew and Luke place the second and third temptations in a different order (Mt 4:1–11; Lk 4:1–13)? The problem is that there are several different possibilities for the student to try to assess! From elsewhere in his Gospel, it's clear that Luke has a special interest in Jerusalem and the temple. So it may be that, in order to highlight this, he reverses the 'original' order (as set out in Matthew) by ending the temptation sequence with the one that deals with Jesus at the temple. On the other hand, we also know that Matthew has a particular interest in hills and mountains (e.g. 5:1; 8:1; 14:23; 15:29; 17:1; 21:1; 28:16). So it could be that Luke's is the original order and that Matthew ends with the temptation that takes place on a high mountain in order to underline *his* emphasis.

Other aspects of composition criticism include looking at the significance of the relationships between neighbouring pericopae, the development of plot lines within the Gospels, the different messages conveyed by the different settings of particular events and the way stories are differently phrased to bring out the particular emphases of the Gospel writers. One of the most famous examples of the latter is in the different versions of the Beatitudes set out by Matthew and Luke. Where Matthew 5:3 has *'Blessed are the poor in spirit, for theirs is the kingdom of heaven'*, Luke 6:20 has *'Blessed are you who are poor, for yours is the kingdom of God'*. Matthew's stress is on spiritual values, while Luke focuses on economic deprivation. Both ideas are found elsewhere in the teaching of Jesus set out in the Gospels, so it isn't that one is true and the other is necessarily false, just that the two Gospel writers choose to highlight different aspects.

Redaction criticism is not, of course, without its weaknesses. For one thing, it often seems to be taken for granted that the process of redaction led the Gospel writers to invent some of their material in order to make it fit in with what they wanted to say. Although this *may* have happened, it is clearly wrong to assume that it definitely *was* the case. Another point is that redaction criticism depends heavily on the four-source hypothesis of Gospel origins. Conclusions based on the supposition that Matthew used Mark would look quite different if the Griesbach hypothesis were correct after all and that Mark is independent of Matthew. It is also a highly subjective discipline, with different scholars producing radically diverse conclusions from the same observations. In addition, redaction critics have sometimes been tempted to see theological significance in every minor change and not allowed sufficiently for the possibility that differences may be purely stylistic. This is where composition criticism can be a useful corrective in helping students to see both the wood *and* the trees. There are also dangers in concentrating on the theological interests of the Gospel writers and the communities they are presumed to be writing for. After all, they may not be aiming everything they write in this direction: they may well have had a genuine interest in passing on historical traditions — whether or not they were immediately relevant to their own situations.

─────────── **Literary criticism** ───────────

We have looked at several ways in which scholars during the earlier part of this century have sought to study the text of the Gospels in particular. More recently, the emphasis has shifted from trying to work out what the New Testament writers were doing back in the first century to studying the impact made by what they wrote on those who read it today. For example, the traditional approach of historical criticism to gaps and repetitions in the text has been to try to tease out the ways in which several earlier sources have been, perhaps rather imperfectly, stuck together by the editors of the final work. But there is another way of approaching such observations which, instead of trying to look behind the text, focus (a) on the text itself and (b) in front of the text. For example, *narrative criticism* asks how gaps, repetitions and other aspects of the text are deliberate techniques which serve to create tension, raise questions and so on in the recounting of a story. *Discourse analysis* looks at how the language of the text functions as it does and how communication takes place with the modern reader. *Reader-response criticism* recognises that when we read the New Testament we do far more than simply absorb the text passively. We interact with what we read to create meaning and fit what we discover into what we already know. Reader-response critics evaluate how the text guides and seeks to persuade us (an area known as *rhetorical criticism*) and how we approach the text. For example, Mark includes two accounts of Jesus performing a miracle in which a large crowd is fed (6:30–44 and 8:1–10). Quite apart from questions about whether two such incidents actually took place is the issue of how the author presents the material and the effect the accounts have on the reader. Given what we have already read in the first passage, the account of the disciples' question – *'But where in this remote place can anyone get enough bread to feed them?'* – in verse 4 of the second passage serves to highlight their foolishness in the reader's mind.

As we have seen, the earlier history of biblical criticism rests on the assumption that the meaning of a text is best understood by discovering the intention of its author. Literary critics suggest that there are other worthwhile methods of finding meaning in the text through examining the encounter between the text and its reader. Thus *genre analysis* seeks, by comparing a given text with other examples of ancient writing, to establish the 'sort of literature' it is and so interpret it without necessarily referring to the intention of the author, which may not be known anyway.

Another branch of literary criticism is known as *structuralism*. This is based on the pioneering work of the Swiss scholar Ferdinand de Saussure (1857–1913), regarded as the founder of modern linguistics.

For those who follow him, the way to derive meaning from a text is not to become unduly preoccupied with its historical development (the 'diachronic' emphasis) but to look at it in terms of the relationships between its elements as we perceive them now (the 'synchronic' emphasis). He illustrates the point from consideration of a game of chess. In order to understand what is going on at any given stage, we only need to know the *present* state of the game and the relation of the pieces to one another on the board. It is not necessary (and may indeed be distracting) to know the *history* of how each player has moved their pieces. This is particularly relevant when considering *semantics*, the study of the meaning of words. Words often change their meaning as time goes by and so it can be seriously misleading to try to derive the meaning of a word from its etymology (i.e. the history of its formation and development). An example from the English language makes the point well. The word 'nice' is thought to be derived from the Latin word *nescius*, meaning 'ignorant'. Now when we describe someone as 'a very nice man' we do not (usually!) wish to imply any deficiency in what he knows. If what we mean is unclear, it must be judged primarily from the other things we are saying about him (synchronic study). Looking also at the history of the word (diachronic study) may help but can just as easily mislead us.

It's not that the history of words is unimportant – as long as we pay attention to the process of change and not leap back to the supposed 'original' meaning as the basic one. Diachronic investigation can also be misused in reverse – as when people try to elucidate the meaning of a New Testament Greek word like *dunamis* (meaning 'power') by suggesting that it carries the explosive connotations of the modern English word 'dynamite'.

Rather than seeking to discover meaning in the text itself, the structuralist works at how the text conveys a permanent structure or meaning through the underlying relationships of its constituent elements. A number of biblical scholars have sought to make use of such methods, though very few have been prepared to share the true structuralist's total rejection of history by abandoning the diachronic approach altogether. It may not be right to concentrate exclusively on historical analysis, but this does not mean that history should be ignored completely.

———— Questions to consider ————

1 How has form criticism been able to increase our understanding and appreciation of the New Testament?
2 On what does redaction criticism concentrate? What insights does this way of looking at the New Testament give us?
3 What do the approaches of literary criticism add to the ways we gain meaning from the New Testament?

10

THE USE OF THE NEW TESTAMENT

The story is told of a man seeking divine guidance for the future who decided to find out what God had to say to him. He fervently believed that the Bible is the word of God and wanted to be guided by its teaching. So he shut his eyes, opened his Bible at random and pointed to a verse. He found himself looking at Matthew 27:5: *'So Judas... went away and hanged himself.'* 'That can't be right,' he thought, 'I'll try again.' This time he was unfortunate enough to arrive at Luke 10:37: *'Go and do likewise.'* He finally gave up when he had one more try and found himself looking at 1 John 5:3: *'This is love for God: to obey his commands. And his commands are not burdensome...'*

In this chapter we will be seeking to go beyond this rather haphazard technique and examine some of the more responsible methods which Christians draw on as they use the New Testament in their daily lives.

It's sometimes suggested that the interpretation of the Bible is really much simpler than scholars allow. 'After all,' someone might say, 'I believe that the Bible is the word of the living God and that he desires to make his truth known to me. What's wrong with reading the Bible just as it is and relying on the inner illumination of the Holy Spirit to guide me?'

Now it's true that many Christians can say that, in their own day-by-day experience, God does indeed answer their prayers and 'speak' to them as they read the Bible. An attitude of expectant listening to God, a commitment to put into practice what they learn and a willingness to learn from the insights of others have proved immensely fruitful for Christians down through the years. For example, here is how the great eighteenth-century preacher George Whitefield writes about his own approach to Bible study in his diary: 'I began to read the Holy Scriptures upon my knees, laying aside all other books, and praying over, if possible, every line and word. This proved meat indeed and drink indeed to my soul. I daily received fresh life, light and power from above.' This dramatic power of the New Testament to affect people's lives profoundly has been described again and again. As the Bible scholar J.B. Phillips said of his work in translating the New Testament, 'I felt rather like an electrician rewiring an ancient house without being able to turn off the mains'. More recently, here is how the writer John White has described its impact: 'Bible study has torn apart my life and remade it. That is to say that God, through his Word, has done so. In the darkest period of my life, when everything seemed hopeless, I would struggle in the grey dawns of many faraway countries to grasp the basic truths of Scripture passages... There are no expressions majestic enough to tell of the glory that I have seen or of the wonder of finding that I, a neurotic, unstable, middle-aged man have my feet firmly planted in heaven and breathe the air of heaven. And all this has come to me through a careful study of the Scripture.'

It's also true that grasping the meaning of what the New Testament says can sometimes be a very straightforward matter. With a clear command like *'Do not be conceited'* (Ro 12:16) the hard part is not so much understanding it as *doing* it. As Mark Twain remarked, 'Most people are bothered by those passages of scripture they *don't* understand, but for me I have always noticed that the passages that bother me are the ones I *do* understand'.

Such an approach, which aims to take seriously the claim that the Bible is the word of a living and actively communicating God, is a vital one for Christian believers to take. But it need not be and arguably should not be the *only* way Christians look at their sacred Scriptures. To do so is to ignore two crucial factors. The first is the possibility that people are not as directly in touch with God as they may think they are. This is clearly demonstrated by the undeniable fact that equally sincere Christians often disagree about what each considers to be the 'plain meaning' of certain texts. Whether we like it or not, it seems that God has not chosen to plant infallible thoughts into our minds about what the Bible means: there is work for us to do in learning to interpret it responsibly.

Even the New Testament itself indicates that problems are likely to face those who want to understand its message: '*Bear in mind that our Lord's patience means salvation, just as our dear brother Paul also wrote to you with the wisdom that God gave him. He writes the same way in all his letters, speaking in them of these matters. His letters contain some things that are hard to understand, which ignorant and unstable people distort, as they do the other Scriptures, to their own destruction*' (2 Pe 3:15–16, my emphasis).

If understanding parts of the New Testament was hard in the first century, it is even more so now. The second factor which complicates the task of interpreting its message is the nature of the Bible itself as a series of historical documents. For those who think of the Bible as simply a human book from long ago this is, of course, self-evident. But it's a feature that those who view the Bible as the word of God can sometimes forget. From a Christian perspective, the truth is that *both* dimensions are important. One way of expressing this is to say that the message of the Bible is both timeless and timely. Timeless in that, as the word of God, it may be said to be eternally relevant. And timely in that, as the word of human beings, it comes from a particular period within history. God has not chosen to enshrine his word in a series of neat propositions and commands, but in the particular circumstances and events set out by its human authors. The New Testament epistles, for example, far from being ordered theological treatises, are occasional letters written in response to specific situations arising among groups of Christians in the first century. In some respects, the experiences of the individuals we read about in the Bible resonate with our own. But in other ways they are quite different. It's rather like watching a black and white film from the 1930s. Some aspects of what we see come across as being very familiar while other features are rather obscure and will only be fully understood with the aid of some historical and linguistic research.

Bridging the gap between the past and the present so what the New Testament authors have written comes alive to its modern readers is the province of what we call *hermeneutics* (from the Greek for 'interpret'). At the other end of the spectrum from those who see the interpretation of the Bible as entirely straightforward are those who assert that the problems involved in overcoming these cultural barriers are insurmountable – that the distance between its world and ours is just too great. But Christians who believe in the Bible as the gift of a God who desires to communicate argue that such pessimism is unfounded and that it is possible to discern the authentic voice of God today.

What it meant then

When looking at the New Testament as Christian Scripture, a fundamental principle of interpretation is that the meaning of the text *now*
must be controlled by what its original author intended it to mean
then. This point is well illustrated by the early history of biblical
interpretation. In the patristic period (from the end of the first century to the end of the eighth century), two particular approaches were
developed, one associated with the Egyptian city of Alexandria and
the other with the Syrian city of Antioch.

The *Alexandrian* school of interpretation owed much to the philosopher Philo (*c*. 30 BCE–*c*. 45 CE). He was a wealthy and influential
Alexandrian Jew who was deeply interested in the insights of the
Greek philosophers, especially Zeno, Pythagoras and Plato. As far as
Philo was concerned, the Jewish Scriptures, especially the first five
books of Moses (known as the Pentateuch), already contain much of
what these Greek philosophers were saying. His method of approaching the Scriptures relies heavily on allegory to discover such meaning.
Rather than be content with what can be discerned from a literal
reading of a passage, allegorical interpretation seeks to go deeper and
discover the hidden meaning below the surface. Among the early
church fathers, Clement and Origen are particularly associated with
this way of approaching the Bible. Here, for example, is how Origen
deals with the account in Matthew 21 of the entry of Jesus into
Jerusalem. He suggests that Jesus represents the word of God and
that Jerusalem stands for the human soul. The donkey fetched by the
disciples represents the Old Testament correctly interpreted, while
the accompanying colt is a hidden reference to the New Testament.
The fact that no-one had ever sat on it before is taken as a reference
to those who had never before submitted to the word of God. Origen
ignores the historical and literal sense of the passage altogether. The
use of allegory in this way makes the task of interpreting the Bible an
entirely subjective matter.

Although it's easy to scoff at this approach, it's worth noting that,
whether we like it or not, many people take a very similar attitude to
the study of the Bible today. It's not for anyone to deny that God can
speak to people through the Bible when they use it in this way. But
history shows that a failure to take seriously the intention of the

original human authors is bound to lead eventually to serious distortions in Christian belief and behaviour.

A complete contrast to this method is seen in the *Antiochene* school, associated with theologians such as Theodore of Mopsuestia (350–428) and John Chrysostom (347–407). Whereas the Alexandrians saw the process of biblical inspiration as an ecstatic phenomenon, the Antiochenes believed that it was a much more rational process, using the background and individuality of the authors. This led to their method of interpretation placing much more significance on the historical context as they sought to understand the sense intended by the original writer of a passage. Allegorical interpretations, though not excluded entirely, were much more restrained and tightly controlled by the context of the passage.

In the West, the Latin Fathers were dominated by the work of Augustine (354–430). For him, some passages were to be interpreted in a literal and historical sense, while others were better understood in terms of an allegorical and spiritual sense. A famous example of the latter is his bizarre interpretation of the parable of the Good Samaritan in Luke 10. The man on the road stands for humanity, assaulted by the devil and his angels, neglected by the representatives of Old Testament religion but rescued and brought to the care of the church by Christ. Such a system may have been a useful hook on which to hang a sermon, but it entirely ignores the original context of the parable.

Biblical scholars in the Middle Ages maintained this distinction between the literal and non-literal means of interpreting Scripture, further subdividing the latter into three senses: the *allegorical* (defining what Christians are to believe), the *tropological* or *moral* (defining how Christians are to behave) and the *anagogical* (defining what Christians are to look forward to in the future). For example, although a reference to water in the Bible could have the literal sense of water, it could also refer to baptism (the allegorical sense), purity of life (the moral sense) or the water of life in the heavenly Jerusalem (the anagogical sense).

As we have seen, these non-literal approaches to Scripture are open to the criticism that interpreters can read whatever they like into passages, a phenomenon sometimes referred to as *eisegesis*. As a guard against such uncontrolled interpretation, Martin Luther established the principle that no non-literal sense can be justified 'unless that same truth is explicitly stated literally somewhere else. Otherwise, Scripture would become a laughing matter'. The Protestant reformers insisted that interpretation of the Bible should begin with the 'plain and literal sense' of Scripture.

This is not the same as taking everything the Bible says literally. In understanding the intention of its original authors, we must take care to appreciate the type and style of the literature they have written. The figurative language of the storyteller and the poet must be appreciated for what it is and not abused by being torn apart and read 'literally'. Our focus must be on the 'natural' sense of the text, be it literal or figurative. Discerning which is which is usually a matter of common sense, taking into account the author's intention and style.

Working towards the discovery of the original meaning of the text is the task of *exegesis*. It's important to realise that this needs to be done with *every* passage, including (and perhaps especially!) those whose meaning seems to be obvious. The massive gap between the Bible writers and ourselves must not be underestimated. For example, what comes into your mind when you come across the word 'church'? Most people immediately think of a religious building in which Christians gather for worship. But such an idea would have been entirely foreign to the New Testament writers. For them, 'church' means a group of people called together by God (which is what the Greek word 'ecclesia' means), not a building. Not to realise this means that we are bound to misunderstand the references to 'church' in passages like Ephesians 3:20–21: *'Now to him who is able to do immeasurably more than all we ask or imagine, according to his power that is at work within us, to him be glory in the church and in Christ Jesus throughout all generations, for ever and ever! Amen'.*

The presuppositions we as readers bring to the text need to be examined, which is one of the reasons why dialogue about the Bible with other people is so important. Such dialogue may be one way, through reading books and commentaries and hearing sermons in church. Two-way dialogue comes as we talk to the preacher afterwards and take part in groups or Bible study and discussion. It's vital to try to take account of the insights of those with whom we would not necessarily expect to agree. Listening to such outsiders helps us to take account of our own unrecognised prejudices and unexamined assumptions.

It's all too easy to wrench passages out of context and arrive at conclusions which would horrify their original authors. Politicians and others in the public eye protest when journalists quote them selectively in a way that can make them appear to have said the complete opposite of what they intended. The New Testament authors often have grounds for the same complaint! It is vitally important to look at the words they use and the statements they make in the context of what they say as a whole. This is why it's a good idea to begin by reading what they wrote at a single sitting. To do this several times and to use several different translations helps to build a good foundation on which to build secure exegesis. It's also important to learn as much as possible about the time and culture of the author and his readers. More specifically, what was it that led to the writing of this particular book? Breaking the text up into smaller sections helps in detailed study, though we need to realise that the chapters and printed paragraph divisions in our Bibles are not original to the text and may be misleading if we assume that they mark breaks in the author's thought.

It is vitally important to look at the words the New Testament authors use and the statements they make in the context of what they say as a whole. But it doesn't stop there. If the whole Bible was written under the over-arching guidance of God, then we can expect its teaching to be consistent throughout. It's often said that Scripture is its own best commentary and it can often be helpful to allow passages whose meaning seems clear to shed light on those which are less easy to understand. Some editions of the Bible are specially designed for this sort of study and include a series of cross-references for each verse. It's also helpful to remember that the Christian Scriptures include the Old Testament as well as the New.

It's important to grasp the perspective which the New Testament has about its relationship with the Old. Many people think that the job of the New Testament is to overturn the message of the Old and start again from scratch and see a basic contradiction between the supposedly angry and vengeful God of the Old Testament and the loving and compassionate God of the New.

But the New Testament writers would have been appalled at such an idea, which certainly isn't supported by the evidence. To begin with, the Old Testament contains some of the most profound statements of the love of God. Take the prophet Zephaniah for example. Here's part of his message from God: *'The* LORD *your God is with you, he is mighty to save. He will take great delight in you, he will quiet you with his love, he will rejoice over you with singing'* (Zep 3:17). And on the other hand, the New Testament certainly doesn't hold back on describing God's anger. Here for example, on the lips of Jesus himself, is John 3:36: *'Whoever believes in the Son has eternal life, but whoever rejects the Son will not see life, for God's wrath remains on him.'*

A further point is the way that New Testament writers turn to the Old Testament to back up what they are saying. We saw this in Chapter 2 with the Gospel of Matthew in particular. But it's not just Matthew. Virtually every New Testament book quotes from or alludes to the Old Testament (the 'Scriptures') and treats what it says as authoritative. One of the ways they argue for the truth of what they write is by seeking to show that the stories about Jesus and the church actually fulfil many of the strands of Old Testament prophecy.

Most significant of all for the Christian believer is the reported attitude of Jesus himself to what we now know as the Old Testament. A key statement is recorded in Matthew 5:17–18: *'Do not think that I have come to abolish the Law or the Prophets; I have not come to abolish them but to fulfil them. I tell you the truth, until heaven and earth disappear, not the smallest letter, not the least stroke of a pen, will by any means disappear from the Law until everything is accomplished.'* According to Jesus, *'the Scripture cannot be broken'* (John 10:35). For other examples of how Jesus used the Old Testament, see Matthew 4:1–11; 22:43–46; Luke 24:25–27, 44–47.

The New Testament perspective, then, is to build on the foundation laid by the Old Testament rather than obliterate it and start again. From a Christian point of view, to regard the Old Testament as outmoded and somewhat inferior to the New is a mistake.

——————— What it means now ———————

For Christian believers, using the Bible is not simply a matter of sorting out what its authors intended to convey to its first readers. We need also to go on and investigate what it means for us now. This is sometimes described as the process of *exposition*. As an example, here is Colossians 4: 1–2: *'Masters, provide your slaves with what is right and fair, because you know that you also have a Master in heaven. Devote yourselves to prayer, being watchful and thankful'.* Given a little thought about how the details might apply specifically to us, the application of the second of these two commands is fairly straightforward. But, given that slavery is no longer an issue for most of the modern world, what are we to do with the first? One response would be to ignore the verse completely and go straight on to something else. Alternatively, we could seek to identify the *principle* that underlies this specific command and think about issues in our own lives to which it applies. For example, what attitudes do we adopt towards those who work for us? Even if we don't employ anyone directly, what about our responsibilities as those who benefit from other people's labour in our role as consumers?

The New Testament itself contains an instructive example of such a principle being developed from a command that does not apply directly. Writing to the Christians at Corinth, the apostle Paul asserts that it is right for Christian leaders to receive material support for the spiritual work they do. Part of his argument goes like this: *'Do I say this merely from a human point of view? Doesn't the Law say the same thing? For it is written in the Law of Moses: "Do not muzzle an ox while it is treading out the grain." Is it about oxen that God is concerned? Surely he says this for us, doesn't he? Yes, this was written for us, because when farmers plough and thresh, they ought to do so in the hope of sharing in the harvest. If we have sown spiritual seed among you, is it too much if we reap a material harvest from you?'* (1 Co 9:8–11). Though direct application of the Law's teaching about oxen (from Deuteronomy 25:4) is clearly inappropriate, Paul applies the principle underlying it to a parallel situation in the life of the church.

2 Timothy 3:15–17 is often cited as a passage which focuses on the practical uses to which the Bible should be put: *'...from infancy you have known the holy Scriptures, which are able to make you wise for salvation through faith in Christ Jesus. All Scripture is God-breathed and is useful for teaching, rebuking, correcting and training in righteousness, so that God's servants may be thoroughly equipped for every good work.'* For Timothy, receiving this letter well before the New Testament was compiled, the 'holy Scriptures' were, of course, what we now know as the Old Testament. But there is some justification for Christians including the New Testament in the category of Scripture (i.e. sacred writings), not only from the church's long history

of doing so but also from within the Bible itself. In the reference from 2 Peter quoted earlier, we saw how the author writes about the way Paul's letters *'contain some things that are hard to understand, which ignorant and unstable people distort, <u>as they do the other Scriptures</u>...'* (2 Pe 3:16, my emphasis).

This is borne out by what 2 Timothy 3 goes on to describe as the basic purpose of the Scriptures. Their job is to make their readers *'wise for salvation through faith in Christ Jesus'* (verse 15). By salvation, it's clear that the writer has in view the whole sweep of God's purposes, including the practical changes in the lives of those who read. The focus of verse 16 is not so much on what the Bible's readers *know* but on who they *are* and what they *do*: *'All Scripture is God-breathed and is useful for teaching, rebuking, correcting and training in righteousness, so that God's servant may be thoroughly equipped for every good work'.*

In doing this, the Bible may be said to deal with two sets of relationship we have. These are illustrated by an answer Jesus gave when questioned by a religious lawyer about which was the greatest commandment in the Jewish law. *Jesus replied: 'Love the Lord your God with all your heart and with all your soul and with all your mind. This is the first and greatest commandment. And the second is like it Love your neighbour as yourself. All the Law and the Prophets hang on these two commandments.'* (Mt 22:37–40).

First, then, the Bible speaks to us about our relationship with God. It focuses on Jesus Christ as the figure in human history who is uniquely qualified to show us and tell us what God is like. It deals with how our relationship with God has been damaged and how it may be restored through what Jesus achieved by his death and resurrection. We find out about how the Holy Spirit acts in the lives of Christians to make God real in their present experience, to bring about change in their lives and to equip them to serve him.

Secondly, the Bible looks at the relationships Christians have with other people, both inside the Christian community and with the world around them. As we have seen, most of the New Testament epistles are addressed, not to *individuals*, but to *communities* of believers gathering together as the church in a particular locality. Jesus told his immediate followers that people would recognise them as his disciples *'if you love one another'* (Jn 13:35), and much of the New Testament is devoted to how this works out in practice.

—— Questions to consider ——

1 What does 'exegesis' mean? Why is it so important?
2 What is it that prevents the interpretation of the New Testament from being straightforward? How may such difficulties be overcome?
3 What would you say the New Testament is for?

APPENDICES

Abbreviations of the books of the Bible

Genesis	Ge	Song of Songs	SS
Exodus	Ex	Isaiah	Isa
Leviticus	Lev	Jeremiah	Jer
Numbers	Nu	Lamentations	La
Deuteronomy	Dt	Ezekiel	Eze
Joshua	Jos	Daniel	Da
Judges	Jdg	Hosea	Hos
Ruth	Ru	Joel	Joel
1 Samuel	1 Sa	Amos	Am
2 Samuel	1 Sa	Obadiah	Ob
1 Kings	1 Ki	Jonah	Jnh
2 Kings	2 Ki	Micah	Mic
1 Chronicles	1 Ch	Nahum	Na
2 Chronicles	2 Ch	Habakkuk	Hab
Ezra	Ezr	Zephaniah	Zep
Nehemiah	Ne	Haggai	Hag
Esther	Est	Zechariah	Zec
Job	Job	Malachi	Mal
Psalms	Ps	Matthew	Mt
Proverbs	Pr	Mark	Mk
Ecclesiastes	Ecc	Luke	Lk

John	Jn	2 Timothy	2 Ti
Acts	Ac	Titus	Tit
Romans	Ro	Philemon	Phm
1 Corinthians	1 Co	Hebrews	Heb
2 Corinthians	2 Co	James	Jas
Galatians	Gal	1 Peter	1 Pe
Ephesians	Eph	2 Peter	2 Pe
Philippians	Php	1 John	1 Jn
Colossians	Col	2 John	2 Jn
1 Thessalonians	1 Th	3 John	3 Jn
2 Thessalonians	2 Th	Jude	Jude
1 Timothy	1 Ti	Revelation	Rev

Table of New Testament weights and measures

Because weights and measures differed according to time and place in the ancient world, the figures in this table are only approximate.

Weight

pint	327 grams
talent	34 kilograms

Length

cubit	0.5 metre
orguia/fathom	1.8 metres
stadion	185 metres
milion/'mile'	1.48 kilometres

Dry capacity

choinix/'quart'	1.1 litres
bushel	8.75 litres
koros	350 litres

Liquid capacity

xestes/'pitcher'	0.5 litre
bat	35 litres
metretes	35 litres

People mentioned in the New Testament

Aaron	Brother of Moses; appointed as Israel's first high priest (Lk 1:5; Ac 7:40; Heb 5:4; 7:11; 9:4).
Abel	Adam and Eve's second son, killed by his brother Abel (Heb 11:4; 12:24).
Abraham	Founder of the Jewish nation, noted for his faith (Ro 4:1–3; Heb 11:8–19; Jas 2:21–23).
Adam	The first man, whose sin led to the fall; contrasted with Christ, whose lack of sin led to salvation (Ro 5:12–21; 1 Co 15:22, 45).
Aeneas	Paralysed man, healed by Peter (Ac 9:33–34).
Agabus	Early church prophet (Ac 11:28; 21:10).
Agrippa	See Herod.
Alexander	1 Son of the Simon who carried Christ's cross (Mk 15:21).
	2 Relative of the high priest Annas (Ac 4:6).
	3 Leading Christian in Ephesus (Ac 19:33–34), perhaps the same as [1].
	4 Convert who gave up his faith (1 Ti 1:20).
	5 Person who harmed Paul (2 Ti 4:14), perhaps the same as [4].
Alphaeus	1 Father of Levi/Matthew (Mk 2:14).
	2 Father of James (Mt 10:3), possibly the same as Cleopas.
Ananias	1 Christian in Jerusalem struck down dead (Ac 5:1–6).
	2 Christian in Damascus who helped Paul (Ac 9 : 10–19; 22:12).
	3 High priest in Jerusalem (Ac 23:2; 24:1).
Andrew	Brother of Peter, one of the 12 apostles (Mt 4:18; Jn 1:40, 44; 6:8).
Andronicus	Relative of Paul (Ro 16:7).
Anna	Prophetess who greeted the birth of Christ (Lk 2:36).
Annas	Jewish high priest who tried Jesus (Lk 3:2; Jn 18:13, 24; Ac 4:6).
Antipas	1 See Herod.
	2 Christian martyr from the church at Pergamum (Rev 2:13).

Apollos	Leading Christian in Ephesus (Ac 18:24; 19:1; 1 Co 1:12; 3:4–6; Tit 3:13).
Aquila	Leading Christian, husband of Priscilla (Ac 18:2, 18, 26; Ro 16:3; 1 Co 16:19).
Archelaus	Son of Herod the Great (Mt 2:22).
Aristarchus	A Macedonian, one of Paul's companions on his third missionary journey (Ac 19:29; 20:4; Col 4:10).
Augustus	Imperial name of Octavian, Roman emperor at the time of Christ's birth (Lk 2:1).
Barabbas	Criminal released by Pilate instead of Christ (Mt 27:15–26).
Barnabas	Originally called Joses (Ac 4:36), one of Paul's companions (Ac 9:27; 11:22–30; Gal 2:1).
Bartholomew	One of the 12 apostles (Mt 10:3), probably the same as Nathanael.
Bartimaeus	Blind beggar healed by Christ (Mk 10:46–52).
Caiaphas	High priest involved in the trial of Jesus (Mt 26:3, 57–68; Jn 1:49).
Cephas	See Peter.
Christ	See Jesus.
Chuza	Steward to Herod Antipas and supporter of Christ (Lk 8:3).
Claudius Caesar	Roman emperor who banished Jews from Rome (Ac 18:2).
Claudius Lysias	Chief Roman officer in Jerusalem (Ac 23:26).
Clement	One of Paul's co-workers at Philippi (Php 4:3).
Cleopas	A disciple met by Jesus on the road to Emmaus (Lk 24:18).
Clopas	Husband of one of the Marys who followed Jesus (Jn 19:25), possibly the same as Alphaeus.
Cornelius	Roman centurion, the first Gentile convert to Christianity (Ac 10:1–31).
Crescens	One of Paul's co-workers at Rome (2 Ti 4:10).
Crispus	Leading Jew at Corinth who became a convert to Christianity (Ac 18:7–8; 1 Co 1:14).
Cyrenius	Governor of Syria at the time of Christ's birth (Lk 2:2).
Damaris	Athenian woman who became a convert to Christianity (Ac 17:34).
David	Israel's greatest king, ancestor of Christ (Mt 1:6).

Demas	Co-worker with Paul who later deserted him (Col 4:14; 2 Ti 4:10; Phm 24).
Demetrius	1 Christian mentioned by John (3 Jn 12).
	2 Leading silversmith in Ephesus who opposed Paul (Ac 19:24–41).
Didymus	See Thomas.
Dionysius	Athenian leader who became a convert to Christianity (Ac 17:34).
Diotrephes	An individual who opposed John (3 Jn 9–10).
Dorcas	Christian woman at Joppa who was raised from the dead (Ac 9:36–42), also known as Tabitha.
Elijah	One of Israel's greatest prophets (Mt 17:3).
Elisha	Prophet who succeeded Elijah (Lk 4:27).
Elizabeth	Wife of Zechariah and mother of John the Baptist (Lk 1:5–57).
Elymas	False prophet at Paphos who opposed Paul and Barnabas (Ac 13:6–12), also known as Bar-jesus.
Epaphras	Christian who founded the church at Colossae (Col 1:7–8; 4:12; Phm 23).
Epaphroditus	Christian from Philippi, sent to Paul in Rome with a gift (Php 2:25–30; 4:18).
Erastus	1 Co–worker with Paul and Timothy (Ac 19:22; 2 Ti 4:20).
	2 Important official at Rome (Ro 16:23).
Eunice	Timothy's mother (Ac 16:1; 2 Ti 1:5).
Euodia	Christian woman at Philippi (Php 4:2).
Eutychus	Young man at Troas who was raised from the dead after falling from a window (Ac 20:6–12).
Felix	Roman governor of Judea who presided over the trial of Paul at Caesarea (Ac 23:23–27; 24:22–27).
Festus	Successor to Felix as governor (Ac 25 & 26).
Gaius	1 Recipient of John's third epistle.
	2 A Macedonian involved in the Ephesian riot, one of Paul's companions (Ac 19:29).
	3 A companion of Paul's from Derbe (Ac 20:4), possibly the same as [2].
	4 A Christian from Corinth, Paul's host (Ro 16:23), possibly the same as the Gaius in 1 Co 1:14.
Gallio	Roman proconsul of Achaia before whom Paul was tried in Corinth (Ac 18:12–17).

Gamaliel	Famous Pharisee, Paul's teacher, and a member of the Sanhedrin (Ac 5:33–40; 22:3).
Hagar	Mother of Abraham's son Ishmael, used to illustrate contrast between law and grace (Gal 4:21–31).
Hermogenes	Christian who deserted Paul (2 Ti 1:5).
Herod	1 Herod the Great, king of Judea when Christ was born (Mt 2:1–22; Lk 1:5).
	2 Herod Antipas, son of [1], tetrarch of Galilee and Perea (Mt 14:1–10; Lk 13:31–32; 23:7–12).
	3 Herod Philip I, son of [1] by Mariamne II, whose wife was lured away from him by [2] (Mt 14:3).
	4 Herod Philip II, son of [1] by Cleopatra, tetrarch of Iturea and Trachonitis (Lk 3:1).
	5 Herod Agrippa I, grandson and heir of [1], tetrarch of Galilee (Ac 12:1–23).
	6 Herod Agrippa II, son and partial heir of [5] (Ac 25:13–26:32).
Herodias	Granddaughter of Herod the Great, wife of Herod Antipas (Mt 14:3–9; Lk 3:19).
Hymenaeus	Early Christian who fell into error (1 Ti 1:20; 2 Ti 2:17).
Isaac	Son of Abraham and Sarah, father of Esau and Jacob.
Isaiah	Old Testament prophet often quoted in the New Testament.
Iscariot	See Judas.
Jacob	Son of Isaac, twin brother to Esau, father of the Jewish nation's 12 tribes.
Jairus	Synagogue ruler from near Capernaum whose daughter was raised from the dead by Jesus (Lk 8:41).
Jambres	Egyptian magician who, according to tradition, opposed Moses (2 Ti 3:8–9), see also Jannes
James	1 Son of Zebedee, brother of John, one of the 12 apostles, leader of the Jerusalem church, killed by Herod Agrippa (Mt 4:21; Mk 5:37; Lk 9:54; Ac 12:2).
	2 Son of Alphaeus, another of the 12 apostles (Mt 10:3; Ac 1:13), probably the same as 'James the younger' (Mk 15:40).

| | 3 | One of Jesus' brothers, leader of the Jerusalem church, author of the Epistle of James (Mt 13 : 55; Ac 12:17; 1 Co 15:7; Gal 1:19; 2:9). |
| | 4 | Father of Judas (not Iscariot), one of the 12 apostles (Lk 6:16; Ac 1:13). |

Jannes — Egyptian magician who, according to tradition, opposed Moses (2 Ti 3:8–9); see also Jambres.

Jason
1 Paul's host in Thessalonica (Ac 17:5–9).
2 Jewish Christian friend of Paul (Ro 16:21).

Jeremiah — Old Testament prophet often quoted in the New Testament.

Jesse — Father of David (Mt 1:5–6).

Jesus
1 Personal name given by Joseph and Mary to their son, later known as Jesus Christ.
2 A Christian, also called Justus, mentioned in Col 4:11.

Joanna
1 One of Christ's ancestors (Lk 3:27).
2 Wife of Chuza, Herod's steward (Lk 8:3; 24:10).

John
1 Son of Zechariah and Elizabeth, cousin of Jesus, known as 'John the Baptist', beheaded by Herod (Mt 3; 11:7–18; 14:1–10).
2 Son of Zebedee, brother of Jas, one of the 12 apostles, traditionally viewed as the author of John's Gospel, Epistles and Revelation (Mt 4: 21; 10:2; Ac 1:13; Gal 2:9).
3 Relative of the high priest Annas (Ac 4:6).
4 See Mark

Joseph
1 Husband of Mary the mother of Jesus (Mt 1:1–24; 2:13; Lk 1:27; 2:4).
2 Jew from Arimathea, in whose tomb Jesus was laid (Mt 27:57–60; Lk 15:43).
3 One of the two men proposed to replace Judas Iscariot (Ac 1:23), also known as Barsabbas or Justus.
4 Three Josephs appear in Luke's list of the ancestors of Christ (Lk 3:24, 26, 30).

Joses
1 One of the brothers of Jesus (Mt 13:55; Mk 6:3).
2 Son of Mary the wife of Clopas (Mt 27:56; Mk 15:40, 47).

Judas/Jude
1 One of the 12 apostles, identified as 'Iscariot' (perhaps indicating his home town of Kerioth),

who betrayed Jesus and subsequently committed suicide (Mt 10:4; 26:14–16, 25, 47–50; 27 : 3–10).

2 One of the brothers of Jesus (Mt 13:55; Mk 6 : 3), thought by many to be the author of the Epistle of Jude.

3 A Galilean rebel (Ac 5:37).

4 Paul's host in Damascus (Ac 9:11).

5 Prophet sent with Silas to Antioch (Ac 15:22–32).

6 See Thaddeus.

Julius	Centurion who delivered Paul to Rome (Ac 27:1–3).
Justus	1 Paul's host in Corinth (Ac 18:7).
	2 See Jesus [2].
	3 See Joseph [3].
Lazarus	1 Brother of Mary and Martha, raised from the dead by Jesus (Jn 11:1–12:17).
	2 A beggar in one of Jesus' parables (Lk 16:19–31).
Levi	1 One of the sons of Jacob whose descendants became the priests of Israel.
	2 Another name for Matthew.
	3 Two Levis appear in Luke's list of the ancestors of Christ (Lk 3:24, 29).
Lois	Grandmother of Timothy (2 Ti 1:5).
Lucius	Prophet or teacher from Cyrene working in Antioch (Ac 13:1), possibly the same as the well-wisher mentioned in Ro 16:21.
Luke	Doctor, co-worker with Paul, author of the third Gospel and the Acts of the Apostles (Col 4:14; 2 Ti 4:11; Phm 24).
Malchus	High priest's servant involved in the arrest of Jesus whose ear was cut off by Peter and subsequently healed miraculously (Jn 18:10).
Mark	Co-worker with Paul and author of the second Gospel (Ac 12:12, 25; 15:37, 39; Col 4:10), sometimes known as John Mark.
Martha	Sister of Mary and Lazarus (Lk 10:38–42; Jn 11:1–39).
Mary	1 Mother of Jesus
	2 Sister of Martha (Lk 10:38–42; Jn 11:1–45).
	3 Woman from Magdala, out of whom Jesus cast seven demons (Mt 27:56, 61; 28:1; Lk 8:2;

Jn 19:25.

4 It's possible that the mother of Joses (Mk 15:47), the mother of James (Lk 24:10), the 'other Mary' (Mt 28:1) and the wife of Clopas (Jn 19:25) are all the same person (Mk 15:40).

5 Mother of Mark (Ac 12:12).

Matthew	One of the 12 apostles, previously a tax collector, also known as Levi, author of the first Gospel (Mt 9:9; 10:3; Mk 2:14).
Matthias	Chosen to replace Judas Iscariot as an apostle (Ac 1:23–26).
Melchizedek	Seen by the writer of the Epistle to the Hebrews as a figure who symbolised certain truths about Jesus (Ge 14:18–20; Ps 110:4, Heb 5–7).
Michael	A chief messenger, or archangel, of God (Da 10:21; 12:1; Jude 9; Rev 12:7).
Moses	Israel's great leader and law giver (Mt 17:1–9).
Nathanael	One of Jesus' disciples, probably the same as Bartholomew (Jn 1:45–49; 21:2; Ac 1:13).
Nicodemus	Pharisee who secretly followed Jesus (Jn 3:1–15; 7:50–52; 19:39–42).
Onesimus	Slave who was sent back to this master Philemon by Paul (Col 4:9; Phm).
Onesiphorus	Friend and ally of Paul (2 Ti 1:16; 4:19).
Paul	Pharisee who persecuted the Christian church but was subsequently converted and became apostle to the Gentiles. Acts tells much of his story and many of the New Testament epistles were written by him.
Peter	A fisherman who was called by Christ to lead the 12 apostles (Mt 4:18–20; 16:15–19; Ac 2), originally called Simon.
Philemon	Christian at Colossae to whom Paul writes about Onesimus, a runaway slave (Phm).
Philetus	False teacher condemned by Paul (2 Ti 2:17).
Philip	1 One of the 12 apostles of Christ (Mt 10:3; Jn 1:44–48; 6:5–9).
	2 Evangelist mentioned several times in Acts (e.g. 6:5; 8:5–13).
	3 See Herod [3] and [4].

Phygellus	One who deserted Paul (2 Ti 1:15).
Pontius Pilate	Roman procurator of Judea who allowed Jesus to be executed even though he had found him not guilty (Mt 27:2–24; Jn 18:28–40).
Porcius Festus	See Festus.
Priscilla	Leading Christian, wife of Aquila (Ac 18:2, 18, 26; Ro 16:3; 1 Co 16:19).
Publius	Governor of Malta when Paul was shipwrecked (Ac 28: 1–10).
Rhoda	Maid in the household of Mary (Ac 12:12–15).
Rufus	1 Son of Simon of Cyrene, probably well known to the first recipients of Mark's Gospel (Mk 15:21).
	2 A Christian in Rome (Ro 16:13), possibly the same as [1].
Salome	1 One of the women who witnessed the crucifixion of Jesus (Mk 15:40; 16:1); possibly the mother of James and John, the sons of Zebedee (Mt 27:56), possibly the sister of Jesus' mother Mary (Jn 19:25).
	2 Daughter of Herodias who danced before Herod (Mt 14:6; Mk 6:22).
Sapphira	Wife of Ananias who, like her husband, was struck down dead (Ac 5:7–11).
Saul	1 First king of Israel.
	2 Original name of Paul.
Sceva	Jewish priest at Ephesus whose seven sons attempted to cast out a demon (Ac 19:14–16).
Sergius Paulus	Roman deputy of Cyprus who was converted to Christianity when Elymas was struck blind (Ac 13:7).
Silas	Companion and co-worker with Paul (Ac 15:22, 32–34; 2 Co 1:19; 1 Th 1:1).
Simeon	1 Second son of Jacob by Leah (Ge 29:33).
	2 Devout Jew who blessed Jesus at the temple soon after his birth (Lk 2:25–34).
	3 An ancestor of Jesus (Lk 3:30).
	4 A prophet or teacher at Antioch (Ac 13:1), surnamed Niger.
	5 Another form of Simon.
Simon	1 Original name of the apostle Peter (Mt 4:18; 16 : 16–17).

2 Another of the 12 apostles, a member of the Zealots (Mt 10:4; Ac 1:13).

3 One of the brothers of Jesus (Mt 13:55; Mk 6:3).

4 A leper in Bethany (Mt 26:6; Mk 14:3).

5 A man from Cyrene who was made to carry Jesus' cross (Mt 27:32; Mk 15:21), possibly the same as Simeon [4].

6 A Pharisee in whose house the feet of Christ were anointed (Lk 7:36–50).

7 The father of Judas Iscariot (Jn 6:71; 12:4; 13:2).

8 A sorcerer who tried to buy the ability to pass on the Holy Spirit (Ac 8:9–24).

9 A tanner at Joppa, host to Peter (Ac 9–10).

Sopater	A colleague of Paul (Ac 20:4), possibly the same as Sosipater (Ro 16:21).
Sosthenes	1 Chief ruler of the synagogue at Corinth (Ac 18:17).
	2 A Christian who joined Paul in writing to the church at Corinth (1 Co 1:1), possibly the same as [1].
Stephanas	One of the first converts to Christianity in Greece (1 Co 1:16; 16:15–17).
Stephen	Chosen as one of the seven deacons (Ac 6:1–6), the first Christian martyr (Ac 6:8–7:60).
Susanna	One of the women who supported Christ in his ministry (Lk 8:3).
Tabitha	See Dorcas.
Tertius	Scribe to whom Paul dictates Romans (Ro 16:22), possibly the same as Silas.
Tertullus	Orator brought in to accuse Paul before Felix (Ac 24:1–8).
Theophilus	The unknown recipient, possibly a Roman official, of Luke's Gospel and Ac (Lk 1:3; Ac 1:1).
Theudas	Leader of an unsuccessful rebellion against Rome (Ac 5:36).
Thomas	One of the 12 apostles of Christ, noted for his scepticism (Mt 10:3; Mk 3:18; Jn 11:16; 14:5; 20:24–29), also known by the Aramaic form of his name, Didymus.
Timothy	Co-worker with Paul from Lystra, son of a Jewish mother, Eunice, and a Greek father (Ac 16:1;

	17:14–15; 1 & 2 Ti).
Titus	Co-worker with Paul entrusted with a mission to Crete (2 Co 2:13; Gal 2:1; Tit).
Trophimus	Ephesian Christian who travelled with Paul to Greece and Jerusalem (Ac 20:4; 21:29; 2 Ti 4:20).
Tychicus	Co-worker with Paul who served as a messenger on several occasions (Ac 20:4; Eph 6:21; 2 Ti 4:12).
Zaccheus	Tax collector from Jericho with whom Jesus stayed on one occasion (Lk 19:1–10).
Zebedee	Galilean fisherman, husband of Salome, father of James and John (Mt 4:21; 27:56; Mk 1:19–20).
Zechariah	Priest, husband of Elizabeth, father of John the Baptist (Lk 1:5–25, 57–79). (There are over two dozen other Zechariahs, all in the Old Testament).

_____ Places mentioned in the _____ New Testament

Abilene	Syrian tetrarchy, about 30 km north-west of Damascus (Lk 3:1).
Aceldama	Field purchased by priests in Jerusalem using the money returned by Judas Iscariot (Mt 27:7; Ac 1:9).
Achaia	District in Greece ruled by the Romans (Ac 18:12; Ro 15:26).
Adramyttium	Port city of Mysia in the north-west of the Roman province of Asia (Ac 27:2).
Aenon	Site where John was baptising (Jn 3:23).
Alexandria	Egypt's capital city for many years, on the Mediterranean coast (Ac 27:6; 28:11–13).
Amphipolis	Chief city of Macedonia (Ac 17:1).
Antioch	1 Syrian city where the followers of Jesus were first called Christians (Ac 11:19–26).
	2 Phyrgian city near the border of Pisidia, visited by Paul and Barnabas (Ac 13:14).
Antipatris	City built by Herod the Great on the Plain of Sharon to which Paul was brought (Ac 23:31).

Areopagus	Another name for Mars Hill in Athens to which Paul was brought (Ac 17).
Armageddon	Site of great final battle (Rev 16:16).
Asia	Roman province whose capital was Ephesus (Ac 19).
Assos	Mysian port on south-west coast of modern Turkey (Ac 20:13).
Athens	Cultural centre and capital of Greek city-state of Attica (Ac 17).
Attalia	Port on south coast of modern Turkey (Ac 14:25).
Berea	Macedonian city visited by Paul (Ac 17:10).
Bethany	1 Site where John the Baptist baptised converts, identified in some manuscripts as Bethabara (Jn 1:28).
	2 Village about 3 km from Jerusalem (Mk 11:1; Lk 19:29; Jn 11:1; 12:1).
Bethesda	Pool near Jerusalem's Sheep Gate (Jn 5:2–3).
Bethlehem	Birthplace of Jesus, about 10 km south of Jerusalem; also known as Ephratah (Ru 4:11; Mt 2:5).
Bethphage	Place near Bethany (Mk 11:1).
Bethsaida	Fishing town in Galilee; home of Philip, Andrew and Peter (Mk 8:22; Jn 1:44).
Bithynia	Roman province in north-west Asia Minor, bordering the Black Sea (Ac 16:7; 1 Pe 1:11).
Caesarea	Coastal city in Palestine and provincial capital built by Herod the Great (Ac 8:40).
Caesarea Philippi	Town at the foot of Mount Hermon (Mt 16:13–20).
Cana	Village in Galilee, 16 km north-east of Nazareth (Jn 2:1; 4:46; 11).
Capernaum	Town on the shore of Galilee (Mt 4:13; Lk 4:31).
Cappadocia	Roman province in eastern Asia Minor (Ac 2:9; 1 Pe 1:1).
Cenchrea	Harbour about 11 km east of Corinth (Ac 18:18; Ro 16:1).
Chorazin	Coastal city on the Sea of Galilee (Mt 11:21).
Cilicia	Roman province in south-east Asia Minor whose capital was Tarsus (Ac 21:39).
Colosse	City in Phrygia (Col 1:2).
Crete	Large island south-east of Greece (Ac 2:11; Tit 1:5).

Cyprus	Mediterranean island about 96 km east of Syria (Ac 4:36; 13:4; 15:39).
Cyrene	City in Libya, probably modern Tripoli (Mt 27:32; Ac 2:10).
Dalmanutha	Galilean fishing village (Mk 8:10).
Dalmatia	Roman province on the east of the Adriatic Sea (Ro 15:19; 2 Ti 4:10).
Damascus	Major city in Syria (Ac 9:2).
Decapolis	Federation of Greek cities south of Galilee and east of the Jordan (Mt 4:25; Mk 5:20; 7:31).
Derbe	City in south-eastern Asia Minor visited by Paul (Ac 14:6–20).
Emmaus	A village about 16 km west of Jerusalem (Lk 24:13).
Ephesus	Roman provincial capital of Asia; an important trading centre and port (Ac 18, 19, 20; Eph 1:1; Rev 2:1–7).
Ephratah	See Bethlehem.
Fair Havens	Harbour in Crete (Ac 27:8).
Gadara	Town in Galilee which became the capital of the Roman district of Perea (Mk 5:1; Lk 8:26).
Galatia	Roman province in central Asia Minor (Ac 16:6; 18:23; Gal 1:2).
Galilee	Region in northern Israel (Lk 3:1; 23:6).
Gennesaret	1 Region to the north-west of the Sea of Galilee (Mt 14:34).
	2 Another name for the Sea of Galilee (Lk 5:1).
Gergesa	Town or district to the east of the Sea of Galilee (Mt 8:28).
Gethsemane	Garden to the east of Jerusalem at the foot of the Mount of Olives (Mt 26:36–56; Jn 18:1).
Golgotha	Hill outside the walls of ancient Jerusalem (Mt 27:33; Jn 19:17).
Hierapolis	Town in the Lycus valley in the province of Phrygia (Col 4:13).
Iconium	Capital of the province of Lycaonia in Asia Minor (Ac 13:51; 14:1).
Illyricum	Roman province on the east coast of the Adriatic Sea (Rom 15:19); later renamed Dalmatia.
Iturea	Small Palestinian province at the foot of Mount

	Hermon (Lk 3:1).
Jerusalem	Capital of the southern kingdom of Judah (Lk 2; 19:28–24; Ac 2).
Joppa	Palestinian coastal town (Ac 9:36).
Jordan	Palestine's major river (Mk 1:5).
Judea	Greek/Roman name for Judah, sometimes including Galilee and Samaria (Lk 3:1; 4:44).
Kidron	Valley between Jerusalem and the Mount of Olives (Jn 18:1).
Kios	Greek island at the entrance to the Gulf of Smyrna (Ac 20:15).
Laodicea	Chief city of Phrygia in the Lycus valley (Col 2:1; 4:15; Rev 1:11; 3:14–22).
Lasea	Seaport of Crete (Ac 27:8).
Lycaonia	Part of Asia Minor between Galatia and Cilicia (Ac 14:6–11).
Lycia	Region in south-western Asia Minor (Ac 27:5).
Lystra	Lycaonian city; Timothy's home town (Ac 14:6–21).
Magdala	Town to the west of the Sea of Galilee (Mt 15:39).
Malta	Island in the Mediterranean (Ac 28:1).
Mars Hill	See Areopagus.
Miletus	Ionian coastal city (Ac 20:15; 2 Ti 4:20).
Mitylene	Principal city on the island of Lesbos off the western coast of Asia Minor (Ac 20:14).
Myra	Lycian town (Ac 27:5).
Mysia	Province in north-western Asia Minor (Ac 16:7).
Nain	Galilean village just south of Mount Tabor (Lk 7:11).
Nazareth	Jesus' home town in Galilee (Mt 4:13; Mk 1:9).
Neapolis	Seaport of Macedonian Philippi (Ac 16:11).
Pamphylia	Southern coastal area in Asia Minor whose main town was Perga (Ac 2:10; 13:13).
Paphos	Town in south-west Cyprus (Ac 13:6–13).
Patara	Seacoast city of south-west Lycia (Ac 21:1).
Patmos	Barren island off the coast of modern Turkey (Rev 1:9).
Perga	See Pamphylia.
Pergamum	City in Mysia in north-west Asia Minor (Rev 2:12–17).
Philadelphia	Town in Lydia in Asia Minor (Rev 3:7–13).
Philippi	Macedonian city, the first in Europe where Paul

	established a church (Ac 16:12; 20:3–6).
Phyrygia	Inland province of Asia Minor (Ac 2:10; 16:6).
Pisidia	Inland district of Asia Minor whose capital was (Pisidian) Antioch (Ac 13:14).
Pontus	District in north-eastern Asia Minor (Ac 2:9; 1 Pe 1:1).
Rhodes	Island located off the coast of south-west Asia Minor (Ac 21:1).
Rome	Capital of the Roman Empire (Ac 2:10; 18:2; 23:11; 28; Rom 1:7, 15).
Salamis	Town on the east end of Cyprus visited by Paul and Barnabas (Ac 13:5).
Salmone	Easternmost point of the island of Crete (Ac 27:7), now known as Cape Sidero.
Samaria	Capital of northern kingdom of Israel (Jn 4:4).
Samos	Greek island off the coast of Ephesus (Ac 20:15).
Samothrace	Small Aegean island off the southern coast of Thrace (Ac 16:11).
Sardis	Capital city of Lydia about 80 km east of Smyrna (Rev 3:1–6).
Seleucia	Syrian seaport 8 km north of the mouth of the Orontes river (Ac 13:4).
Sidon	Ancient Canaanite city (Lk 4:26).
Siloam	1 Pool in Jerusalem at the south end of Hezekiah's tunnel (Jn 9:7). 2 The site of a tower which collapsed (Lk 13:4).
Smyrna	City on the western coast of Asia Minor (Rev 2:8–11), about 65 km north of Ephesus.
Solomon's Porch	Colonnade on the east side of the temple (Jn 10:23; Ac 3:11).
Sychar	Samaritan town where Jacob's well was situated (Jn 4:5).
Syracuse	City on the east coast of Sicily (Ac 28:12).
Syria	Roman province of which Palestine was part (Ac 15:23).
Tarsus	See Cilicia.
Thessalonica	Macedonian coastal city in northern Greece (Ac 17; 1 & 2 Th).
Trachonitis	Roman province between Damascus and Jordan (Lk 3:1).

Troas
Coastal city in Mysia (Ac 16:8; 20:5–6; 2 Co 2:12; 2 Ti 4:13).

Zion
One of the hills on which Jerusalem stands; also symbolic of heaven (Rev 14:14).

Read through the New Testament in a year – twice!

January	1	Matthew 1,2			
	2	3,4		29	6,7
	3	5		30	8
	4	6		31	9
	5	7,8	February	1	10
	6	9		2	11
	7	10		3	12,13
	8	11		4	James 1,2
	9	12		5	3–5
	10	13		6	1 Peter 1
	11	14		7	2,3
	12	15		8	4,5
	13	16, 17		9	2 Peter 1–3
	14	18		10	1 John 1,2
	15	19		11	3
	16	20		12	4,5
	17	21		13	2 & 3 John
	18	22		14	Jude
	19	23		15	Mark 1
	20	24		16	2,3
	21	25		17	4
	22	26		18	5
	23	27		19	6
	24	28		20	7
	25	Hebrews 1		21	8
	26	2		22	9
	27	3,4		23	10
	28	5		24	11
				25	12

	26	13	3	3,4
	27	14	4	Colossians 1,2
	28	15,16	5	3,4
	29	Romans 1,2	6	1
March	1	3,4	Thessalonians 1,2	
	2	5,6	7	3,4
	3	7,8	8	5
	4	9,10	9	2
	5	11,12	Thessalonians 1–3	
	6	13,14	10	1 Timothy 1,2
	7	15,16	11	3,4
	8	1 Corinthians 1,2	12	5,6
			13	2 Timothy 1,2
	9	3,4	14	3,4
	10	5,6	15	Titus 1–3
	11	7	16	Philemon
	12	8,9	17	Luke 1
	13	10,11	18	2
	14	12–14	19	3
	15	15	20	4
	16	16	21	5
	17	2 Corinthians 1,2	22	6
			23	7
	18	3	24	8
	19	4,5	25	9
	20	6,7	26	10
	21	8,9	27	11
	22	10	28	12
	23	11,12	29	13,14
	24	13	30	15,16
	25	Galatians 1,2	May	1	17
	26	3,4	2	18
	27	5,6	3	19
	28	Ephesians 1,2	4	20
	29	3	5	21
	30	4	6	22
	31	5	7	23
April	1	6	8	24
	2	Philippians 1,2	9	Acts 1,2
			10	3,4

11	5		20	9,10
12	6,7		21	11,12
13	8		22	13
14	9		23	14,15
15	10		24	16
16	11,12		25	17
17	13		26	18
18	14,15		27	19
19	16		28	20
20	17,18		29	21
21	19		30	2
22	20	July	1	Matthew 1,2
23	21,22		2	3,4
24	23,24		3	5
25	25,26		4	6
26	27		5	7
27	28		6	8
28	John 1		7	9
29	2,3		8	10
30	4		9	11
31	5		10	12
June 1	6		11	13
2	7		12	14
3	8		13	15
4	9		14	16,17
5	10		15	18,19
6	11		16	20
7	12		17	21
8	13		18	22
9	14		19	23
10	15,16		20	24
11	17		21	25
12	18		22	26
13	19		23	27
14	20,21		24	28
15	Revelation 1,2		25	Hebrews 1,2
16	3		26	3,4
17	4,5		27	5,6
18	6		28	7
19	7,8		29	8,9

	30	10	
	31	11	
August	1	12,13	
	2	James 1,2	
	3	3–5	
	4	1 Peter 1,2	
	5	3	
	6	4,5	
	7	2 Peter 1–3	
	8	1 John 1,2	
	9	3,4	
	10	5	
	11	2 & 3 John	
	12	Jude	
	13	Mark 1	
	14	2,3	
	15	4	
	16	5	
	17	6	
	18	7	
	19	8	
	20	9	
	21	10	
	22	11	
	23	12	
	24	13	
	25	14	
	26	15,16	
	27	Romans 1	
	28	2	
	29	3,4	
	30	5	
	31	6	
September	1	7,8	
	2	9,10	
	3	11	
	4	12,13	
	5	14,15	
	6	16	
	7	1 Corinthians 1,2	

8	3
9	4
10	5,6
11	7
12	8,9
13	10,11
14	12–14
15	15
16	16
17	2 Corinthians 1,2
18	3
19	4,5
20	6,7
21	8–10
22	11,12
23	13
24	Galatians 1
25	2
26	3,4
27	5,6
28	Ephesians 1,2
29	3
30	4,5

October	1	6
	2	Philippians 1,2
	3	3,4
	4	Colossians 1
	5	2
	6	3,4
	7	1 Thessalonians 1–3
	8	4,5
	9	2 Thessalonians 1
	10	2,3
	11	1 Timothy 1,2
	12	3,4
	13	5,6
	14	2 Timothy 1,2

	15	3,4	
	16	Titus 1–3	
	17	Philemon	
	18	Luke 1	
	19	2	
	20	3	
	21	4	
	22	5	
	23	6	
	24	7	
	25	8	
	26	9	
	27	10	
	28	11	
	29	12	
	30	13	
	31	14	
November	1	15	
	2	16	
	3	17	
	4	18	
	5	19	
	6	20	
	7	21	
	8	22	
	9	23	
	10	24	
	11	Acts 1,2	
	12	3,4	
	13	5	
	14	6,7	
	15	8	
	16	9	
	17	10	
	18	11,12	
	19	13	
	20	14,15	
	21	16	
	22	17,18	
	23	19	

24	20	
25	21,22	
26	23,24	
27	25	
28	26	
29	27	
30	28	
December	1	John 1
	2	2
	3	3
	4	4
	5	5
	6	6
	7	7
	8	8
	9	9
	10	10
	11	11
	12	12
	13	13
	14	14,15
	15	16
	16	17
	17	18
	18	19
	19	20
	20	21
	21	Revelation 1,2
	22	3,4
	23	5,6
	24	7,8
	25	9,10
	26	11,12
	27	13,14
	28	15,16
	29	17,18
	30	19,20
	31	21,22

SOME FURTHER READING

New Testament background

New Testament Background, F.F. Bruce (Pickering & Inglis, 1982).
The Life and Times of Jesus the Messiah, Alfred Edersheim, Eerdmans, 1971.
New Testament Survey, Merrill C. Tenney (IVP), 1985.
Handbook of Life in Bible Times, J.A. Thompson (IVP, 1986).
New Bible Atlas (IVP, 1985).

New Testament texts and translations

Manuscripts and the Text of the New Testament, Keith Elliott & Ian Moir (T & T Clark, 1995).
The Text of the New Testament, Bruce M. Metzger (OUP, 1992).
The Making of the New Testament, Arthur G. Patzia (Apollos, 1995).

New Testament study

The Historical Reliability of the Gospels, Craig Blomberg (IVP, 1987).
The Message of the New Testament, F.F. Bruce (Paternoster, 1972).
Beginning New Testament Study, Bruce Chilton (SPCK, 1986).
Hearing the New Testament, ed. Joel B. Green (Eerdmans/ Paternoster, 1995).
Pauline Pieces, Morna Hooker (Epworth, 1979).
New Testament Interpretation, ed. I. Howard Marshall (Paternoster, 1977).
Biblical Interpretation, Robert Morgan with John Barton (OUP, 1988).
The Interpretation of the New Testament, Stephen Neill and Tom Wright (OUP, 1988).
Studying the Synoptic Gospels, E.P. Sanders & Margaret Davies (SCM, 1989).
The Gospels and Jesus, Graham Stanton (OUP, 1986).
The New Testament and the People of God, N.T. Wright (SPCK, 1992).

New Testament use

The Bible User's Manual, ed. John F. Balchin, David H. Field &
Tremper Longman III (Inter-Varsity Press/Scripture Union, 1991).
How to Read the Bible for All Its Worth, Gordon D. Fee & Douglas
Stuart (Scripture Union, 1983).
Taking the Guesswork out of Applying the Bible, Jack Kuhatschek
(IVP, 1991).

The Eastern Mediterranean in New Testament times

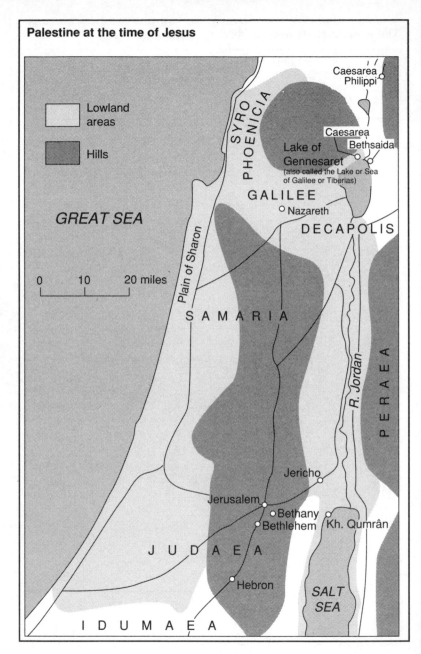

Palestine at the time of Jesus

Lowland areas

Hills

GREAT SEA

SYRO PHOENICIA

Caesarea Philippi

Caesarea

Bethsaida

Lake of Gennesaret (also called the Lake or Sea of Galilee or Tiberias)

GALILEE

o Nazareth

DECAPOLIS

Plain of Sharon

0   10   20 miles

SAMARIA

R. Jordan

PERAEA

Jericho

Jerusalem

Bethany

Bethlehem   Kh. Qumrân

JUDAEA

Hebron

SALT SEA

IDUMAEA

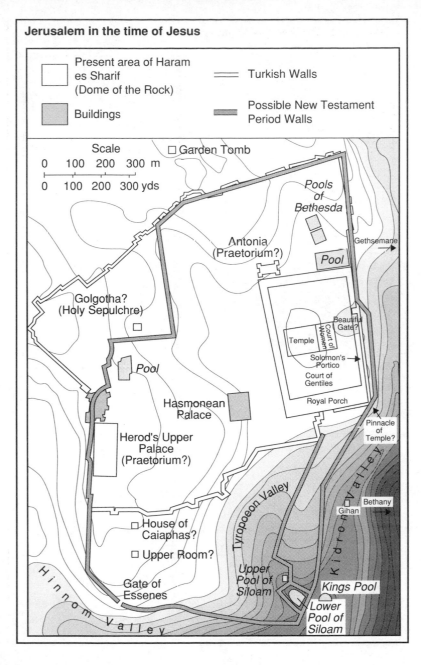

Jerusalem in the time of Jesus

Present area of Haram
es Sharif
(Dome of the Rock)

Buildings

Turkish Walls

Possible New Testament
Period Walls

Scale

0   100   200   300 m

0   100   200   300 yds

Garden Tomb

Pools
of
Bethesda

Antonia
(Praetorium?)

Pool

Gethsemane

Golgotha?
(Holy Sepulchre)

Beautiful
Gate?

Court of
Women

Temple

Solomon's
Portico

Court of
Gentiles

Royal Porch

Pool

Hasmonean
Palace

Herod's Upper
Palace
(Praetorium?)

Pinnacle
of
Temple?

Tyropoeon Valley

Kidron Valley

Gihan

Bethany

House of
Caiaphas?

Upper Room?

Gate of
Essenes

Hinnom Valley

Upper
Pool of
Siloam

Kings Pool

Lower
Pool of
Siloam

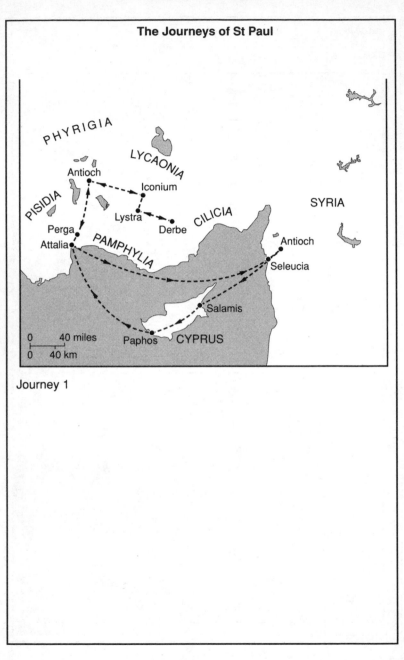

Journey 1

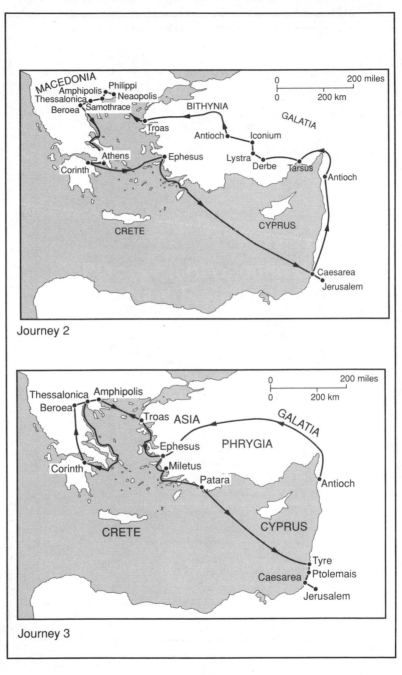

Journey 2

Journey 3

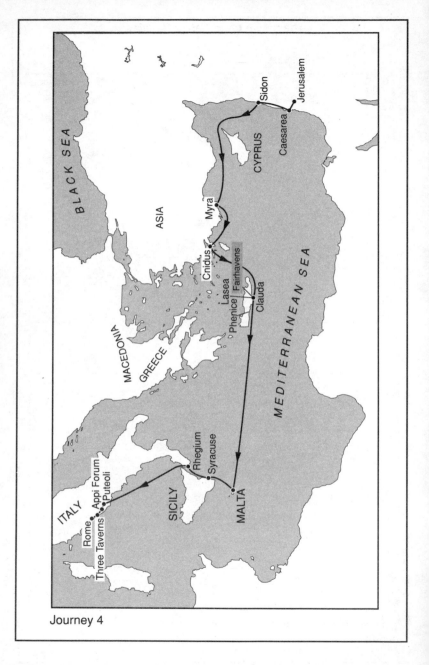

Journey 4

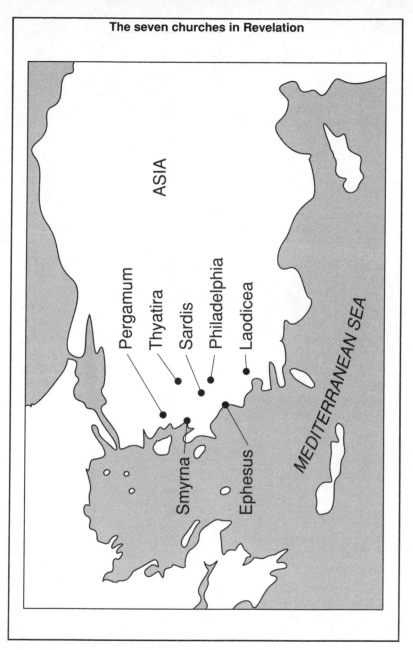

The seven churches in Revelation

INDEX

(See also the list of people mentioned in the New Testament on pages 180–9 and places mentioned in the New Testament on pages 189–94.)

Other related titles

🔲 TEACH YOURSELF

CHRISTIANITY

John Young

This book gives an introduction to Christianity as a living religion. Starting from the person, teaching and impact of Jesus, it describes the beliefs and practices of Christians and outlines some of the key features of the Church's two-thousand-year history. Christianity has deeply influenced Western culture, so a final section looks at some of its artistic, musical, architectural and literary inheritance.

The book includes sections on:

- prayer, worship and Christian experience
- modern movements within the church
- Christian faith in a scientific age
- facing death
- church, society, medical ethics and other faiths

This is a book to stimulate reflection on the Christian faith, both for practising Christians and for the general reader who wants to know more about his world-wide faith.

John Young is a Canon of York Minster and a member of the General Synod. He has written twelve books, including *Know Your Faith* and *The Case Against Christ* (Hodder & Stoughton). This book also features chapters by other experts on the Christian faith.